English Literature for Schools

SELECTIONS FROM
THE SPECTATOR

ADDISON

SELECTIONS FROM
THE SPECTATOR

Edited with Introduction and Notes

by

J. H. LOBBAN, M.A.

Cambridge:
at the University Press
1952

CAMBRIDGE
UNIVERSITY PRESS

University Printing House, Cambridge CB2 8BS, United Kingdom

Cambridge University Press is part of the University of Cambridge.

It furthers the University's mission by disseminating knowledge in the pursuit of education, learning and research at the highest international levels of excellence.

www.cambridge.org
Information on this title: www.cambridge.org/9781316612569

© Cambridge University Press 1952

First edition 1909
Reprinted 1914, 1920, 1925, 1928, 1929, 1933, 1936, 1946, 1950, 1952
First paperback edition 2016

A catalogue record for this publication is available from the British Library

ISBN 978-1-316-61256-9 Paperback

PREFACE

THE following selection of Addison's essays from *The Spectator* is given in chronological order. Only in this way is it possible in a selection to convey something of the desultory charm of the complete work, and artificial grouping may well be left to the discretion and to the requirements of the teacher. As it is necessary for the understanding of the Coverley papers, Steele's account of the Club is given in an appendix.

In the brief notes to this edition I have acknowledged various obligations. I am specially indebted to the careful reprint of *The Spectator* edited and annotated by Professor Gregory Smith.

J. H. L.

LONDON
1st July, 1909.

CONTENTS

		PAGE
	Introduction	ix
I.	Mr Spectator	1
II.	Stage Realism	5
III.	The Aim of *The Spectator* . . .	9
IV.	Nicolini and the Lions	13
V.	Malicious Wit	17
VI.	Valetudinarians	21
VII.	Meditations in the Abbey . . .	25
VIII.	The Scope of Satire	28
IX.	A Lady's Library	32
X.	Stage Murder	36
XI.	French Fopperies	42
XII.	On Friendship	45
XIII.	The Ballad of Chevy Chase (I) . .	49
XIV.	The Ballad of Chevy Chase (II) . .	55
XV.	Appearances Deceptive	62
XVI.	Ladies' Head-Dresses	66
XVII.	Fans	69
XVIII.	Pedants	73
XIX.	Sir Roger's Country-House . . .	76
XX.	Will Wimble	80
XXI.	Sir Roger in Church	83
XXII.	The Value of Exercise	86
XXIII.	Sir Roger and Witchcraft . . .	90
XXIV.	Sir Roger on the Bench	93
XXV.	Periodical Essays	97
XXVI.	Sir Roger and the Gipsies . . .	101
XXVII.	Town and Country	104
XXVIII.	The Genius of the English Language .	108

		PAGE
XXIX.	The Vision of Mirzah	112
XXX.	Inconstancy	117
XXXI.	A Grinning Match	120
XXXII.	On Charity	124
XXXIII.	Wit and Wisdom	129
XXXIV.	The Trunk-Maker	133
XXXV.	Female Orators	137
XXXVI.	On Ridicule	141
XXXVII.	The Cries of London	145
XXXVIII.	The Philosophy of Hoods	149
XXXIX.	Sir Roger comes to Town	153
XL.	Milton (I)	156
XLI.	Milton (II)	162
XLII.	Sir Roger visits the Abbey	170
XLIII.	Sir Roger at the Play	174
XLIV.	On Cheerfulness	178
XLV.	Coffee-House Politicians	182
XLVI.	On Fine Taste	186
XLVII.	Wealth and Poverty	190
XLVIII.	Qualifications for Office	194
XLIX.	Gardens	197
L.	Coffee-House Opinion	201
LI.	Uncharitable Judgment	205
LII.	On Giving Advice	209
LIII.	The Death of Sir Roger	212
LIV.	Project of a new Club	215
LV.	On Egotism	218
LVI.	On Contentment	221
LVII.	False Criticism	226
	APPENDIX	230
	NOTES	236

INTRODUCTION

THE opening sentence of *The Spectator* is interesting from more than one point of view. It is thoroughly Addisonian, and strikes the key-note of what is best in the essays that follow. One might search far without encountering a finer example in miniature of Addison's delicate irony or of what is now to us the pleasing archaism of his style. But to the writer upon Addison the concluding thrust of his first sentence comes home with special directness, and warns him to pass rapidly over those "Particulars...that conduce very much to the right understanding of an Author." The fear of seeming to fall into *Mr Spectator's* little trap by taking his advice seriously would alone set very brief limits to an outline of his life. The course of that life is itself another reason for brevity. During the last thirteen years of his life Addison held many important political offices. But the greatness that was thrust upon him interests us little now. To think of Addison as a Secretary of State and of Sir Richard Steele as a Commissioner of Stamps imposes a distinct strain on the reconstructive imagination. These facts still interest men of letters and make them think wistfully of the age of Queen Anne. It may be said, however, without any disrespect, that the thought of Steele's and Addison's appearance in the political world fills us with the same misgiving as that to which *Mr Spectator* pleads guilty when he saw to his surprise that his old friend, Sir Roger, was getting up to speak at the assizes. "I was in some pain for him till I found he had acquitted himself of two or three sentences with a look of much business and great intrepidity." When we read of these things, we instinctively join the group of "the gentlemen of the county gathering about my old friend and striving who should compliment him most," and sympathizing with the awe-struck rustics who "gazed upon him at a distance, not a little admiring his courage that was not afraid to speak to the judge."

Addison was born on May 1, 1672, at Milston, Wiltshire, where his father, Lancelot Addison, was rector. He received his earlier education at Amesbury and Salisbury, and when he was eleven years old his father became Dean of Lichfield. After a short time at Lichfield Grammar School— the school of his chief successor in the list of English Essayists—Addison was sent to Charter-house where he made his eventful friendship with Richard Steele. In 1687 he entered Queen's College, Oxford, and two years later—owing, it is said, to the excellence of some Latin verses—he obtained a demyship at Magdalen. He was elected to a Fellowship in 1698 and retained it, without taking orders, for thirteen years.

Addison's literary career began in 1693, the year in which he took his M.A. degree. His *Account of the Greatest English Poets* gave no promise of the reputation to come. The feeble couplets contain much that is of the nature of an awful example to critics. They convict Addison of a narrow range of reading and of a willingness to indulge in what

Lamb called damning at a venture. Thus Chaucer is described as a rude barbarian who

> jests in his unpolished strain,
> And tries to make his readers laugh in vain,

and the *Faerie Queene* is dismissed as a " mystic tale" that

> Can charm an understanding age no more.

A complimentary poem to Dryden had the result of gaining the dictator's favour, and soon Addison was being invited by Tonson, the publisher, to cooperate in various undertakings. His early writings it is safe to say would be forgotten now but for the interest reflected on them by his subsequent achievements. In their day, however, they seemed of sufficient merit to attract the attention of those in high places. With the Revolution came the chance for the miscellaneous writer, and leaders of party were eager to secure the services of promising recruits. How great was this eagerness is strikingly shown by the fortune of Addison. Somers and Halifax not only wished to obtain his literary help : they were willing to train him for the work. Accordingly in 1699 Addison set out on his tour on the continent with a government pension of £300 a year. He visited France, Italy, Germany, Austria, and Holland, with results far greater than the actual literary products of this period show. Addison was ostensibly qualifying for the service of King William, but the pension was really being put to more valuable use in training Mr Spectator to be a citizen of the world.

The accession of Queen Anne brought the downfall of Halifax and the stoppage of Addison's pension. He now began his way homewards, arriving in England in the Autumn of 1703, shortly after the death of his father. His prospects at this time seemed black enough, but presently he was destined to find himself the hero of a fairy tale in literary history. The story has lent itself to picturesque embroidery, but the plainest statement of the facts is sufficiently romantic. The victory of Blenheim found no competent government eulogist. Godolphin in despair sought the advice of Halifax. Halifax spoke of Mr Addison, but hinted that he was not likely to serve a party that " had neither the justice nor the generosity to make it worth his while." Godolphin, acting on this hint, despatched his Chancellor of the Exchequer to interview Addison and to promise him a Commissionership if he would undertake the task. The result was *The Campaign* and the beginning of Addison's triumphant progress towards the Cabinet. Of the intrinsic merits of the poem it is unnecessary to speak. It is a piece of commission work skilfully executed, and had it any value now poetically it would have doubtless been correspondingly a failure in its own day as a piece of metrical journalism. Tradition tells us of Godolphin's delight at the famous " Angel simile " where Marlborough

Rides in the whirlwind and directs the storm.

In 1706 Godolphin made good his promises by advancing Addison to be Under-Secretary of State, and when two years later he followed Lord Sunderland into retirement, he was almost immediately appointed Secretary to Wharton, the Lord Lieutenant of Ireland, a fellow-member of the Kit-Cat Club to which Addison had been elected on his return from the continent. While in Ireland Addison formed a strong friendship with Swift which survived the latter's defection to the Tory party. *The Whig Examiner* was undertaken in the Government's defence in 1710, but only ran for five numbers, and Addison displayed little of the polemical vigour shown by Swift when he began to assail the Whigs in *The Examiner*. The fall of the Whig Ministry in 1710 cost Addison his place, and in the following year he had to resign his Fellowship. His fortunes, however, had prospered so greatly that he was able in 1711 to buy an estate near Rugby for £10,000. To this prosperity no doubt the success of *The Tatler* and of *The Spectator* contributed.

In 1707 Steele was made editor of the *London Gazette*, and two years later, while Addison was in Ireland, he founded *The Tatler*, "a paper which should observe upon the manners of the pleasurable as well as the busy part of mankind." On its first appearance on April 12, 1709, *The Tatler* was at once recognized as a new and brilliant departure. The paper was divided into five heads—gallantry, poetry, learning, politics, and "editorial." *The Tatler* itself had its pioneers and at first it was only a periodical in the making. It gained in uniformity as it proceeded, and it is likely enough that this was due to the influence of Addison who is said to have discovered the identity of Mr Bickerstaff in the fifth number. The project appears to have delighted Addison who saw in it the perfect medium for his satire. Nothing could be more definite than the way in which Addison at once found himself as an essayist. Steele hailed his co-operation with his old enthusiasm and when the paper had run its brilliant course of nearly two years paid a generous tribute to his friend's "genius, humour, wit, and learning" and described himself as "like a distressed prince who calls in a powerful neighbour to his aid; I was undone by my own auxiliary; when I had once called him in, I could not subsist without dependence on him." Steele is never worse as a critic than when he writes of himself, and to accept his statement literally is to overlook all the facts of the case and to deny to friendship the pleasure of hyperbole. Generosity as well as irony is in need of intelligent interpretation. It is sufficient here to indicate that the happy thought was Steele's, that he wrote four *Tatlers* to Addison's one, and that his good-humoured "lucubrations" with their fine sympathy and insight probably did more to create a new circle of readers than the highly polished sarcasms of his auxiliary. Many years afterwards, when that auxiliary was dead, Steele again bore generous testimony to the value of his assistance. But he was goaded into adding the perfectly just observation, "whatever Steele owes to Mr Addison, the public owes Addison to Steele."

The short life of *The Tatler* was not due to any want of appreciation. It had undergone modifications of its original plan, and Steele and Addison thought it better to start anew. After an interval of two months *The Spectator* began its memorable career of five hundred and ten numbers. Of these all but forty-five papers were the work of Steele and Addison whose own shares were very nearly equal. The lead was taken by Addison who describes Mr Spectator and announces his intention of being a "looker-on." In the second number Steele drew the members of the Spectator Club and thus has the credit of furnishing the *dramatis personae* of our greatest periodical. These two opening essays are of special importance. They are the key to all the rest of the papers that bear on the Club and enable us to see that the essays were not rigorously edited. They were not carved and cut into consistency. Steele and Addison and others handled the characters in their own ways, and the marvel is that they succeeded in drawing portraits so vivid and convincing. The inconsistencies, for example, in the delineation of Sir Roger de Coverley are such as would be easily pardoned even had they been the work of a single hand. While for various purposes the work of its contributors must be valued separately, it cannot be too strongly urged that *The Spectator* is the joint achievement of Steele and Addison. To read the essays of either in isolation is to forgo the charm of the whole. What that charm is may not easily be defined. A single essay can illustrate the irony of Addison or the humour and sentiment of Steele, but no number of essays by the hand of either can adequately represent *The Spectator*.

The essays in *The Spectator* fall into a few easily defined groups of which three are of outstanding interest and importance—the Coverley papers, the critical essays, and the " comedy of manners." In view of the professed object of *The Spectator*—to bring "philosophy out of closets and libraries, schools and colleges, to dwell in clubs and assemblies, at tea-tables and in coffee-houses "—the last group is the most important of all. In the truest sense of the words, the term, "comedy of manners," is ludicrously inapplicable to the post-Restoration drama, but it would be difficult to find a better title for this section of the work of Steele and Addison. Using entirely different weapons they have the same object in view—to combat ignorance and affectation and folly and impurity. Steele has many claims to be regarded as a great journalist, but none more notable than his resolve to write for and about women. This side of *The Spectator's* satire puzzled some of his contemporaries. Swift tells Stella, "I will not meddle with the *Spectator*, let him *fair sex* it to the world's end." The essays on the fair sex need no initials to betray their

authorship. Those marked by the letters C.L.I.O.
are as obviously the work of the bachelor don as
those signed R. and T. are from the hand of the
writer of Prue's love-letters and of the immortal
compliment, "to love her is a liberal education."
Of the effect of this side of *The Spectator's* mission
we have many incontestable proofs: none more
famous than the words of the poet, John Gay. "It
is impossible to conceive the effect his writings
have had on the town; how many thousand follies
they have either quite banished or given a very
great check to; how entirely they have convinced
our fops and young fellows of the value and
advantage of learning." These papers were esteemed in their own day as both entertaining and
educative. Their power of entertainment is peren-
nial and they have now acquired an historical
value as the best of all sidelights on the London of
Queen Anne.

His irony and his urbanity are the two most
prominent traits in the essays of Addison. The
former is of a kind almost *sui generis.* To define
its specific difference, it is needful to remember
that irony literally means dissembling. In dramatic
or tragic or Sophoclean irony, Fate is the dissembler.
The actors in the tragedy are hoodwinked by a
deceptive prosperity and it is in the very moment
of apparent safety that they are overtaken by ruin.
Socratic irony, on the other hand, is the feigning of
ignorance. The master leads the novice step by
step into a pitfall of contradiction. In a similar
manner Addison uses the device of feigning
sympathy. There is nothing of the censor or
moralist in the way he approaches his victim. The
more ridiculous the folly he attacks, the greater is
his air of pretended concernment and sympathy.
The irony is all the more deadly that it is delivered

under the guise of friendship, and his "gay malevolence" was capable of leaving a wound more
lasting than the angry blows of Swift. But here
it is necessary to recall the other great quality of
Addison's writing—its fine taste and urbanity. It
was the type and not the individual that he
assailed. His object he tells us was to reprehend
"those vices which are too trivial for the chastisement
of the law, and too fantastical for the cognizance of
the pulpit...All agreed that I should be at liberty to
carry the war into what quarters I pleased ; provided
I continued to combat with criminals in a body,
and to assault the vice without hurting the person...
I must entreat every particular person who does
me the honour to be a reader of this paper, never
to think himself, or any one of his friends or
enemies, aimed at in what is said ; for I promise
him never to draw a faulty character which does
not fit at least a thousand people ; or to publish a
single paper that is not written in the spirit of
benevolence and with a love of mankind." This
claim Addison vindicated. Far-fetched attempts
have been made to identify some of his characters,
but these are really as little individual as the
"characters" of the Jacobean writers which
Addison's so far excel in point of vitality and
verisimilitude. There is sometimes the suggestion
of party bias in the portraiture but never the
personal rancour of Pope.

With the close of *The Spectator* Addison's best
literary work was done. The fierceness of party
strife invested his tragedy *Cato* with an interest
that has not survived, and the play is now
remembered chiefly as an awful example of
classical frigidity and correctness and by reason
of Voltaire's eulogy of its author as "the first
English writer who composed a regular tragedy."

Johnson's criticism of *Cato* reveals an amusing conflict between common sense and respect for classical tradition. It is "unquestionably the noblest production of Addison's genius…Every critical reader must remark that Addison has, with a scrupulosity almost unexampled on the English stage, confined himself in time to a single day, and in place to rigorous unity." So much for "the rules." But when we come to the characterisation Johnson tells us that *Cato* is " rather a poem in dialogue than a drama, rather a succession of just sentiments in elegant language, than a representation of natural affections or of any state probable or possible in human life…Of the agents we have no care; we consider not what they are doing or what they are suffering; we wish only to know what they have to say. Cato is a being above our solicitude; a man of whom the gods take care, and whom we leave to their care with heedless confidence." In this deliverance we seem to detect an amusing (because a perfectly unintentional) instance of Addison's being attacked with his own weapon.

After the death of Queen Anne Addison resumed his political career, returning to his former post as Irish Secretary and in 1717 becoming a Secretary of State. The latter office he held for less than a year when he was obliged to resign on account of failing health. In 1716 he married the Countess of Warwick, "marrying discord with a noble wife." The tradition of his unhappiness is of doubtful value and a large discount has to be allowed for the persistent enmity of Pope. In 1719 he suffered from repeated attacks of asthma and died in the summer of that year in Holland House, one of his last literary labours being a controversy with his old schoolfellow and confederate, Steele. Two years later, Steele, in his preface to *The*

Drummer, paid a noble tribute to his friend. " I am indeed much more proud of his continued friendship than I should be of the fame of being thought the author of any writings which he himself is capable of producing. I remember when I finished *The Tender Husband*, I told him there was nothing I so ardently wished as that we might sometime or other publish a work written by us both, which should bear the name of the Monument, in memory of our friendship." Steele's loyal heart could have wished no more lasting memorial than *The Spectator*.

Fortune, as we have seen, was very kind to Addison. It brought him laurels, scarcely deserved, as a poet and as a dramatist and as a politician. It brought him his chance, through the agency of Steele, of revealing his real gifts as a great master of English prose, as one of the foremost of our English humorists. On one occasion, however, fortune deserted him, and brought upon him the malignity of Pope who remains unique in our literature for his satanic skill in giving immortality to his malice. The story is a tangled one and does not concern us here. As in every similar episode of his life Pope seems deliberately to have obscured the issue with a view to justifying himself. The famous description of Atticus in the *Epistle to Arbuthnot* shows Pope's skill and malice at their best and worst.

> Were there one whose fires
> True genius kindles, and fair fame inspires ;
> Blest with each talent and each art to please,
> And born to write, converse, and live with ease :
> Should such a man, too fond to live alone,
> Bear, like the Turk, no brother near the throne,
> View him with scornful, yet with jealous eyes,
> And hate for arts that caused himself to rise ;
> Damn with faint praise, assent with civil leer,
> And without sneering, teach the rest to sneer ;

> Willing to wound, and yet afraid to strike,
> Just hint a fault, and hesitate dislike;
> Alike reserved to blame or to commend,
> A timorous foe, and a suspicious friend;
> Dreading e'en fools, by flatterers besieged,
> And so obliging that he ne'er obliged;
> Like Cato gave his little senate laws,
> And sit attentive to his own applause,
> While Wits and Templars ev'ry sentence raise
> And wonder with a foolish face of praise:
> Who but must laugh, if such a man there be?
> Who would not weep if Atticus were he?

The lines have become so familiar, and have in part been found so capable of general application, that one is apt to overlook their particular significance and skill as a portrait of Addison. Their sting is the more deadly because every line contains a half truth. Misanthropy and introspection gave Pope a truly diabolical insight into human weakness. Addison doubtless enjoyed his sovereignty at Button's, and his reserved manner might well be construed as patronising condescension. The irony of his writings is likely to have had its counterpart in his speech, and if we assume this hypothesis we can see the precise amount of truth and exaggeration in Pope's description.—To

> Damn with faint praise, assent with civil leer,
> And without sneering, teach the rest to sneer—

that is a brilliant definition of Addisonian irony as viewed by hostile eyes, but how inadequate as a full description of the methods of Mr Spectator! There is just sufficient truth in the couplet to make us beware of using such adjectives as "gentle" in describing Addison's style. The word is as inapplicable here as it is in the case of Charles Lamb. Addison's irony is gentle only because it is general and is veiled by humour. Had he chosen to be bitter and particular, neither Swift nor Pope would have been so formidable an assailant.

" We have not the least doubt that if Addison had written a novel, on an extensive plan, it would have been superior to any that we possess." This is one of Macaulay's most typical flights into the thin air of generalisation. There is no reason for thinking that Steele and Addison could have constructed and carried forward a complete plot. The Coverley papers are evidence to the contrary at the same time that they firmly establish the right of Steele and Addison to rank among the most important pioneers of the English novel. The fame of Addison does not require support from probabilities. He helped to perfect a new kind in English literature and revealed to his successors, of whom none has excelled him, the full possibilities of humorous satire.

J. H. L.

ESSAYS OF ADDISON FROM
THE SPECTATOR

MR SPECTATOR

Non fumum ex fulgore, sed ex fumo dare lucem
Cogitat, ut speciosa dehinc miracula promat.
HOR. Ars. Poet. ver. 143.

One with a flash begins, and ends in smoke ;
Another out of smoke brings glorious light,
And (without raising expectation high)
Surprises us with dazzling miracles. ROSCOMMON.

I HAVE observed, that a reader seldom peruses a
book with pleasure, till he knows whether the writer
of it be a black or a fair man, of a mild or choleric
disposition, married or a bachelor, with other particulars of the like nature, that conduce very much to
the right understanding of an author. To gratify
this curiosity, which is so natural in a reader, I design this paper and my next as prefatory discourses
to my following writings, and shall give some account
in them of the several persons that are engaged in this
work. As the chief trouble of compiling, digesting, and
correcting will fall to my share, I must do myself the
justice to open the work with my own history.

I was born to a small hereditary estate, which,
according to the tradition of the village where it lies,
was bounded by the same hedges and ditches in
William the Conqueror's time that it is at present,
and has been delivered down from father to son,

whole and entire, without the loss or acquisition of a single field or meadow, during the space of six hundred years. There runs a story in the family, that, when my mother was gone with child of me about three months, she dreamed that she was brought to bed of a judge. Whether this might proceed from a law-suit which was then depending in the family, or my father's being a justice of the peace, I cannot determine; for I am not so vain as to think it presaged any dignity that I should arrive at in future life, though that was the interpretation which the neighbourhood put upon it. The gravity of my behaviour at my first appearance in the world, and at the time that I sucked, seemed to favour my mother's dream; for, as she has often told me, I threw away my rattle before I was two months old, and would not make use of my coral until they had taken away the bells from it.

As for the rest of my infancy, there being nothing in it remarkable, I shall pass over it in silence. I find that, during my nonage, I had the reputation of a very sullen youth, but was always a favourite of my school-master, who used to say, "that my parts were solid, and would wear well." I had not been long at the university, before I distinguished myself by a most profound silence; for during the space of eight years, excepting in the public exercises of the college, I scarce uttered the quantity of a hundred words; and indeed do not remember that I ever spoke three sentences together in my whole life. Whilst I was in this learned body, I applied myself with so much diligence to my studies, that there are very few celebrated books, either in the learned or the modern tongues, which I am not acquainted with.

Upon the death of my father, I was resolved to travel into foreign countries, and therefore left the university with the character of an odd, unaccountable fellow, that had a great deal of learning, if I would but show it. An insatiable thirst after knowledge carried me into all the countries of Europe in which there was any thing new or strange to be seen;

nay, to such a degree was my curiosity raised, that having read the controversies of some great men concerning the antiquities of Egypt, I made a voyage to Grand Cairo on purpose to take the measure of a pyramid; and as soon as I had set myself right in that particular, returned to my native country with great satisfaction.

I have passed my latter years in this city, where I am frequently seen in most public places, though there are not above half a dozen of my select friends that know me; of whom my next paper shall give a more particular account. There is no place of general resort wherein I do not often make my appearance. Sometimes I am seen thrusting my head into a round of politicians at Will's, and listening with great attention to the narratives that are made in those little circular audiences. Sometimes I smoke a pipe at Child's, and while I seem attentive to nothing but the Postman, overhear the conversation of every table in the room. I appear on Sunday nights at St James's coffee-house, and sometimes join the little committee of politics in the inner room, as one who comes there to hear and improve. My face is likewise very well known at the Grecian, the Cocoa-tree, and in the theatres both of Drury-lane and the Haymarket. I have been taken for a merchant upon the exchange for above these ten years, and sometimes pass for a Jew in the assembly of stock-jobbers at Jonathan's. In short, wherever I see a cluster of people, I always mix with them, though I never open my lips but in my own club.

Thus I live in the world rather as a Spectator of mankind than as one of the species, by which means I have made myself a speculative statesman, soldier, merchant, and artisan, without ever meddling with any practical part in life. I am very well versed in the theory of a husband, or a father, and can discern the errors in the economy, business, and diversions of others, better than those who are engaged in them; as standers-by discover blots, which are apt to escape those who are in the game. I never espoused any party with violence, and am resolved to observe a strict neutrality between the Whigs and Tories, unless I shall be forced to declare myself by the hostilities of either side. In short, I have acted in all the parts of my life as a looker-on, which is the character I intend to preserve in this paper.

I have given the reader just so much of my history and character, as to let him see I am not altogether unqualified for the business I have undertaken. As for other particulars in my life and adventures, I shall insert them in following papers, as I shall see occasion. In the meantime, when I consider how much I have seen, read, and heard, I begin to blame my own taciturnity; and since I have neither time nor inclination to communicate the fulness of my heart in speech, I am resolved to do it in writing, and to print myself out, if possible, before I die. I have been often told by my friends, that it is pity so many useful discoveries which I have made should be in the possession of a silent man. For this reason, therefore, I shall publish a sheet-full of thoughts every morning, for the benefit of my contemporaries; and if I can in any way contribute to the diversion or improvement of the country in which I live, I shall leave it when I am summoned out of it, with the secret satisfaction of thinking that I have not lived in vain.

There are three very material points which I have not spoken to in this paper: and which, for several important reasons, I must keep to myself, at least for some time: I mean an account of my name, age, and lodgings. I must confess, I would gratify my reader in any thing that is reasonable; but as for these three particulars, though I am sensible they might tend very much to the embellishment of my paper, I cannot yet come to a resolution of communicating them to the public. They would indeed draw me out of that obscurity which I have enjoyed for many years, and expose me in public places to several salutes and civilities, which have been always very disagreeable to me; for the greatest pain I can suffer, is the being talked to, and being stared at. It is for this reason, likewise, that I keep my complexion and dress as very great secrets; though it is not impossible but I may make discoveries of both in the progress of the work I have undertaken.

After having been thus particular upon myself, I shall in to-morrow's paper give an account of those gentlemen who are concerned with me in this work: for, as I have before intimated, a plan of it is laid and concerted (as all other matters of importance are) in a club. However, as my friends have engaged me to stand in the front, those who have a mind to correspond with me may direct their letters to the Spectator, at Mr Buckley's, in Little Britain. For I must further acquaint the reader, that though our club meets only on Tuesdays and Thursdays, we have appointed a committee to sit every night for the inspection of all such papers as may contribute to the advancement of the public weal.

STAGE REALISM

Spectatum admissi risum teneatis?

HOR. *Ars. Poet.* ver. 5.

Admitted to the sight, would you not laugh?

AN opera may be allowed to be extravagantly lavish in its decorations, as its only design is to gratify the senses, and keep up an indolent attention in the audience. Common sense however requires, that there should be nothing in the scenes and machines which may appear childish and absurd. How would the wits of King Charles's time have laughed to have seen Nicolini exposed to a tempest in robes of ermine, and sailing in an open boat upon a sea of pasteboard? What a field of raillery would they have been led into, had they been entertained with painted dragons spitting wildfire, enchanted chariots drawn by Flanders mares, and real cascades in artificial landscapes? A little skill in criticism would inform us, that shadows and realities ought not to be mixed together in the same piece; and that the scenes which are designed as the representations of nature should be filled with resemblances, and not with the things themselves. If one would represent a wide champaign country filled with herds and flocks, it would be ridiculous to draw the country only upon the scenes, and to crowd several parts of the stage with sheep and oxen. This is joining together inconsistencies, and making the decoration partly real, and partly imaginary. I would recommend what I have here said to the directors, as well as to the admirers, of our modern opera.

As I was walking in the streets about a fortnight ago, I saw an ordinary fellow carrying a cage full of little birds upon his shoulder; and, as I was wondering with myself what use he would put them to, he was met very luckily by an acquaintance, who had the same curiosity. Upon his asking what he had upon his shoulder, he told him that he had been buying sparrows for the opera. "Sparrows for the opera," says his friend, licking his lips; "what! are they to be roasted?"—"No, no," says the other, "they are to enter towards the end of the first act, and to fly about the stage."

This strange dialogue awakened my curiosity so far, that I immediately bought the opera, by which means I perceived the sparrows were to act the part of singing birds in a delightful grove; though upon a nearer inquiry I found the sparrows put the same trick upon the audience that Sir Martin Mar-all practised upon his mistress; for though they flew in sight, the music proceeded from a concert of flageolets and bird-calls, which were planted behind the scenes. At the same time I made this discovery, I found by the discourse of the actors, that there were great designs on foot for the improvement of the opera; that it had been proposed to break down a part of the wall, and to surprise the audience with a party of a hundred horse, and that there was actually a project of bringing the New-river into the house, to be employed in jetteaus and water-works. This project, as I have since heard, is post-poned till the summer season, when it is thought the coolness that proceeds from fountains and cascades will be more acceptable and refreshing to people of quality. In the meantime, to find out a more agree-able entertainment for the winter season, the opera of Rinaldo is filled with thunder and lightning, illumina-tions and fire-works, which the audience may look upon without catching cold, and indeed without much danger of being burnt; for there are several engines filled with water, and ready to play at a minute's warning, in case any such accident should happen. However, as I have a very great friendship for the owner of this theatre, I hope that he has been wise enough to insure his house before he would let this opera be acted in it.

It is no wonder that those scenes should be very surprising, which were contrived by two poets of different nations, and raised by two magicians of dif-ferent sexes. Armida (as we are told in the argument) was an Amazonian enchantress, and poor Signior Cassani (as we learn from the persons represented) a Christian conjurer (*Mago Christiano*). I must con-fess I am very much puzzled to find how an Amazon should be versed in the black art, or how a good Christian, for such is the part of the magician, should deal with the devil.

To consider the poet after the conjurers, I shall give you a taste of the Italian from the first lines of his preface: "*Eccoti, benigno lettore, un parto di poche sere, che se ben nato di notte, non è però aborto di tenebre, mà si farà conoscere figlio d' Apollo con qualche raggio di Parnasso*": "Behold, gentle reader, the birth of a few evenings, which, though it be the off-spring of the night, is not the abortive of darkness, but will make itself known to be the son of Apollo, with a certain ray of Parnassus." He afterwards proceeds to call Minheer Hendel the Orpheus of our age, and to acquaint us, in the same sublimity of style, that he composed this opera in a fortnight. Such are the wits to whose tastes we so ambitiously conform ourselves. The truth of it is, the finest writers among the modern Italians express themselves in such a florid form of words, and such tedious circumlocutions, as are used by none but pedants in our own country; and at the same time fill their writings with such poor imaginations and conceits, as our youths are ashamed of before they have been two years at the university. Some may be apt to think that it is the difference of genius which produces this difference in the works of the two nations; but to show that there is nothing in this, if we look into the writings of the old Italians, such as Cicero and Virgil, we shall find that the English writers, in their way of thinking and expressing themselves, resemble those authors much more than the modern Italians pretend to do And as for the poet himself, from whom the dreams of this opera are taken, I must entirely agree with Monsieur Boileau, that one verse in Virgil is worth all the clinquant or tinsel of Tasso.

But to return to the sparrows: there have been so many flights of them let loose in this opera, that it is feared the house will never get rid of them; and that in other plays they may make their entrance in very wrong and improper scenes, so as to be seen flying in a lady's bed-chamber, or perching upon a king's throne —besides the inconveniences which the heads of the audience may sometimes suffer from them. I am credibly informed, that there was once a design of casting into an opera the story of Whittington and his Cat, and that, in order to it there had been got to- gether a great quantity of mice; but Mr Rich, the proprietor of the playhouse, very prudently considered that it would be impossible for the cat to kill them all, and that consequently the princes of the stage might be as much infested with mice, as the prince of the island was before the cat's arrival upon it; for which reason he would not permit it to be acted in his house.

And indeed I cannot blame him; for, as he said very well upon that occasion, I do not hear that any of the performers in our opera pretend to equal the famous pied piper, who made all the mice of a great town in Germany follow his music, and by that means cleared the place of those little noxious animals.

Before I dismiss this paper, I must inform my reader, that I hear there is a treaty on foot between London and Wise (who will be appointed gardeners of the play-house) to furnish the opera of Rinaldo and Armida with an orange-grove: and that the next time it is acted, the singing-birds will be personated by tom-tits, the undertakers being resolved to spare neither pains nor money for the gratification of the audience.

THE AIM OF *THE SPECTATOR*

Non aliter quam qui adverso vix flumine lembum
Remigiis subigit ; si brachia forte remisit,
Atque illum in præceps prono rapit alveus amni.
VIRG. Georg. i. 201.

So the boat's brawny crew the current stem,
And, slow advancing, struggle with the stream :
But if they slack their hands, or cease to strive,
Then down the flood with headlong haste they drive.
DRYDEN.

IT is with much satisfaction that I hear this great city inquiring day by day after these my papers, and receiving my morning lectures with a becoming serious-ness and attention. My publisher tells me, that there are already three thousand of them distributed every day: so that if I allow twenty readers to every paper, which I look upon as a modest computation, I may reckon about threescore thousand disciples in London and Westminster, who I hope will take care to distin-guish themselves from the thoughtless herd of their ignorant and inattentive brethren. Since I have raised to myself so great an audience, I shall spare no pains to make their instruction agreeable, and their diversion useful. For which reasons I shall endeavour to enliven morality with wit, and to temper wit with morality, that my readers may, if possible, both ways find their account in the speculation of the day. And to the end that their virtue and discretion may not be short, transient, intermitting starts of thought, I have resolved to refresh their memories from day to day, till I have recovered them out of that desperate state of vice and folly, into which the age is fallen. The mind that lies fallow for a single day, sprouts up in follies that are only to be killed by a constant and assiduous culture. It was said of Socrates, that he brought Philosophy down from heaven, to inhabit among men; and I shall be ambitious to have it said of me, that I have brought Philosophy out of closets and libraries, schools and colleges, to dwell in clubs and assemblies, at tea-tables, and in coffee-houses.

I would therefore in a very particular manner re-commend these my speculations to all well-regulated families, that set apart an hour in every morning for tea and bread and butter; and would earnestly advise them for their good to order this paper to be punctually served up, and to be looked upon as a part of the tea-equipage.

Sir Francis Bacon observes, that a well-written book, compared with its rivals and antagonists, is like Moses's serpent, that immediately swallowed up and devoured those of the Egyptians. I shall not be so vain as to think, that where the Spectator appears, the other public prints will vanish: but shall leave it to my reader's consideration, whether it is not much better to be let into the knowledge of one's self, than to hear what passes in Muscovy or Poland: and to amuse ourselves with such writings as tend to the wearing out of ignorance, passion, and prejudice, than such as naturally conduce to inflame hatreds, and make enmities irreconcileable.

In the next place I would recommend this paper to the daily perusal of those gentlemen whom I cannot but consider as my good brothers and allies, I mean the fraternity of Spectators, who live in the world without having any thing to do in it; and either by the affluence of their fortunes, or laziness of their dispositions, have no other business with the rest of mankind, but to look upon them. Under this class of men are comprehended all contemplative tradesmen, titular physicians, Fellows of the Royal Society, Templars that are not given to be contentious, and statesmen that are out of business; in short, every one that considers the world as a theatre, and desires to form a right judgment of those who are the actors on it.

There is another set of men that I must likewise lay a claim to, whom I have lately called the blanks of society, as being altogether unfurnished with ideas, till the business and conversation of the day has supplied them. I have often considered these poor souls with an eye of great commiseration, when I have heard them asking the first man they have met with, whether there was any news stirring? and by that means gathering together materials for thinking. These needy persons do not know what to talk of, till about twelve o'clock in the morning; for by that time they are pretty good judges of the weather, know which way the wind sets, and whether the Dutch mail be come in. As they lie at the mercy of the first man they meet, and are grave or impertinent all the day long, according to the notions which they have imbibed in the morning, I would earnestly entreat them not to stir out of their chambers till they have read this paper, and do promise them that I will daily instil into them such sound and wholesome sentiments, as shall have a good effect on their conversation for the ensuing twelve hours.

But there are none to whom this paper will be more useful than to the female world. I have often thought there has not been sufficient pains taken in finding out proper employment and diversions for the fair ones. Their amusements seem contrived for them, rather as they are women, than as they are reasonable creatures;

and are more adapted to the sex than to the species. The toilet is their great scene of business, and the right adjusting of their hair the principal employment of their lives. The sorting of a suit of ribbons is reckoned a very good morning's work; and if they make an excursion to a mercer's or a toy-shop, so great a fatigue makes them unfit for any thing else all the day after. Their more serious occupations are sewing and embroidery, and their greatest drudgery the preparation of jellies and sweetmeats. This, I say, is the state of ordinary women; though I know there are multitudes of those of a more elevated life and conversation, that move in an exalted sphere of knowledge and virtue, that join all the beauties of the mind to the ornaments of dress, and inspire a kind of awe and respect, as well as love, into their male beholders. I hope to increase the number of these by publishing this daily paper, which I shall always endeavour to make an innocent if not an improving entertainment, and by that means, at least, divert the minds of my female readers from greater trifles. At the same time, as I would fain give some finishing touches to those which are already the most beautiful pieces in human nature, I shall endeavour to point out all those imperfections that are the blemishes, as well as those virtues which are the embellishments of the sex. In the meanwhile, I hope these my gentle readers, who have so much time on their hands, will not grudge throwing away a quarter of an hour in a day on this paper, since they may do it without any hindrance to business.

I know several of my friends and well-wishers are in great pain for me, lest I should not be able to keep up the spirit of a paper which I oblige myself to furnish every day; but to make them easy in this particular, I will promise them faithfully to give it over as soon as I grow dull. This I know will be matter of great raillery to the small wits, who will frequently put me in mind of my promise, desire me to keep my word, assure me that it is high time to give over, with many other little pleasantries of the like nature, which men of a little smart genius cannot forbear throwing out against their best friends, when they have such a handle given them of being witty. But let them remember, that I do hereby enter my caveat against this piece of raillery.

NICOLINI AND THE LIONS

Dic mihi, si fias tu leo, qualis eris? MART.

Were you a lion, how would you behave?

THERE is nothing that of late years has afforded matter of greater amusement to the town than Signior Nicolini's combat with a lion in the Haymarket, which has been very often exhibited to the general satisfaction of most of the nobility and gentry in the kingdom of Great Britain. Upon the first rumour of this intended combat, it was confidently affirmed, and is still believed by many in both galleries, that there would be a tame lion sent from the tower every opera night, in order to be killed by Hydaspes: this report, though altogether groundless, so universally prevailed in the upper regions of the play-house, that some of the most refined politicians in those parts of the audience gave it out in a whisper, that the lion was a cousin-german of the tiger who made his appearance in King William's days, and that the stage would be supplied with lions at the public expense during the whole session. Many likewise were the conjectures of the treatment which this lion was to meet with from the hands of Signior Nicolini; some supposed that he was to subdue him in recitativo, as Orpheus used to serve the wild beasts in his time, and afterwards to knock him on the head; some fancied that the lion would not pretend to lay his paws upon the hero, by reason of the received opinion, that a lion will not hurt a virgin. Several,

who pretended to have seen the opera in Italy, had
informed their friends, that the lion was to act a part
in High Dutch, and roar twice or thrice to a thorough
bass, before he fell at the feet of Hydaspes. To clear
up a matter that was so variously reported, I have
made it my business to examine whether this pretended lion is really the savage he appears to be, or
only a counterfeit.

But before I communicate my discoveries, I must
acquaint the reader, that upon my walking behind
the scenes last winter, as I was thinking on something else, I accidentally jostled against a monstrous
animal that extremely startled me, and upon my
nearer survey of it, appeared to be a lion rampant.
The lion, seeing me very much surprised, told me,
in a gentle voice, that I might come by him if I
pleased: "for," says he, "I do not intend to hurt
anybody." I thanked him very kindly, and passed
by him: and in a little time after, saw him leap upon
the stage, and act his part with very great applause.
It has been observed by several, that the lion has
changed his manner of acting twice or thrice since
his first appearance; which will not seem strange,
when I acquaint my reader that the lion has been
changed upon the audience three several times. The
first lion was a candle-snuffer, who being a fellow of
a testy choleric temper, overdid his part, and would
not suffer himself to be killed so easily as he ought
to have done; besides, it was observed of him, that
he grew more surly every time that he came out of
the lion; and having dropped some words in ordinary
conversation, as if he had not fought his best, that he
suffered himself to be thrown upon his back in the
scuffle, and that he would wrestle with Mr Nicolini
for what he pleased out of his lion's skin, it was
thought proper to discard him: and it is verily believed to this day, that had he been brought upon the
stage another time, he would certainly have done
mischief. Besides, it was objected against the first
lion, that he reared himself so high upon his hinder

paws, and walked in so erect a posture, that he looked
more like an old man than a lion.

The second lion was a tailor by trade, who belonged to the playhouse, and had the character of a
mild and peaceable man in his profession. If the
former was too furious, this was too sheepish for his
part; inasmuch, that after a short modest walk upon
the stage, he would fall at the first touch of Hydaspes,
without grappling with him, and giving him an opportunity of showing his variety of Italian trips. It is
said, indeed, that he once gave him a rip in his flesh-
colour doublet: but this was only to make work for
himself, in his private character of a tailor. I must
not omit, that it was this second lion who treated me
with so much humanity behind the scenes.

The acting lion at present is, as I am informed, a
country gentleman, who does it for his diversion, but
desires his name may be concealed. He says very
handsomely in his own excuse, that he does not act
from gain, that he indulges an innocent pleasure in
it; and that it is better to pass away an evening in
this manner, than in gaming and in drinking: but at
the same time says, with a very agreeable raillery
upon himself, that if his name should be known, the
ill-natured world might call him, "the ass in the lion's
skin." This gentleman's temper is made out of such
a happy mixture of the mild and the choleric, that
he outdoes both his predecessors, and has drawn together greater audiences than have been known in the
memory of man.

I must not conclude my narrative, without taking
notice of a groundless report that has been raised to
a gentleman's disadvantage, of whom I must declare
myself an admirer; namely, that Signior Nicolini and
the lion have been seen sitting peaceably by one
another, and smoking a pipe together behind the
scenes; by which their common enemies would in-
sinuate, that it is but a sham combat which they
represent upon the stage: but upon inquiry I find,
that if any such correspondence has passed between

them, it was not till the combat was over, when the
lion was to be looked upon as dead, according to the
received rules of the drama.   Besides, this is what
is practised every day in Westminster Hall, where
nothing is more usual than to see a couple of lawyers,
who have been tearing each other to pieces in the
court, embracing one another as soon as they are out
of it.

I would not be thought, in any part of this relation, to reflect upon Signior Nicolini, who in acting
this part only complies with the wretched taste of his
audience; he knows very well, that the lion has many
more admirers than himself; as they say of the famous
equestrian statue on the Pont-Neuf at Paris, that
more people go to see the horse, than the king who
sits upon it.   On the contrary, it gives me a just
indignation to see a person whose action gives new
majesty to kings, resolution to heroes, and softness to
lovers, thus sinking from the greatness of his behaviour, and degraded into the character of the London
Prentice.   I have often wished, that our tragedians
would copy after this great master in action.   Could
they make the same use of their arms and legs, and
inform their faces with as significant looks and passions, how glorious would an English tragedy appear
with that action which is capable of giving dignity to
the forced thoughts, cold conceits, and unnatural
expressions of an Italian opera!   In the meantime,
I have related this combat of the lion, to show what
are at present the reigning entertainments of the
politer part of Great Britain.

Audiences have often been reproached by writers
for the coarseness of their taste, but our present
grievance does not seem to be the want of a good
taste, but of common sense.

MALICIOUS WIT

Sævit atrox Volscens, nec teli conspicit usquam
Auctorem, nec quo se ardens immittere possit.
VIRG. Æn. ix. 420.

Fierce Volscens foams with rage, and gazing round,
Descry'd not him who gave the fatal wound ;
Nor knew to fix revenge. DRYDEN.

THERE is nothing that more betrays a base ungenerous spirit than the giving of secret stabs to a
man's reputation; lampoons and satires, that are
written with wit and spirit, are like poisoned darts,
which not only inflict a wound, but make it incurable.
For this reason I am very much troubled when I see
the talents of humour and ridicule in the possession
of an ill-natured man. There cannot be a greater
gratification to a barbarous and inhuman wit, than to
stir up sorrow in the heart of a private person, to
raise uneasiness among near relations, and to expose
whole families to derision, at the same time that he
remains unseen and undiscovered. If, besides the
accomplishments of being witty and ill-natured, a
man is vicious into the bargain, he is one of the most
mischievous creatures that can enter into a civil
society. His satire will then chiefly fall upon those
who ought to be the most exempt from it. Virtue,
merit, and every thing that is praiseworthy, will be
made the subject of ridicule and buffoonery. It is
impossible to enumerate the evils which arise from
these arrows that fly in the dark; and I knew no
other excuse that is or can be made for them, than
that the wounds they give are only imaginary, and
produce nothing more than a secret shame or sorrow
in the mind of the suffering person. It must indeed
be confessed, that a lampoon or a satire do not carry
in them robbery or murder, but at the same time how
many are there that would not rather lose a considerable sum of money, or even life itself, than be set up
as a mark of infamy and derision ? and in this case

a man should consider, that an injury is not to be measured by the notions of him that gives, but of him that receives it.

Those who can put the best countenance upon the outrages of this nature which are offered them, are not without their secret anguish. I have often observed a passage in Socrates's behaviour at his death, in a light wherein none of the critics have considered it. That excellent man entertaining his friends, a little before he drank the bowl of poison, with a discourse on the immortality of the soul, at his entering upon it says that he does not believe any, the most comic genius, can censure him for talking upon such a subject at such a time. This passage, I think, evidently glances upon Aristophanes, who writ a comedy on purpose to ridicule the discourses of that divine philosopher. It has been observed by many writers, that Socrates was so little moved at this piece of buffoonery, that he was several times present at its being acted upon the stage, and never expressed the least resentment of it. But with submission, I think the remark I have here made shows us, that this unworthy treatment made an impression upon his mind, though he had been too wise to discover it.

When Julius Cæsar was lampooned by Catullus, he invited him to supper, and treated him with such a generous civility, that he made the poet his friend ever after. Cardinal Mazarine gave the same kind of treatment to the learned Quillet, who had reflected upon his eminence in a famous Latin poem. The cardinal sent for him, and, after some kind expostulations upon what he had written, assured him of his esteem, and dismissed him with a promise of the next good abbey that should fall, which he accordingly conferred upon him in a few months after. This had so good an effect upon the author, that he dedicated the second edition of his book to the cardinal, after having expunged the passages which had given him offence.

Sextus Quintus was not of so generous and for-
giving a temper. Upon his being made pope, the
statue of Pasquin was one night dressed in a very
dirty shirt, with an excuse written under it, that he
was forced to wear foul linen, because his laundress
was made a princess. This was a reflection upon
the Pope's sister, who, before the promotion of her
brother, was in those mean circumstances that Pasquin represented her. As this pasquinade made a
great noise in Rome, the pope offered a considerable
sum of money to any person that should discover
the author of it. The author relying upon his holiness's generosity, as also on some private overtures
which he had received from him, made the discovery
himself; upon which the pope gave him the reward
he had promised, but at the same time, to disable
the satirist for the future, ordered his tongue to be
cut out, and both his hands to be chopped off.
Aretine is too trite an instance. Everyone knows
that all the kings of Europe were his tributaries.
Nay, there is a letter of his extant, in which he makes
his boasts that he had laid the Sophy of Persia under
contribution.

Though, in the various examples which I have
here drawn together, these several great men behaved themselves very differently towards the wits
of the age who had reproached them; they all of
them plainly showed that they were very sensible of
their reproaches, and consequently that they received
them as very great injuries. For my own part, I
would never trust a man that I thought was capable
of giving these secret wounds; and cannot but think
that he would hurt the person whose reputation he
thus assaults, in his body or in his fortune, could he
do it with the same security. There is, indeed,
something very barbarous and inhuman in the ordinary scribblers of lampoons. An innocent young
lady shall be exposed for an unhappy feature; a
father of a family turned to ridicule for some
domestic calamity; a wife made uneasy all her life

for a misinterpreted word or action; nay, a good, a temperate, and a just man shall be put out of countenance by the representation of those qualities that should do him honour. So pernicious a thing is wit, when it is not tempered with virtue and humanity.

I have indeed heard of heedless, inconsiderate writers, that without any malice have sacrificed the reputation of their friends and acquaintance to a certain levity of temper, and a silly ambition of distinguishing themselves by a spirit of raillery and satire: as if it were not infinitely more honourable to be a good-natured man than a wit. Where there is this little petulant humour in an author, he is often very mischievous without designing to be so. For which reason, I always lay it down as a rule, that an indiscreet man is more hurtful than an ill-natured one; for as the latter will only attack his enemies, and those he wishes ill to; the other injures indifferently both friends and foes. I cannot forbear on this occasion transcribing a fable out of Sir Roger l'Estrange, which accidentally lies before me. "A company of waggish boys were watching of frogs at the side of a pond, and still as any of them put up their heads, they would be pelting them down again with stones. 'Children,' says one of the frogs, 'you never consider, that though this may be play to you, it is death to us.'"

As this week is in a manner set apart and dedicated to serious thoughts, I shall indulge myself in such speculations as may not be altogether unsuitable to the season; and in the meantime, as the settling in ourselves a charitable frame of mind is a work very proper for the time, I have in this paper endeavoured to expose that particular breach of charity which has been generally overlooked by divines, because they are but few who can be guilty of it.

VALETUDINARIANS

Ægrescitque medendo.   VIRG. Æn. xii. 46.

And sickens by the very means of health.

THE following letter will explain itself, and needs no apology.

" SIR,

" I am one of that sickly tribe who are commonly known by the name of valetudinarians; and do confess to you, that I first contracted this ill habit of body, or rather of mind, by the study of physic. I no sooner began to peruse books of this nature, but I found my pulse was irregular; and scarce ever read the account of any disease that I did not fancy myself afflicted with. Dr Sydenham's learned treatise of fevers threw me into a lingering hectic, which hung upon me all the while I was reading that excellent piece. I then applied myself to the study of several authors who have written upon phthisical distempers, and by that means fell into a consumption; till at length, growing very fat, I was in a manner shamed out of that imagination. Not long after this I found in myself all the symptoms of the gout, except pain; but was cured of it by a treatise upon the gravel, written by a very ingenious author, who (as it is usual for physicians to convert one distemper into another) eased me of the gout by giving me the stone. I at length studied myself into a complication of distempers; but, accidentally taking into my hand that ingenious discourse written by Sanctorius, I was resolved to direct myself by a scheme of rules, which I had collected from his observations. The learned world are very well acquainted with that gentleman's invention; who, for the better carrying on his experiments, contrived a certain mathematical chair, which was so artificially hung upon springs, that it would weigh any thing as well as a pair of scales. By this means he discovered how many ounces of his food passed by perspiration, what quantity of it was turned into nourishment, and how much went away by the other channels and distributions of nature.

"Having provided myself with this chair, I used to study, eat, drink, and sleep in it; insomuch that I may be said, for these last three years, to have lived in a pair of scales. I compute myself, when I am in full health, to be precisely two hundredweight, falling short of it about a pound after a day's fast, and exceeding it as much after a very full meal; so that it is my continual employment to trim the balance between these two volatile pounds in my constitution. In my ordinary meals I fetch myself up to two hundred weight and half a pound; and if, after having dined, I find myself fall short of it, I drink so much small beer, or eat such a quantity of bread, as is sufficient to make me weight. In my greatest excesses, I do not transgress more than the other half-pound; which, for my health's sake, I do the first Monday in every month. As soon as I find myself duly poised after dinner, I walk till I have perspired five ounces and four scruples; and when I discover, by my chair, that I am so far reduced, I fall to my books, and study away three ounces more. As for the remaining parts of the pound, I keep no account of them. I do not dine and sup by the clock, but by my chair; for when that informs me my pound of food is exhausted, I conclude myself to be hungry, and lay in another with all diligence. In my days of abstinence I lose a pound and a half, and on solemn fasts am two pounds lighter than on the other days of the year.

"I allow myself, one night with another, a quarter of a pound of sleep, within a few grains more or less; and if, upon my rising, I find that I have not consumed my whole quantity, I take out the rest in my chair. Upon an exact calculation of what I expended and received the last year, which I always register in a book, I find the medium to be two hundredweight, so that I cannot discover that I am impaired one ounce in my health during a whole twelvemonth.

And yet, Sir, notwithstanding this my great care to ballast myself equally every day, and to keep my body in its proper poise, so it is, that I find myself in a sick and languishing condition. My complexion is grown very sallow, my pulse low, and my body hydropical. Let me therefore beg you, Sir, to consider me as your patient, and to give me more certain rules to walk by than those I have already observed, and you will very much oblige

" Your humble servant."

This letter puts me in mind of an Italian epitaph written on the monument of a valetudinarian : " *Stavo ben, ma per star meglio, sto qui* ": which it is impossible to translate. The fear of death often proves mortal, and sets people on methods to save their lives which infallibly destroy them. This is a reflection made by some historians, upon observing that there are many more thousands killed in a flight, than in a battle; and may be applied to those multitudes of imaginary sick persons that break their constitutions by physic, and throw themselves into the arms of death by endeavouring to escape it. This method is not only dangerous, but below the practice of a reasonable creature. To consult the preservation of life, as the only end of it—to make our health our business—to engage in no action that is not part of a regimen, or course of physic—are purposes so abject, so mean, so unworthy human nature, that a generous soul would rather die than submit to them. Besides, that a continual anxiety for life vitiates all the relishes of it, and casts a gloom over the whole face of nature; as it is impossible we should take delight in any thing that we are every moment afraid of losing.

I do not mean, by what I have here said, that I think any one to blame for taking due care of their health. On the contrary, as cheerfulness of mind, and capacity for business, are in a great measure the effects of a well-tempered constitution, a man cannot be at too much pains to cultivate and preserve it.

But this care, which we are prompted to, not only by common sense, but by duty and instinct, should never engage us in groundless fears, melancholy apprehensions, and imaginary distempers, which are natural to every man who is more anxious to live, than how to live. In short, the preservation of life should be only a secondary concern, and the direction of it our principal. If we have this frame of mind, we shall take the best means to preserve life, without being over-solicitous about the event; and shall arrive at that point of felicity which Martial has mentioned as the perfection of happiness, of neither fearing nor wishing for death.

In answer to the gentleman, who tempers his health by ounces and by scruples, and instead of complying with those natural solicitations of hunger and thirst, drowsiness, or love of exercise, governs himself by the prescriptions of his chair, I shall tell him a short fable. Jupiter, says the mythologist, to reward the piety of a certain countryman, promised to give him whatever he would ask. The countryman desired that he might have the management of the weather in his own estate. He obtained his request, and immediately distributed rain, snow, and sunshine, among his several fields, as he thought the nature of the soil required. At the end of the year, when he expected to see a more than ordinary crop, his harvest fell infinitely short of that of his neighbours. Upon which (says the fable) he desired Jupiter to take the weather again into his own hands, or that otherwise he should utterly ruin himself.

MEDITATIONS IN THE ABBEY

Pallida mors æquo pulsat pede pauperum tabernas
  Regumque turres. O beate Sexti,
Vitæ summa brevis spem nos vetat inchoare longam.
  Jam te premet nox, fabulæque manes,
Et domus exilis Plutonia.   HOR. *Od.* i. iv. 13.

With equal foot, rich friend, impartial fate
Knocks at the cottage and the palace gate;
Life's span forbids thee to extend thy cares,
And stretch thy hopes beyond thy years;
Night soon will seize, and you must quickly go
To storied ghosts, and Pluto's house below.
                         CREECH.

WHEN I am in a serious humour, I very often walk by myself in Westminster Abbey: where the gloominess of the place, and the use to which it is applied, with the solemnity of the building, and the condition of the people who lie in it, are apt to fill the mind with a kind of melancholy, or rather thoughtfulness that is not disagreeable. I yesterday passed a whole afternoon in the church-yard, the cloisters, and the church, amusing myself with the tombstones and inscriptions that I met with in those several regions of the dead. Most of them recorded nothing else of the buried person, but that he was born upon one day, and died upon another; the whole history of his life being comprehended in those two circumstances that are common to all mankind. I could not but look upon these registers of existence, whether of brass or marble, as a kind of satire upon the departed persons; who had left no other memorial of them, but that they were born, and that they died. They put me in mind of several persons mentioned in the battles of heroic poems, who have sounding names given them, for no other reason but that they may be killed, and are celebrated for nothing but being knocked on the head.

   Γλαῦκόν τε Μέδοντά τε Θερσίλοχόν τε.   HOM.

   Glaucumque, Medontaque, Thersilochumque.   VIRG.

The life of these men is finely described in holy writ by " the path of an arrow," which is immediately closed up and lost.

Upon my going into the church, I entertained myself with the digging of a grave; and saw in every shovel-full of it that was thrown up, the fragment of a bone or skull intermixed with a kind of fresh mouldering earth that some time or other had a place in the composition of a human body. Upon this I began to consider with myself what innumerable multitudes of people lay confused together under the pavement of that ancient cathedral; how men and women, friends and enemies, priests and soldiers, monks and prebendaries, were crumbled amongst one another, and blended together in the same common mass; how beauty, strength, and youth, with old age, weakness, and deformity, lay undistinguished in the same promiscuous heap of matter.

After having thus surveyed the great magazine of mortality, as it were, in the lump, I examined it more particularly by the accounts which I found on several of the monuments which are raised in every quarter of that ancient fabric. Some of them were covered with such extravagant epitaphs, that if it were possible for the dead person to be acquainted with them, he would blush at the praises which his friends have bestowed upon him. There are others so excessively modest, that they deliver the character of the person departed in Greek or Hebrew, and by that means are not understood once in a twelvemonth. In the poetical quarter, I found there were poets who had no monuments, and monuments which had no poets. I observed, indeed, that the present war has filled the church with many of these uninhabited monuments, which had been erected to the memory of persons whose bodies were perhaps buried in the plains of Blenheim, or in the bosom of the ocean.

I could not but be very much delighted with several modern epitaphs, which are written with great elegance of expression and justness of thought, and therefore do honour to the living as well as the dead. As a foreigner is very apt to conceive an idea of the ignorance or politeness of a nation from the turn of their public monuments and inscriptions, they should be submitted to the perusal of men of learning and genius before they are put in execution. Sir Cloudesley Shovel's monument has very often given me great offence. Instead of the brave rough English admiral, which was the distinguishing character of that plain gallant man, he is represented on his tomb by the figure of a beau, dressed in a long periwig, and reposing himself upon velvet cushions, under a canopy of state. The inscription is answerable to the monument; for instead of celebrating the many remarkable actions he had performed in the service of his country, it acquaints us only with the manner of his death, in which it was impossible for him to reap any honour. The Dutch, whom we are apt to despise for want of genius, show an infinitely greater taste of antiquity and politeness in their buildings and works of this nature than what we meet with in those of our own country. The monuments of their admirals, which have been erected at the public expense, represent them like themselves, and are adorned with rostral crowns and naval ornaments, with beautiful festoons of sea-weed, shells, and coral.

But to return to our subject. I have left the repository of our English kings for the contemplation of another day, when I shall find my mind disposed for so serious an amusement. I know that entertainments of this nature are apt to raise dark and dismal thoughts in timorous minds and gloomy imaginations; but for my own part, though I am always serious, I do not know what it is to be melancholy; and can therefore take a view of nature in her deep and solemn scenes with the same pleasure as in her most gay and delightful ones. By this means I can improve myself with those objects which others consider with terror. When I look upon the tombs of the great, every motion of envy dies in me; when I read the epitaphs

of the beautiful, every inordinate desire goes out;
when I meet with the grief of parents upon a tomb-
stone, my heart melts with compassion; when I see
the tomb of the parents themselves, I consider the
vanity of grieving for those whom we must quickly
follow.   When I see kings lying by those who deposed
them, when I consider rival wits placed side by side,
or the holy men that divided the world with their contests and disputes, I reflect with sorrow and astonishment on the little competitions, factions, and debates
of mankind.   When I read the several dates of the
tombs, of some that died yesterday, and some six
hundred years ago, I consider that great day when
we shall all of us be contemporaries, and make our
appearance together.

THE SCOPE OF SATIRE

Parcit
Cognatis maculis similis fera.   JUV. *Sat.* xv. 159.

From spotted skins the leopard does refrain.   TATE.

THE club of which I am a member, is very luckily
composed of such persons as are engaged in different
ways of life, and deputed as it were out of the most
conspicuous classes of mankind.   By this means I
am furnished with the greatest variety of hints and
materials, and know every thing that passes in the
different quarters and divisions, not only of this
great city, but of the whole kingdom.   My readers
too have the satisfaction to find that there is no rank
or degree among them who have not their representative in this club, and that there is always somebody
present who will take care of their respective interests,
that nothing may be written or published to the
prejudice or infringement of their just rights and
privileges.

I last night sat very late in company with this

select body of friends, who entertained me with several remarks which they and others had made upon these my speculations, as also with the various success which they had met with among their several ranks and degrees of readers. Will Honeycomb told me, in the softest manner he could, that there were some ladies (but for your comfort, says Will, they are not those of the most wit) that were offended at the liberties I had taken with the opera and the puppet-show; that some of them were likewise very much surprised, that I should think such serious points as the dress and equipage of persons of quality proper subjects for raillery.

He was going on, when Sir Andrew Freeport took him up short, and told him, that the papers he hinted at, had done great good in the city, and that all their wives and daughters were the better for them; and farther added, that the whole city thought themselves very much obliged to me for declaring my generous intentions to scourge vice and folly as they appear in a multitude, without condescending to be a publisher of particular intrigues. " In short," says Sir Andrew, " if you avoid that foolish beaten road of falling upon aldermen and citizens, and employ your pen upon the vanity and luxury of courts, your paper must needs be of general use."

Upon this, my friend the Templar told Sir Andrew, that he wondered to hear a man of his sense talk after that manner; that the city had always been the province for satire; and that the wits of king Charles's time jested upon nothing else during his whole reign. He then showed, by the examples of Horace, Juvenal, Boileau, and the best writers of every age, that the follies of the stage and court had never been accounted too sacred for ridicule, how great soever the persons might be that patronised them. " But after all," says he, " I think your raillery has made too great an excursion, in attacking several persons of the inns of court; and I do not believe you can show me any precedent for your behaviour in that particular."

My good friend Sir Roger de Coverley, who had said nothing all this while, began his speech with a pish! and told us, that he wondered to see so many men of sense so very serious upon fooleries. "Let our good friend," says he, "attack every one that deserves it; I would only advise you, Mr Spectator," applying himself to me, "to take care how you meddle with country 'squires. They are the ornaments of the English nation; men of good heads and sound bodies! and, let me tell you, some of them take it ill of you, that you mention fox-hunters with so little respect."

Captain Sentry spoke very sparingly on this occasion. What he said was only to commend my prudence in not touching upon the army, and advised me to continue to act discreetly in that point.

By this time I found every subject of my speculations was taken away from me, by one or other of the club: and began to think myself in the condition of the good man that had one wife who took a dislike to his grey hair, and another to his black, till by their picking out what each of them had an aversion to, they left his head altogether bald and naked.

While I was thus musing with myself, my worthy friend the clergyman, who, very luckily for me, was at the club that night, undertook my cause. He told us, that he wondered any order of persons should think themselves too considerable to be advised. That it was not quality, but innocence, which exempted men from reproof. That vice and folly ought to be attacked wherever they could be met with, and especially when they were placed in high and conspicuous stations of life. He farther added, that my paper would only serve to aggravate the pains of poverty, if it chiefly exposed those who are already depressed, and in some measure turned into ridicule, by the meanness of their conditions and circumstances. He afterward proceeded to take notice of the great use this paper might be of to the public, by reprehending those vices which are too trivial for the chastisement of the law, and too fantastical for the cognizance of the pulpit. He then advised me to prosecute my undertaking with cheerfulness, and assured me, that whoever might be displeased with me, I should be approved by all those whose praises do honour to the persons on whom they are bestowed.

The whole club pay a particular deference to the discourse of this gentleman, and are drawn into what he says as much by the candid ingenuous manner with which he delivers himself, as by the strength of argument and force of reason which he makes use of. Will Honeycomb immediately agreed, that what he had said was right; and that, for his part, he would not insist upon the quarter which he had demanded for the ladies. Sir Andrew gave up the city with the same frankness. The Templar would not stand out, and was followed by Sir Roger and the Captain; who all agreed that I should be at liberty to carry the war into what quarter I pleased; provided I continued to combat with criminals in a body, and to assault the vice without hurting the person.

This debate, which was held for the good of mankind, put me in mind of that which the Roman triumvirate were formerly engaged in for their destruction. Every man at first stood hard for his friend, till they found that by this means they should spoil their proscription; and at length, making a sacrifice of all their acquaintance and relations, furnished out a very decent execution.

Having thus taken my resolutions to march on boldly in the cause of virtue and good sense, and to annoy their adversaries in whatever degree or rank of men they may be found; I shall be deaf for the future to all the remonstrances that shall be made to me on this account. If Punch grows extravagant, I shall reprimand him very freely. If the stage becomes a nursery of folly and impertinence, I shall not be afraid to animadvert upon it. In short, if I meet with any thing in city, court, or country, that shocks modesty or good manners, I shall use my utmost endeavours to make an example of it. I must, however, entreat every particular person, who does me the honour to be a reader of this paper, never to think himself, or any one of his friends or enemies, aimed at in what is said; for I promise him, never to draw a faulty character which does not fit at least a thousand people; or to publish a single paper, that is not written in the spirit of benevolence, and with a love of mankind.

A LADY'S LIBRARY

Non illa colo calathisve Minervæ
Femineas assueta manus.   VIRG. *Æn.* vii. 805.

Unbred to spinning, in the loom unskill'd.   DRYDEN.

SOME months ago, my friend Sir Roger, being in the country, enclosed a letter to me, directed to a certain lady whom I shall here call by the name of Leonora—and as it contained matters of consequence, desired me to deliver it to her with my own hand. Accordingly I waited upon her ladyship pretty early in the morning, and was desired by her woman to walk into her lady's library, till such time as she was in readiness to receive me. The very sound of a lady's library gave me a great curiosity to see it; and as it was some time before the lady came to me, I had an opportunity of turning over a great many of her books, which were ranged together in a very beautiful order. At the end of the folios (which were finely bound and gilt) were great jars of china, placed one above another in a very noble piece of architecture. The quartos were separated from the octavos by a pile of smaller vessels, which rose in a delightful pyramid. The octavos were bounded by tea-dishes of all shapes, colours, and sizes, which were so disposed on a wooden frame, that they looked like one continued pillar indented with the finest strokes of sculpture, and stained with the greatest variety of dyes. That part of the library which was designed for the reception of plays

and pamphlets, and other loose papers, was enclosed
in a kind of square, consisting of one of the prettiest
grotesque works that I ever saw, and made up of
scaramouches, lions, monkeys, mandarins, trees,
shells, and a thousand other odd figures in china-
ware. In the midst of the room was a little japan
table, with a quire of gilt paper upon it, and on the
paper a silver snuff-box made in the shape of a little
book. I found there were several other counterfeit
books upon the upper shelves, which were carved in
wood, and served only to fill up the numbers like fagots
in the muster of a regiment. I was wonderfully pleased
with such a mixed kind of furniture, as seemed very
suitable both to the lady and the scholar, and did not
know at first whether I should fancy myself in a grotto
or in a library.

Upon my looking into the books, I found there
were some few which the lady had bought for her
own use, but that most of them had been got together, either because she had heard them praised, or
because she had seen the authors of them. Among
several that I examined, I very well remember these
that follow:

Ogleby's Virgil.
Dryden's Juvenal.
Cassandra.
Cleopatra.
Astræa.
Sir Isaac Newton's Works.
The Grand Cyrus; with a pin stuck in one of the
    middle leaves.
Pembroke's Arcadia.
Locke on Human Understanding, with a paper of
    patches in it.
A Spelling-book.
A Dictionary for the explanation of hard words.
Sherlock upon Death.
The fifteen Comforts of Matrimony.
Sir William Temple's Essays.

Father Malebranche's Search after Truth, translated into English.

A book of Novels.

The Academy of Compliments.

Culpepper's Midwifery.

The Ladies' Calling.

Tales in Verse by Mr Durfey: bound in red leather, gilt on the back, and doubled down in several places.

All the Classic Authors in Wood.

A set of Elzevirs by the same Hand.

Clelia: which opened of itself in the place that describes two lovers in a bower.

Baker's Chronicle.

Advice to a Daughter.

The New Atalantis, with a Key to it.

Mr Steele's Christian Hero.

A Prayer-book: with a bottle of Hungary Water by the side of it.

Dr Sacheverell's Speech.

Fielding's Trial.

Seneca's Morals.

Taylor's Holy Living and Dying.

La Ferte's Instructions for Country Dances.

I was taking a catalogue in my pocket-book of these and several other authors, when Leonora entered, and upon my presenting her with a letter from the knight, told me, with an unspeakable grace, that she hoped Sir Roger was in good health; I answered yes, for I hate long speeches, and after a bow or two retired.

Leonora was formerly a celebrated beauty, and is still a very lovely woman. She has been a widow for two or three years, and being unfortunate in her first marriage, has taken a resolution never to venture upon a second. She has no children to take care of, and leaves the management of her estate to my good friend Sir Roger. But as the mind naturally sinks into a kind of lethargy, and falls asleep, that is not agitated

by some favourite pleasures and pursuits, Leonora has
turned all the passion of her sex into a love of books
and retirement. She converses chiefly with men (as
she has often said herself), but it is only in their writings, and admits of very few male visitants, except my
friend Sir Roger, whom she hears with great pleasure,
and without scandal. As her reading has lain very
much among romances, it has given her a very particular turn of thinking, and discovers itself even in her
house, her gardens, and her furniture. Sir Roger has
entertained me an hour together with a description of
her country-seat, which is situated in a kind of wilderness, about a hundred miles distant from London, and
looks like a little enchanted palace. The rocks about
her are shaped into artificial grottos covered with
woodbines and jessamines. The woods are cut into
shady walks, twisted into bowers, and filled with cages
of turtles. The springs are made to run among pebbles,
and by that means taught to murmur very agreeably.
They are likewise collected into a beautiful lake that
is inhabited by a couple of swans, and empties itself
by a little rivulet which runs through a green meadow,
and is known in the family by the name of The Purling
Stream. The knight likewise tells me, that this lady
preserves her game better than any of the gentlemen
in the country, not (says Sir Roger) that she sets so
great a value upon her partridges and pheasants, as
upon her larks and nightingales. For she says that
every bird which is killed in her ground, will spoil a
concert, and that she shall certainly miss him the next
year.

When I think how oddly this lady is improved by
learning, I look upon her with a mixture of admiration
and pity. Amidst these innocent entertainments which
she has formed to herself, how much more valuable
does she appear than those of her sex, who employ
themselves in diversions that are less reasonable,
though more in fashion? What improvements would
a woman have made, who is so susceptible of impressions from what she reads, had she been guided by

such books as have a tendency to enlighten the understanding and rectify the passions, as well as to those which are of little more use than to divert the imagination?

But the manner of a lady's employing herself usefully in reading, shall be the subject of another paper, in which I design to recommend such particular books as may be proper for the improvement of the sex. And as this is a subject of very nice nature, I shall desire my correspondents to give me their thoughts upon it.

STAGE MURDER

Tu, quid ego et populus mecum desideret, audi.
HOR. *Ars. Poet.* ver. 123.

Now hear what every auditor expects. ROSCOMMON.

AMONG the several artifices which are put in practice by the poets to fill the minds of an audience with terror, the first place is due to thunder and lightning, which are often made use of at the descending of a god, or the rising of a ghost, at the vanishing of a devil, or at the death of a tyrant. I have known a bell introduced into several tragedies with good effect; and have seen the whole assembly in a very great alarm all the while it has been ringing. But there is nothing which delights and terrifies our English theatre so much as a ghost, especially when he appears in a bloody shirt. A spectre has very often saved a play, though he has done nothing but stalked across the stage, or rose through a cleft of it, and sunk again without speaking one word. There may be a proper season for these several terrors; and when they only come in as aids and assistances to the poet, they are not only to be excused, but to be applauded. Thus the sounding of the clock in *Venice Preserved* makes the hearts of the whole audience

quake; and conveys a stronger terror to the mind
than it is possible for words to do. The appearance
of the ghost in *Hamlet* is a master-piece in its kind,
and wrought up with all the circumstances that can
create either attention or horror. The mind of the
reader is wonderfully prepared for his reception by
the discourses that precede it. His dumb behaviour
at his first entrance strikes the imagination very
strongly; but every time he enters, he is still more
terrifying. Who can read the speech with which
young Hamlet accosts him without trembling?

> HOR.   Look, my lord, it comes!
> HAM.   Angels and ministers of grace defend us!
> Be thou a spirit of health, or goblin damn'd:
> Bring with thee airs from heav'n, or blasts from hell,
> Be thy events wicked or charitable;
> Thou com'st in such a questionable shape
> That I will speak to thee. I'll call thee Hamlet,
> King, Father, Royal Dane. Oh! answer me.
> Let me not burst in ignorance; but tell
> Why thy canoniz'd bones, hearsed in death,
> Have burst their cerements? Why the sepulchre
> Wherein we saw thee quietly inurn'd,
> Hath op'd his ponderous and marble jaws
> To cast thee up again? What may this mean?
> That thou, dead corse, again in complete steel
> Revisit'st thus the glimpses of the moon,
> Making night hideous?

I do not therefore find fault with the artifices above
mentioned, when they are introduced with skill, and
accompanied by proportionable sentiments and expressions in the writing.

For the moving of pity, our principal machine is
the handkerchief; and indeed, in our common tragedies, we should not know very often that the persons
are in distress by any thing they say, if they did not
from time to time apply their handkerchiefs to their
eyes. Far be it from me to think of banishing this
instrument of sorrow from the stage; I know a
tragedy could not subsist without it; all that I would

contend for, is to keep it from being misapplied. In a word, I would have the actor's tongue sympathise with his eyes.

A disconsolate mother, with a child in her hand, has frequently drawn compassion from the audience, and has therefore gained a place in several tragedies. A modern writer, that observed how this had took in other plays, being resolved to double the distress, and melt his audience twice as much as those before him had done, brought a princess upon the stage with a little boy in one hand, and a girl in the other. This too had a very good effect. A third poet being resolved to outwrite all his predecessors, a few years ago introduced three children with great success: and as I am informed, a young gentleman, who is fully determined to break the most obdurate hearts, has a tragedy by him, where the first person that appears upon the stage is an afflicted widow in her mourning weeds, with half a dozen fatherless children attending her, like those that usually hang about the figure of Charity. Thus several incidents that are beautiful in a good writer, become ridiculous by falling into the hands of a bad one.

But among all our methods of moving pity or terror, there is none so absurd and barbarous, and which more exposes us to the contempt and ridicule of our neighbours, than that dreadful butchering of one another, which is so very frequent upon the English stage. To delight in seeing men stabbed, poisoned, racked, or impaled, is certainly the sign of a cruel temper: and as this is often practised before the British audience, several French critics, who think these are grateful spectacles to us, take occasion from them to represent us as a people that delight in blood. It is indeed very odd, to see our stage strewed with carcases in the last scenes of a tragedy, and to observe in the wardrobe of the playhouse several daggers, poniards, wheels, bowls for poison, and many other instruments of death. Murders and executions are always transacted behind the scenes in the French

theatre; which in general is very agreeable to the
manners of a polite and civilised people: but as there
are no exceptions to this rule on the French stage, it
leads them into absurdities almost as ridiculous as
that which falls under our present censure. I remember in the famous play of *Corneille*, written upon the
subject of the Horatii and Curiatii; the fierce young
hero who had overcome the Curiatii one after another
(instead of being congratulated by his sister for his
victory, being upbraided by her for having slain her
lover), in the height of his passion and resentment
kills her. If any thing could extenuate so brutal an
action, it would be the doing of it on a sudden, before
the sentiments of nature, reason, or manhood, could
take place in him. However, to avoid public blood-
shed, as soon as his passion is wrought to its height,
he follows his sister the whole length of the stage,
and forbears killing her till they are both withdrawn
behind the scenes. I must confess, had he murdered
her before the audience, the indecency might have
been greater; but as it is, it appears very unnatural,
and looks like killing in cold blood. To give my
opinion upon this case, the fact ought not to have been
represented, but to have been told, if there was any
occasion for it.

It may not be unacceptable to the reader to see how
Sophocles has conducted a tragedy under the like
delicate circumstances. Orestes was under the same
condition with Hamlet in Shakspeare, his mother
having murdered his father, and taken possession of
his kingdom in conspiracy with her adulterer. That
young prince, therefore, being determined to revenge
his father's death upon those who filled his throne,
conveys himself by a beautiful stratagem into his
mother's apartment, with a resolution to kill her.
But because such a spectacle would have been too
shocking to the audience, this dreadful resolution is
executed behind the scenes: the mother is heard
calling out to her son for mercy; and the son answering
her, that she showed no mercy to his father; after

which she shrieks out that she is wounded, and by
what follows we find that she is slain. I do not
remember that in any of our plays there are speeches
made behind the scenes, though there are other
instances of this nature to be met with in those of
the ancients: and I believe my reader will agree with
me, that there is something infinitely more affecting
in this dreadful dialogue between the mother and her
son behind the scenes, than could have been in any
thing transacted before the audience. Orestes immediately after meets the usurper at the entrance of
his palace; and by a very happy thought of the poet,
avoids killing him before the audience, by telling him
that he should live some time in his present bitterness
of soul before he would dispatch him, and by ordering
him to retire into that part of the palace where he had
slain his father, whose murder he would revenge in
the very same place where it was committed. By this
means the poet observes that decency, which Horace
afterward established by a rule, of forbearing to
commit parricides or unnatural murders before the
audience.

Nec pueros coram populo Medea trucidet.
Ars. Poet. ver. 185.

Let not Medea draw her murd'ring knife,
And spill her children's blood upon the stage.
ROSCOMMON.

The French have therefore refined too much upon
Horace's rule, who never designed to banish all kinds
of death from the stage; but only such as had too
much horror in them, and which would have a better
effect upon the audience when transacted behind the
scenes. I would therefore recommend to my countrymen the practice of the ancient poets, who were very
sparing of their public executions, and rather chose
to perform them behind the scenes, if it could be done
with as great an effect upon the audience. At the
same time I must observe, that though the devoted
persons of the tragedy were seldom slain before the

audience, which has generally something ridiculous in it, their bodies were often produced after their death, which has always something melancholy or terrifying: so that the killing on the stage does not seem to have been avoided only as an indecency, but also as an improbability.

Nec pueros coram populo Medea trucidet;
Aut humana palam coquat exta nefarius Atreus;
Aut in avem Progne vertatur, Cadmus in anguem;
Quodcunque ostendis mihi sic, incredulus odi.

HOR. *Ars. Poet.* ver. 185.

Medea must not draw her murd'ring knife,
Nor Atreus there his horrid feast prepare;
Cadmus and Progne's metamorphoses,
(She to a swallow turn'd, he to a snake;)
And whatsoever contradicts my sense,
I hate to see, and never can believe.   ROSCOMMON.

I have now gone through the several dramatic inventions which are made use of by the ignorant poets to supply the place of tragedy, and by the skilful to improve it; some of which I would wish entirely rejected, and the rest to be used with caution. It would be an endless task to consider comedy in the same light, and to mention the innumerable shifts that small wits put in practice to raise a laugh. Bullock in a short coat, and Norris in a long one, seldom fail of this effect. In ordinary comedies, a broad and a narrow-brimmed hat are different characters. Sometimes the wit of the scene lies in a shoulder-belt, and sometimes in a pair of whiskers. A lover running about the stage with his head peeping out of a barrel, was thought a very good jest in King Charles the Second's time; and invented by one of the first wits of that age. But because ridicule is not so delicate as compassion, and because the objects that make us laugh are infinitely more numerous than those that make us weep, there is much greater latitude for comic than tragic artifices, and by consequence a much greater indulgence to be allowed them.

FRENCH FOPPERIES

Natio comœda est.   JUV. *Sat.* iii. 100.

The nation is a company of players.

THERE is nothing which I desire more than a safe and honourable peace, though at the same time I am very apprehensive of many ill consequences that may attend it. I do not mean in regard to our politics, but to our manners. What an inundation of ribbons and brocades will break in upon us! What peals of laughter and impertinence shall we be exposed to! For the prevention of these great evils I could heartily wish that there was an act of parliament for prohibiting the importation of French fopperies.

The female inhabitants of our island have already received very strong impressions from this ludicrous nation, though by the length of the war (as there is no evil which has not some good attending it) they are pretty well worn out and forgotten. I remember the time when some of our well-bred countrywomen kept their valet de chambre, because, forsooth, a man was much more handy about them than one of their own sex. I myself have seen one of these male Abigails tripping about the room with a looking-glass in his hand, and combing his lady's hair a whole morning together.

About the time that several of our sex were taken into this kind of service, the ladies likewise brought up the fashion of receiving visits in their beds. It was then looked upon as a piece of ill-breeding for a woman to refuse to see a man because she was not stirring; and a porter would have been thought unfit for his place, that could have made so awkward an excuse. As I love to see every thing that is new, I once prevailed upon my friend Will Honeycomb to carry me along with him to one of these travelled ladies, desiring him, at the same time, to present me as a foreigner who could not speak English, that so

I might not be obliged to bear a part in the discourse. The lady, though willing to appear undrest, had put on her best looks, and painted herself for our reception. Her hair appeared in a very nice disorder, as the nightgown which was thrown upon her shoulders was ruffled with great care. For my part, I am so shocked with every thing which looks immodest in the fair sex, that I could not forbear taking off my eye from her when she moved in bed, and was in the greatest confusion imaginable every time she stirred a leg or an arm. As the coquettes who introduced this custom grew old they left it off by degrees, well knowing that a woman of threescore may kick and tumble her heart out without making any impression.

Sempronia is at present the most professed admirer of the French nation, but is so modest as to admit her visitants no farther than her toilet. It is a very odd sight that beautiful creature makes, when she is talking politics with her tresses flowing about her shoulders, and examining that face in the glass which does such execution upon all the male standers-by. How prettily does she divide her discourse between her woman and her visitants! What sprightly transitions does she make from an opera or a sermon to an ivory comb or a pincushion! How have I been pleased to see her interrupted in an account of her travels, by a message to her footman; and holding her tongue in the midst of a moral reflection, by applying the tip of it to a patch!

There is nothing which exposes a woman to greater dangers, than that gaiety and airiness of temper which are natural to most of the sex. It should be therefore the concern of every wise and virtuous woman to keep this sprightliness from degenerating into levity. On the contrary, the whole discourse and behaviour of the French is to make the sex more fantastical, or (as they are pleased to term it) more awakened, than is consistent either with virtue or discretion. To speak loud in public assemblies, to let everyone hear you talk of things that should only be mentioned in private or in whisper, are looked upon as parts of a refined education. At the same time a blush is unfashionable, and silence more ill-bred than any thing that can be spoken. In short, discretion and modesty, which in all other ages and countries have been regarded as the greatest ornaments of the fair sex, are considered as the ingredients of a narrow conversation, and family behaviour.

Some years ago I was at the tragedy of *Macbeth*, and unfortunately placed myself under a woman of quality that is since dead, who, as I found by the noise she made, was newly returned from France. A little before the rising of the curtain, she broke out into a loud soliloquy, "When will the dear witches enter?" and immediately upon their first appearance, asked a lady that sat three boxes from her on her right hand, if those witches were not charming creatures. A little after, as Betterton was in one of the finest speeches of the play, she shook her fan at another lady who sat as far on her left hand, and told her with a whisper that might be heard all over the pit, "We must not expect to see Balloon to-night." Not long after, calling out to a young baronet by his name, who sat three seats before me, she asked him whether Macbeth's wife was still alive ; and before he could give an answer, fell a talking of the ghost of Banquo. She had by this time formed a little audience to herself, and fixed the attention of all about her. But as I had a mind to hear the play, I got out of the sphere of her impertinence, and planted myself in one of the remotest corners of the pit.

This pretty childishness of behaviour is one of the most refined parts of coquetry, and is not to be attained in perfection by ladies that do not travel for their improvement. A natural and unconstrained behaviour has something in it so agreeable, that it is no wonder to see people endeavouring after it. But at the same time it is so very hard to hit, when it is not born with us, that people often make themselves ridiculous in attempting it.

A very ingenious French author tells us, that the ladies of the court of France in his time thought it ill-breeding, and a kind of female pedantry, to pronounce a hard word right; for which reason they took frequent occasion to use hard words, that they might show a politeness in murdering them. He farther adds, that a lady of some quality at court having accidentally made use of a hard word in a proper place, and pronounced it right, the whole assembly was out of countenance for her.

I must however be so just to own, that there are many ladies who have travelled several thousands of miles without being the worse for it, and have brought home with them all the modesty, discretion, and good sense that they went abroad with. As, on the contrary, there are great numbers of travelled ladies who have lived all their days within the smoke of London. I have known a woman that never was out of the parish of St James's, betray as many foreign fopperies in her carriage, as she could have gleaned in half the countries of Europe.

ON FRIENDSHIP

Nos duo turba sumus.   OVID. *Met.* i. 355.

We two are a multitude.

ONE would think that the larger the company is in which we are engaged, the greater variety of thoughts and subjects would be started in discourse; but instead of this, we find that conversation is never so much straitened and confined as in numerous assemblies. When a multitude meet together on any subject of discourse, their debates are taken up chiefly with forms and general positions; nay, if we come into a more contracted assembly of men and women, the talk generally runs upon the weather, fashion, news,

and the like public topics. In proportion as conversation gets into clubs and knots of friends, it descends
into particulars, and grows more free and communica-
tive: but the most open, instructive, and unreserved
discourse, is that which passes between two persons
who are familiar and intimate friends. On these occasions, a man gives a loose to every passion and every
thought that is uppermost, discovers his most retired
opinions of persons and things, tries the beauty and
strength of his sentiments, and exposes his whole soul
to the examination of his friend.

Tully was the first who observed, that friendship
improves happiness and abates misery, by the doubling
of our joy, and dividing of our grief; a thought in which
he hath been followed by all the essayers upon friendship that have written since his time. Sir Francis
Bacon has finely described other advantages, or, as he
calls them, fruits of friendship; and, indeed, there is
no subject of morality which has been better handled
and more exhausted than this. Among the several
fine things which have been spoken of it, I shall beg
leave to quote some out of a very ancient author,
whose book would be regarded by our modern wits as
one of the most shining tracts of morality that is extant, if it appeared under the name of a Confucius, or of
any celebrated Grecian philosopher: I mean the little
apocryphal treatise, entitled The Wisdom of the Son
of Sirach. How finely has he described the art of
making friends by an obliging and affable behaviour!—
and laid down that precept, which a late excellent
author has delivered as his own, That we should have
many well-wishers, but few friends. "Sweet language
will multiply friends; and a fair-speaking tongue will
increase kind greetings. Be in peace with many, nevertheless have but one counsellor of a thousand." With
what prudence does he caution us in the choice of our
friends! And with what strokes of nature (I could
almost say of humour) has he described the behaviour
of a treacherous and self-interested friend! "If thou
wouldst get a friend, prove him first, and be not hasty

to credit him: for some man is a friend for his own occasion, and will not abide in the day of thy trouble. And there is a friend, who being turned to enmity and strife, will discover thy reproach." Again, "Some friend is a companion at the table, and will not continue in the day of thy affliction: but in thy prosperity he will be as thyself, and will be bold over thy servants. If thou be brought low he will be against thee, and hide himself from thy face." What can be more strong and pointed than the following verse? "Separate thyself from thine enemies, and take heed of thy friends." In the next words he particularizes one of those fruits of friendship which is described at length by the two famous authors above mentioned, and falls into a general eulogium of friendship, which is very just as well as very sublime. "A faithful friend is a strong defence; and he that hath found such a one hath found a treasure. Nothing doth countervail a faithful friend, and his excellency is invaluable. A faithful friend is the medicine of life; and they that fear the Lord shall find him. Whoso feareth the Lord shall direct his friendship aright; for as he is, so shall his neighbour (that is his friend) be also." I do not remember to have met with any saying that has pleased me more than that of a friend's being the medicine of life, to express the efficacy of friendship in healing the pains and anguish which naturally cleave to our existence in this world; and am wonderfully pleased with the turn in the last sentence, that a virtuous man shall as a blessing meet with a friend who is as virtuous as himself. There is another saying in the same author, which would have been very much admired in a heathen writer: "Forsake not an old friend, for the new is not comparable to him: a new friend is as new wine; when it is old thou shalt drink it with pleasure." With what strength of allusion, and force of thought, has he described the breaches and violations of friendship?—"Whoso casteth a stone at the birds frayeth them away; and he that upbraideth

his friend, breaketh friendship.   Though thou drawest
a sword at a friend, yet despair not, for there may be
a returning to favour.   If thou hast opened thy mouth
against thy friend, fear not, for there may be a reconciliation ; except for upbraiding, or pride, or disclosing
of secrets, or a treacherous wound; for, for these
things every friend will depart."   We may observe in
this and several other precepts in this author, those
little familiar instances and illustrations which are so
much admired in the moral writings of Horace and
Epictetus.   There are very beautiful instances of this
nature in the following passages, which are likewise
written on the same subject: "Whoso discovereth
secrets loseth his credit, and shall never find a friend
to his mind.   Love thy friend, and be faithful to him;
but if thou bewrayeth his secret, follow no more after
him : for as a man hath destroyed his enemy, so hast
thou lost the love of thy friend; as one that letteth a
bird go out of his hand, so hast thou let thy friend go,
and shall not get him again: follow after him no more,
for he is too far off; he is as a roe escaped out of the
snare.   As for a wound it may be bound up, and after
reviling there may be a reconciliation; but he that
bewrayeth secrets is without hope."

Among the several qualifications of a good friend,
this wise man has very justly singled out constancy
and faithfulness, as the principal: to these, others
have added virtue, knowledge, discretion, equality in
age and fortune, and, as Cicero calls it, *Morum comitas*,
"a pleasantness of temper."   If I were to give my
opinion upon such an exhausted subject, I should join
to these other qualifications, a certain equability or
evenness of behaviour.   A man often contracts a friendship with one whom perhaps he does not find out till
after a year's conversation; when on a sudden some
latent ill-humour breaks out upon him, which he never
discovered or suspected at his first entering into an
intimacy with him.   There are several persons who in
some certain periods of their lives are inexpressibly

agreeable, and in others as odious and detestable. Martial has given us a very pretty picture of one of this species in the following epigram:

> Difficilis, facilis, jucundus, acerbus es idem,
> Nec tecum possum vivere, nec sine te. *Epig.* xii. 47.

> In all thy humours, whether grave or mellow,
> Thou'rt such a touchy, testy, pleasant fellow;
> Hast so much wit, and mirth, and spleen about thee,
> There is no living with thee, nor without thee.

It is very unlucky for a man to be entangled in a friendship with one, who, by these changes and vicissitudes of humour, is sometimes amiable and sometimes odious: and as most men are at some times in admirable frame and disposition of mind, it should be one of the greatest tasks of wisdom to keep ourselves well when we are so, and never to go out of that which is the agreeable part of our character.

THE BALLAD OF CHEVY-CHASE (I)

> Interdum vulgus rectum videt.   HOR. *Ep.* i. ii. 63.
> Sometimes the vulgar see and judge aright.

WHEN I travelled, I took a particular delight in hearing the songs and fables that are come from father to son, and are most in vogue among the common people of the countries through which I passed; for it is impossible that any thing should be universally tasted and approved by a multitude, though they are only the rabble of a nation, which hath not in it some peculiar aptness to please and gratify the mind of man. Human nature is the same in all reasonable creatures; and whatever falls in with it, will meet with admirers amongst readers of all qualities and conditions. Moliere, as we are told by Monsieur Boileau, used to read all his comedies to an old woman who was his housekeeper,

as she sat with him at her work by the chimney-corner;
and could foretell the success of his play in the theatre,
from the reception it met at his fire-side—for he tells
us the audience always followed the old woman, and
never failed to laugh in the same place.

I know nothing which more shows the essential
and inherent perfection of simplicity of thought, above
that which I call the Gothic manner in writing, than
this—that the first pleases all kinds of palates, and
the latter only such as have formed to themselves a
wrong artificial taste upon little fanciful authors and
writers of epigram.   Homer, Virgil, or Milton, so far
as the language of their poems is understood, will
please a reader of plain common sense, who would
neither relish nor comprehend an epigram of Martial,
or a poem of Cowley; so, on the contrary, an ordinary
song or ballad that is the delight of the common
people, cannot fail to please all such readers as are
not unqualified for the entertainment by their affectation or ignorance; and the reason is plain—because
the same paintings of nature which recommend it to
the most ordinary reader will appear beautiful to the
most refined.

The old song of Chevy-Chase is the favourite ballad
of the common people of England; and Ben Jonson
used to say, he had rather have been the author of it
than of all his works.   Sir Philip Sidney, in his discourse of Poetry, speaks of it in the following words:
"I never heard the old song of Percy and Douglas,
that I found not my heart more moved than with a
trumpet: and yet it is sung by some blind crowder
with no rougher voice than rude style; which being
so evil apparelled in the dust and cobweb of that un-
civil age, what would it work trimmed in the gorgeous
eloquence of Pindar?"   For my own part, I am so
professed an admirer of this antiquated song, that I
shall give my reader a critique upon it, without any
farther apology for so doing.

The greatest modern critics have laid it down as a
rule, That an heroic poem should be founded upon

some important precept of morality, adapted to the constitution of the country in which the poet writes. Homer and Virgil have formed their plans in this view. As Greece was a collection of many governments who suffered very much among themselves, and gave the Persian emperor, who was their common enemy, many advantages over them by their mutual jealousies and animosities, Homer, in order to establish among them a union which was so necessary for their safety, grounds his poem upon the discords of the several Grecian princes who were engaged in a confederacy against an Asiatic prince, and the several advantages which the enemy gained by such discords. At the time the poem we are now treating of was written, the dissensions of the barons, who were then so many petty princes, ran very high, whether they quarrelled among themselves, or with their neighbours, and produced unspeakable calamities to the country. The poet, to deter men from such unnatural contentions, describes a bloody battle and dreadful scene of death, occasioned by the mutual feuds which reigned in the families of an English and Scotch nobleman. That he designed this for the instruction of his poem, we may learn from his four last lines, in which, after the example of the modern tragedians, he draws from it a precept for the benefit of his readers:

> God save the king, and bless the land
> In plenty, joy, and peace;
> And grant henceforth that foul debate
> 'Twixt noblemen may cease.

The next point observed by the greatest heroic poets, hath been to celebrate persons and actions which do honour to their country: thus Virgil's hero was the founder of Rome, Homer's a prince of Greece; and for this reason Valerius Flaccus and Statius, who were both Romans, might be justly derided for having chosen the expedition of the Golden Fleece, and the Wars of Thebes, for the subjects of their epic writings.

4—2

The poet before us has not only found out a hero in his own country, but raises the reputation of it by several incidents.   The English are the first who take the field, and the last who quit it.   The English bring only fifteen hundred to the battle; the Scotch two thousand.   The English keep the field with fifty-three; the Scotch retire with fifty-five: all the rest on each side being slain in battle.   But the most remarkable circumstance of this kind is the different manner in which the Scotch and English kings receive the news of this fight, and of the great men's deaths who commanded in it:

> This news was brought to Edinburgh,
>   Where Scotland's king did reign,
> That brave Earl Douglas suddenly
>   Was with an arrow slain.
>
> O heavy news, King James did say,
>   Scotland can witness be,
> I have not any captain more
>   Of such account as he.
>
> Like tidings to King Henry came
>   Within as short a space,
> That Percy of Northumberland
>   Was slain in Chevy-Chace.
>
> Now God be with him, said our king,
>   Sith 'twill no better be,
> I trust I have within my realm
>   Five hundred good as he.
>
> Yet shall not Scot nor Scotland say,
>   But I will vengeance take,
> And be revenged on them all
>   For brave Lord Percy's sake.
>
> This vow full well the king perform'd
>   After on Humble-down,
> In one day fifty knights were slain,
>   With lords of great renown.
>
> And of the rest of small account
>   Did many thousands die, &c.

At the same time that our poet shows a laudable partiality to his countrymen, he represents the Scots after a manner not unbecoming so bold and brave a people:

> Earl Douglas on a milk-white steed,
>   Most like a baron bold,
> Rode foremost of the company,
>   Whose armour shone like gold.

His sentiments and actions are every way suitable to a hero. One of us two, says he, must die: I am an earl as well as yourself, so that you can have no pretence for refusing the combat: however, says he, it is pity, and indeed would be a sin, that so many innocent men should perish for our sakes; rather let you and I end our quarrel in a single fight:

> Ere thus I will out-braved be,
>   One of us two shall die;
> I know thee well, an earl thou art,
>   Lord Percy, so am I.
>
> But trust me, Percy, pity it were
>   And great offence to kill
> Any of these our harmless men,
>   For they have done no ill.
>
> Let thou and I the battle try,
>   And set our men aside;
> Accurst be he, Lord Percy said,
>   By whom this is deny'd.

When these brave men had distinguished themselves in the battle, and in single combat with each other, in the midst of a generous parley, full of heroic sentiments, the Scotch earl falls; and with his dying words encourages his men to revenge his death, representing to them, as the most bitter circumstance of it, that his rival saw him fall:

> With that there came an arrow keen
>   Out of an English bow,
> Which struck Earl Douglas to the heart
>   A deep and deadly blow.

> Who never spoke more words than these,
>   Fight on, my merry-men all,
> For why, my life is at an end,
>   Lord Percy sees my fall.

Merry-men, in the language of those times, is no more than a cheerful word for companions and fellow-soldiers. A passage in the eleventh book of Virgil's Æneid is very much to be admired, where Camilla, in her last agonies, instead of weeping over the wound she had received, as one might have expected from a warrior of her sex, considers only (like the hero of whom we are now speaking) how the battle should be continued after her death:

> Tum sic expirans, &c.   *Æn*. xi. 820.

> A gathering mist o'erclouds her cheerful eyes,
> And from her cheeks the rosy colour flies,
> Then turns to her, whom, of her female train,
> She trusted most, and thus she speaks with pain:
> "Acca, 'tis past! he swims before my sight,
> Inexorable Death; and claims his right.
> Bear my last words to Turnus; fly with speed,
> And bid him timely to my charge succeed:
> Repel the Trojans, and the town relieve:
> Farewell——."   DRYDEN.

Turnus did not die in so heroic a manner, though our poet seems to have had his eye upon Turnus's speech in the last verse:

> Lord Percy sees my fall.

> ——Vicisti, et victum tendere palmas
> Ausonii videre.   *Æn*. xii. 936.

> The Latin chiefs have seen me beg my life.
>   DRYDEN.

Earl Percy's lamentation over his enemy is generous, beautiful, and passionate: I must only caution the reader not to let the simplicity of the style, which one may well pardon in so old a poet, prejudice him against the greatness of the thought:

Then leaving life, Earl Percy took
   The dead man by the hand,
And said, Earl Douglas, for thy life
   Would I had lost my land.

O Christ! my very heart doth bleed
   With sorrow for thy sake;
For sure a more renowned knight
   Mischance did never take.

The beautiful line, "Taking the dead man by the
hand," will put the reader in mind of Æneas's behaviour
towards Lausus, whom he himself had slain as he
came to the rescue of his aged father:

At vero ut vultum vidit morientis, et ora,
Ora modis Anchisiades pallentia miris;
Ingemuit, miserans graviter, dextramque tetendit.
                    Æn. x. 821.

The pious prince beheld young Lausus dead;
He griev'd, he wept, then grasp'd his hand, and said, &c.
                    DRYDEN.

I shall take another opportunity to consider the
other parts of this old song.

THE BALLAD OF CHEVY-CHASE (II)

Pendent opera interrupta.   VIRG. *Æn.* iv. 88.
The works unfinished and neglected lie.

IN my last Monday's paper I gave some general
instances of those beautiful strokes which please the
reader in the old song of Chevy-Chase; I shall here,
according to my promise, be more particular, and
show that the sentiments in that ballad are extremely
natural and poetical, and full of the majestic simplicity
which we admire in the greatest of the ancient poets;
for which reason I shall quote several passages of it,
in which the thought is altogether the same with what

we meet in several passages of the Æneid; not that I would infer from thence, that the poet (whoever he was) proposed to himself any imitation of those passages, but that he was directed to keep them in general by the same kind of poetical genius, and by the same copyings after nature.

Had this old song been filled with epigrammatical turns and points of wit, it might perhaps have pleased the wrong taste of some readers; but it would never have become the delight of the common people, nor have warmed the heart of Sir Philip Sidney like the sound of a trumpet; it is only nature that can have this effect, and please those tastes which are the most unprejudiced, or the most refined. I must, however, beg leave to dissent from so great an authority as that of Sir Philip Sidney, in the judgment which he has passed as to the rude style and evil apparel of this antiquated song; for there are several parts in it where not only the thought, but the language is majestic, and the numbers sonorous; at least the apparel is much more gorgeous than many of the poets made use of in Queen Elizabeth's time, as the reader will see in several of the following quotations.

What can be greater than either the thought or the expression in that stanza,

> To drive the deer with hound and horn
>   Earl Percy took his way!
> The child may rue that is unborn
>   The hunting of that day!

This way of considering the misfortunes which this battle would bring upon posterity, not only on those who were born immediately after the battle, and lost their fathers in it, but on those also who perished in future battles which took their rise from this quarrel of the two earls, is wonderfully beautiful, and conformable to the way of thinking among the ancient poets.

Audiet pugnas vitio parentum
Rara juventus.   HOR. *Od.* I. ii. 23.

Posterity, thinn'd by their fathers' crimes,
Shall read with grief the story of their times.

What can be more sounding and poetical, or resemble
more the majestic simplicity of the ancients, than the
following stanzas?

> The stout Earl of Northumberland
>   A vow to God did make,
> His pleasure in the Scottish woods
>   Three summer's days to take:
>
> With fifteen hundred bowmen bold,
>   All chosen men of might,
> Who knew full well, in time of need,
>   To aim their shafts aright.
>
> The hounds ran swiftly through the woods
>   The nimble deer to take:
> And with their cries the hills and dales
>   An echo shrill did make.

——Vocat ingenti clamore Cithæron
Taygetique canes, domitrixque Epidaurus equorum:
Et vox assensu nemorum ingeminata remugit. *Georg.* iii. 43.

Cithæron loudly calls me to my way;
Thy hounds, Taygetus, open and pursue the prey:
High Epidaurus urges on my speed,
Fam'd for his hills, and for his horses' breed:
From hills and dales the cheerful cries rebound;
For Echo hunts along, and propagates the sound. DRYDEN.

> Lo, yonder doth Earl Douglas come,
>   His men in armour bright;
> Full twenty hundred Scottish spears,
>   All marching in our sight.
>
> All men of pleasant Tividale,
>   Fast by the river Tweed, &c.

The country of the Scotch warriors, described in these
two last verses, has a fine romantic situation, and
affords a couple of smooth words for verse. If the
reader compares the foregoing six lines of the song

with the following Latin verses, he will see how much
they are written in the spirit of Virgil :

> Adversi campo apparent, hastasque reductis
> Protendunt longe dextris ; et spicula vibrant:—
> Quique altum Præneste viri, quique arva Gabinæ
> Junonis, gelidumque Anienem, et roscida rivis
> Hernica saxa colunt :—qui rosea rura Velini,
> Qui Tetricæ horrentes rupes, montemque Severum,
> Casperiamque colunt, Forulosque et flumen Himellæ :
> Qui Tiberim Fabarimque bibunt.
>
> *Æn*. xi. 605, vii. 682, 712.

> Advancing in a line, they couch their spears——
> ——Præneste sends a chosen band,
> With those who plough Saturnia's Gabine land:
> Besides the succours which cold Anien yields ;
> The rocks of Hernicus——besides a band,
> That followed from Velinum's dewy land——
> And mountaineers that from Severus came :
> And from the craggy cliffs of Tetrica ;
> And those where yellow Tiber takes his way,
> And where Himella's wanton waters play :
> Casperia sends her arms, with those that lie
> By Fabaris, and fruitful Foruli.   DRYDEN.

But to proceed :

> Earl Douglas on a milk-white steed,
>   Most like a baron bold,
> Rode foremost of the company—
>   Whose armour shone like gold.

> Turnus ut antevolans tardum præcesserat agmen, &c.
> Vidisti, quo Turnus equo, quibus ibat in armis
> Aureus.   *Æn*. ix. 47, 269.

> Our English archers bent their bows,
>   Their hearts were good and true ;
> At the first flight of arrows sent,
>   Full threescore Scots they slew.

> They clos'd full fast on every side,
>   No slackness there was found ;
> And many a gallant gentleman
>   Lay gasping on the ground.

> With that there came an arrow keen
>   Out of an English bow,
> Which struck Earl Douglas to the heart,
>   A deep and deadly blow.

Æneas was wounded after the same manner by an unknown hand in the midst of a parley.

> Has inter voces, media inter talia verba,
> Ecce viro stridens alis allapsa sagitta est,
> Incertum qua pulsa manu.   *Æn.* xii. 318.

> Thus, while he spake, unmindful of defence,
> A winged arrow struck the pious prince;
> But whether from a human hand it came,
> Or hostile god, is left unknown by fame.   DRYDEN.

But of all the descriptive parts of this song, there are none more beautiful than the four following stanzas, which have a great force and spirit in them, and are filled with very natural circumstances.   The thought in the third stanza was never touched by any other poet, and is such a one as would have shined in Homer or in Virgil:

> So thus did both these nobles die,
>   Whose courage none could stain;
> An English archer then perceiv'd
>   The noble Earl was slain.

> He had a bow bent in his hand,
>   Made of a trusty tree,
> An arrow of a cloth-yard long,
>   Unto the head drew he.

> Against Sir Hugh Montgomery
>   So right his shaft he set,
> The grey-goose wing that was thereon
>   In his heart blood was wet.

> This fight did last from break of day
>   Till setting of the sun;
> For when they rang the ev'ning bell
>   The battle scarce was done.

One may observe, likewise, that in the catalogue of the slain, the author has followed the example of the

greatest ancient poets, not only in giving a long list of
the dead, but by diversifying it with little characters
of particular persons.

> And with Earl Douglas there was slain
>   Sir Hugh Montgomery,
> Sir Charles Carrel, that from the field
>   One foot would never fly:
>
> Sir Charles Murrel of Ratcliffe too,
>   His sister's son was he;
> Sir David Lamb so well esteem'd,
>   Yet saved could not be.

The familiar sound in these names destroys the
majesty of the description; for this reason I do
not mention this part of the poem but to show
the natural cast of thought which appears in it,
as the two last verses look almost like a translation of
Virgil.

> ————Cadit et Ripheus justissimus unus
> Qui fuit in Teucris et servantissimus æqui.
> Diis aliter visum.   *Æn.* ii. 426.
>
> Then Ripheus fell in the unequal fight,
> Just of his word, observant of the right:
> Heav'n thought not so.   DRYDEN.

In the catalogue of the English who fell, Wither-
ington's behaviour is in the same manner particularized very artfully, as the reader is prepared for
it by that account which is given of him in the
beginning of the battle; though I am satisfied your
little buffoon readers (who have seen that passage
ridiculed in Hudibras) will not be able to take the
beauty of it; for which reason I dare not so much as
quote it.

> Then stept a gallant squire forth,
>   Witherington was his name,
> Who said, I would not have it told
>   To Henry our king for shame,
>
> That e'er my captain fought on foot,
>   And I stood looking on.

We meet with the same heroic sentiment in Virgil.

Non pudet, O Rutuli, pro cunctis talibus unam
Objectare animam? numerone an viribus æqui
Non sumus?   *Æn.* xii. 229.

For shame, Rutilians, can you bear the sight
Of one expos'd for all, in single fight?
Can we before the face of heav'n confess
Our courage colder, or our numbers less? DRYDEN.

What can be more natural, or more moving, than the
circumstances in which he describes the behaviour of
those women who had lost their husbands on this
fatal day?

Next day did many widows come
    Their husbands to bewail;
They wash'd their wounds in brinish tears,
    But all would not prevail.

Their bodies bathed in purple blood,
    They bore with them away;
They kiss'd them dead a thousand times,
    When they were clad in clay.

Thus we see how the thoughts of this poem, which
naturally arise from the subject, are always simple,
and sometimes exquisitely noble; that the language is
often very sounding, and that the whole is written
with a true poetical spirit.

If this song had been written in the Gothic manner,
which is the delight of all our little wits whether
writers or readers, it would not have hit the taste of
so many ages, and have pleased the readers of all
ranks and conditions. I shall only beg pardon for
such a profusion of Latin quotations, which I should
not have made use of, but that I feared my own judgment would have looked too singular on such a subject,
had not I supported it by the practice and authority
of Virgil.

APPEARANCES DECEPTIVE

Heu quam difficile est crimen non prodere vultu!
OVID, *Met.* ii. 447.

How in the looks does conscious guilt appear!
ADDISON.

THERE are several arts, which all men are in some
measure masters of, without having been at the pains
of learning them.   Every one that speaks or reasons
is a grammarian and a logician, though he may be
wholly unacquainted with the rules of grammar or
logic, as they are delivered in books and systems.   In
the same manner, every one is in some degree a
master of that art which is generally distinguished by
the name of Physiognomy: and naturally forms to
himself the character or fortune of a stranger, from
the features and lineaments of his face.   We are no
sooner presented to any one we never saw before, but
we are immediately struck with the idea of a proud,
a reserved, an affable, or a good-natured man; and
upon our first going into a company of strangers,
our benevolence or aversion, awe or contempt, rises
naturally towards several particular persons, before
we have heard them speak a single word, or so much
as know who they are.

Every passion gives a particular cast to the countenance, and is apt to discover itself in some feature
or other.   I have seen an eye curse for half an hour
together, and an eye-brow call a man a scoundrel.
Nothing is more common than for lovers to complain,
resent, languish, despair, and die, in dumb-show.   For
my own part, I am so apt to frame a notion of every
man's humour or circumstances by his looks, that
I have sometimes employed myself from Charing-
Cross to the Royal Exchange in drawing the characters
of those who have passed by me.   When I see a man
with a sour rivelled face, I cannot forbear pitying his

wife: and when I meet with an open ingenuous
countenance, think on the happiness of his friends,
his family, and relations.

I cannot recollect the author of a famous saying
to a stranger, who stood silent in his company,
"Speak, that I may see thee." But, with submission,
I think we may be better known by our looks than by
our words, and that a man's speech is much more
easily disguised than his countenance. In this case,
however, I think the air of the whole face is much
more expressive than the lines of it. The truth of it
is, the air is generally nothing else but the inward
disposition of the mind made visible.

Those who have established physiognomy into an
art, and laid down rules of judging men's tempers by
their faces, have regarded the features much more
than the air. Martial has a pretty epigram on this
subject:

> Crine ruber, niger ore, brevis pede, lumine læsus:
> Rem magnam præstas, Zoile, si bonus es.
>
> *Epig.* xii. 54.

> Thy beard and head are of a different die;
> Short of one foot, distorted in an eye:
> With all these tokens of a knave complete,
> Should'st thou be honest, thou'rt a devilish cheat.

I have seen a very ingenious author on this subject, who founds his speculations on the supposition,
that as a man hath in the mould of his face a remote
likeness to that of an ox, a sheep, a lion, a hog, or
any other creature; he hath the same resemblance
in the frame of his mind, and is subject to those
passions which are predominant in the creature that
appears in his countenance. Accordingly he gives
the prints of several faces that are of a different
mould, and by a little overcharging the likeness,
discovers the figures of these several kinds of brutal
faces in human features. I remember, in the life of
the famous Prince of Condé, the writer observes, the
face of that prince was like the face of an eagle, and

that the prince was very well pleased to be told so. In this case therefore we may be sure, that he had in his mind some general implicit notion of this art of physiognomy which I have just now mentioned; and that when his courtiers told him his face was made like an eagle's, he understood them in the same manner as if they had told him, there was something in his looks, which showed him to be strong, active, piercing, and of a royal descent. Whether or no the different motions of the animal spirits, in different passions, may have any effect on the mould of the face when the lineaments are pliable and tender, or whether the same kind of souls require the same kind of habitations, I shall leave to the consideration of the curious. In the meantime I think nothing can be more glorious than for a man to give the lie to his face, and to be an honest, just, good-natured man, in spite of all those marks and signatures which nature seems to have set upon him for the contrary. This very often happens among those who, instead of being exasperated by their own looks, or envying the looks of others, apply themselves entirely to the cultivating of their minds, and getting those beauties which are more lasting, and more ornamental. I have seen many an amiable piece of deformity; and have observed a certain cheerfulness in as bad a system of features as ever was clapped together, which hath appeared more lovely than all the blooming charms of an insolent beauty. There is a double praise due to virtue, when it is lodged in a body that seems to have been prepared for the reception of vice; in many such cases the soul and the body do not seem to be fellows.

Socrates was an extraordinary instance of this nature. There chanced to be a great physiognomist in his time at Athens, who had made strange discoveries of men's tempers and inclinations by their outward appearances. Socrates's disciples, that they might put this artist to the trial, carried him to their master, whom he had never seen before, and did not

know he was then in company with him. After a
short examination of his face, the physiognomist
pronounced him the most lewd, libidinous, drunken
old fellow that he had ever met with in his whole
life. Upon which the disciples all burst out a-
laughing, as thinking they had detected the false-
hood and vanity of his art. But Socrates told them,
that the principles of his art might be very true,
notwithstanding his present mistake; for that he
himself was naturally inclined to those particular
vices which the physiognomist had discovered in his
countenance, but that he had conquered the strong
dispositions he was born with, by the dictates of
philosophy.

We are indeed told by an ancient author, that
Socrates very much resembled Silenus in his face;
which we find to have been very rightly observed
from the statues and busts of both, that are still
extant; as well as on several antique seals and pre-
cious stones, which are frequently enough to be met
with in the cabinets of the curious. But however
observations of this nature may sometimes hold, a
wise man should be particularly cautious how he
gives credit to a man's outward appearance. It is an
irreparable injustice we are guilty of towards one
another, when we are prejudiced by the looks and
features of those whom we do not know. How often
do we conceive hatred against a person of worth, or
fancy a man to be proud or ill-natured by his aspect,
whom we think we cannot esteem too much when we
are acquainted with his real character? Dr Moore,
in his admirable System of Ethics, reckons this
particular inclination to take a prejudice against a
man for his looks, among the smaller vices in morality,
and, if I remember, gives it the name of a *prosopolepsia.*

LADIES' HEAD-DRESSES

Tanta est quærendi cura decoris.

JUV. *Sat.* vi. 500

So studiously their persons they adorn.

THERE is not so variable a thing in nature as a lady's head-dress. Within my own memory, I have known it rise and fall above thirty degrees. About ten years ago it shot up to a very great height, insomuch that the female part of our species were much taller than the men. The women were of such an enormous stature, that "we appeared as grasshoppers before them." At present the whole sex is in a manner dwarfed, and shrunk into a race of beauties that seems almost another species. I remember several ladies, who were once very near seven foot high, that at present want some inches of five. How they came to be thus curtailed I cannot learn; whether the whole sex be at present under any penance which we know nothing of; or whether they have cast their head-dresses in order to surprise us with something in that kind which shall be entirely new; or whether some of the tallest of the sex, being too cunning for the rest, have contrived this method to make themselves appear sizeable—is still a secret; though I find most are of opinion, they are at present like trees new lopped and pruned, that will certainly sprout up and flourish with greater heads than before. For my own part, as I do not love to be insulted by women who are taller than myself, I admire the sex much more in their present humiliation, which has reduced them to their natural dimensions, than when they had extended their persons and lengthened themselves out into formidable and gigantic figures. I am not for adding to the beautiful edifices of nature, nor for raising any whimsical superstructure upon her plans: I must therefore repeat it, that I am highly pleased with the coiffure now in fashion, and think it shows the good sense which at present very much reigns among the valuable part of the sex. One may observe that women in all ages have taken more pains than men to adorn the outside of their heads; and indeed I very much admire, that those female architects, who raise such wonderful structures out of ribands, lace, and wire, have not been recorded for their respective inventions. It is certain there have been as many orders in these kinds of building, as in those which have been made of marble. Sometimes they rise in the shape of a pyramid, sometimes like a tower, and sometimes like a steeple. In Juvenal's time the building grew by several orders and stories, as he has very humorously described it:

> Tot premit ordinibus, tot adhuc compagibus altum
> Ædificat caput; Andromachen a fronte videbis;
> Post minor est; aliam credas.
>
> JUV. *Sat.* vi. 501.

> With curls on curls they build her head before,
> And mount it with a formidable tow'r;
> A giantess she seems; but look behind,
> And then she dwindles to the pigmy kind.
>
> DRYDEN.

But I do not remember in any part of my reading, that the head-dress aspired to so great an extravagance as in the fourteenth century; when it was built up in a couple of cones or spires, which stood so exceedingly high on each side of the head, that a woman, who was but a pigmy without her head-dress, appeared like a colossus upon putting it on. Monsieur Paradin says, "that these old-fashioned fontanges rose an ell above the head; that they were pointed like steeples, and had long loose pieces of crape fastened to the tops of them, which were curiously fringed, and hung down their backs like streamers."

The women might possibly have carried this Gothic building much higher, had not a famous monk,

Thomas Conecte by name, attacked it with great zeal and resolution. This holy man travelled from place to place to preach down this monstrous commode; and succeeded so well in it, that, as the magicians sacrificed their books to the flames upon the preaching of an apostle, many of the women threw down their head-dresses in the middle of the sermon, and made a bonfire of them within sight of the pulpit. He was so renowned as well for the sanctity of his life as his manner of preaching, that he had often a congregation of twenty thousand people; the men placing themselves on the one side of his pulpit, and the women on the other, that appeared (to use the similitude of an ingenious writer) like a forest of cedars with their heads reaching to the clouds. He so warmed and animated the people against this monstrous ornament, that it lay under a kind of persecution; and whenever it appeared in public, was pelted down by the rabble, who flung stones at the persons that wore it. But notwithstanding this prodigy vanished while the preacher was among them, it began to appear again some months after his departure, or, to tell it in Monsieur Paradin's own words, "the women that, like snails in a fright, had drawn in their horns, shot them out again as soon as the danger was over." This extravagance of the women's head-dresses in that age, is taken notice of by Monsieur d'Argentré in his history of Bretagne, and by other historians, as well as the person I have here quoted.

It is usually observed, that a good reign is the only proper time for making laws against the exorbitance of power; in the same manner an excessive head-dress may be attacked the most effectually when the fashion is against it. I do therefore recommend this paper to my female readers by way of prevention.

I would desire the fair sex to consider how impossible it is for them to add any thing that can be ornamental to what is already the master-piece of nature. The head has the most beautiful appearance, as well as the highest station, in a human figure. Nature has laid out all her art in beautifying the face; she has touched it with vermilion, planted in it a double row of ivory, made it the seat of smiles and blushes, lighted it up and enlivened it with the brightness of the eyes, hung it on each side with curious organs of sense, given it airs and graces that cannot be described, and surrounded it with such a flowing shade of hair as sets all its beauties in the most agreeable light. In short, she seems to have designed the head as the cupola to the most glorious of her works: and when we load it with such a pile of supernumerary ornaments, we destroy the symmetry of the human figure, and foolishly contrive to call off the eye from great and real beauties, to childish gew· gaws, ribands, and bone-lace.

FANS

Lusus animo debent aliquando dari,
Ad cogitandum melior ut redeat sibi.
                          PHÆDR. *Fab.* xiv. 3.

The mind ought sometimes to be diverted, that it may return the better to thinking.

I DO not know whether to call the following letter a satire upon coquettes, or a representation of their several fantastical accomplishments, or what other title to give it; but, as it is, I shall communicate it to the public. It will sufficiently explain its own intentions, so that I shall give it my reader at length, without either preface or postscript.

"MR SPECTATOR,

"Women are armed with fans as men with swords, and sometimes do more execution with them. To the end, therefore, that ladies may be entire mistresses

of the weapon they bear, I have erected an academy
for the training up of young women in the exercise of
the fan, according to the most fashionable airs and
motions that are now practised at court. The ladies
who carry fans under me are drawn up twice a day in
my great hall, where they are instructed in the use of
their arms, and exercised by the following words of
command: Handle your fans, Unfurl your fans,
Discharge your fans, Ground your fans, Recover your
fans, Flutter your fans. By the right observation of
these few plain words of command, a woman of a
tolerable genius, who will apply herself diligently to
her exercise for the space of but one half-year, shall
be able to give her fan all the graces that can possibly
enter into that little modish machine.

"But to the end that my readers may form to
themselves a right notion of this exercise, I beg leave
to explain it to them in all its parts. When my
female regiment is drawn up in array, with every one
her weapon in her hand, upon my giving the word to
Handle their fans, each of them shakes her fan at me
with a smile, then gives her right-hand woman a tap
upon the shoulder, then presses her lips with the
extremity of her fan, then lets her arms fall in an easy
motion, and stands in readiness to receive the next
word of command. All this is done with a close fan,
and is generally learned in the first week.

"The next motion is that of Unfurling the fan,
in which are comprehended several little flirts and
vibrations, as also gradual and deliberate openings,
with many voluntary fallings asunder in the fan itself,
that are seldom learned under a month's practice.
This part of the exercise pleases the spectators more
than any other, as it discovers on a sudden an infinite
number of cupids, garlands, altars, birds, beasts, rain-
bows, and the like agreeable figures that display
themselves to view—whilst every one in the regiment
holds a picture in her hand.

"Upon my giving the word to Discharge their
fans, they give one general crack that may be heard

at a considerable distance when the wind sets fair. This is one of the most difficult parts of the exercise: but I have several ladies with me, who at their first entrance could not give a pop loud enough to be heard at the farther end of a room, who can now discharge a fan in such a manner, that it shall make a report like a pocket-pistol. I have likewise taken care (in order to hinder young women from letting off their fans in wrong places or on unsuitable occasions) to show upon what subject the crack of a fan may come in properly: I have likewise invented a fan, with which a girl of sixteen, by the help of a little wind which is enclosed about one of the largest sticks, can make as loud a crack as a woman of fifty with an ordinary fan.

"When the fans are thus discharged, the word of command, in course, is to Ground their fans. This teaches a lady to quit her fan gracefully when she throws it aside in order to take up a pack of cards, adjust a curl of hair, replace a falling pin, or apply herself to any other matter of importance. This part of the exercise, as it only consists in tossing a fan with an air upon a long table (which stands by for that purpose), may be learned in two days' time as well as in a twelvemonth.

"When my female regiment is thus disarmed, I generally let them walk about the room for some time; when, on a sudden (like ladies that look upon their watches after a long visit), they all of them hasten to their arms, catch them up in a hurry, and place themselves in their proper stations, upon my calling out, Recover your fans. This part of the exercise is not difficult, provided a woman applies her thoughts to it.

"The Fluttering of the fan is the last, and indeed the master-piece of the whole exercise; but if a lady does not mis-spend her time, she may make herself mistress of it in three months. I generally lay aside the dog-days and the hot time of the summer for the teaching this part of the exercise; for as soon as ever

I pronounce, Flutter your fans, the place is filled with so many zephyrs and gentle breezes as are very refreshing in that season of the year, though they might be dangerous to ladies of a tender constitution in any other.

"There is an infinite variety of motions to be made use of in the flutter of a fan. There is the angry flutter, the modest flutter, the timorous flutter, and the amorous flutter. Not to be tedious, there is scarce any emotion in the mind which does not produce a suitable agitation in the fan; insomuch, that if I only see the fan of a disciplined lady, I know very well whether she laughs, frowns, or blushes. I have seen a fan so very angry, that it would have been dangerous for the absent lover who provoked it to have come within the wind of it; and at other times so very languishing, that I have been glad for the lady's sake the lover was at a sufficient distance from it. I need not add, that a fan is either a prude or coquette, according to the nature of the person who bears it. To conclude my letter, I must acquaint you that I have from my own observation compiled a little treatise for the use of my scholars, entitled, The Passions of the Fan; which I will communicate to you, if you think it may be of use to the public. I shall have a general review on Thursday next; to which you shall be very welcome if you will honour it with your presence.

I am, &c.

"P.S. I teach young gentlemen the whole art of gallanting a fan.

"N.B. I have several little plain fans made for this use, to avoid expense."

PEDANTS

Id arbitror
Adprime in vita esse utile, ut nequid nimis.
TER. *Andr.* Act. i, Sc. i.

I take it to be a principal rule of life, not to be too much addicted to any one thing.

Too much of any thing, is good for nothing. ENG. PROV.

My friend Will Honeycomb values himself very much upon what he calls the knowledge of mankind, which has cost him many disasters in his youth; for Will reckons every misfortune that he has met with among the women, and every rencounter among the men, as parts of his education; and fancies he should never have been the man he is, had he not broke windows, knocked down constables, disturbed honest people with his midnight serenades, and beat up the lowest quarters, when he was a young fellow. The engaging in adventures of this nature Will calls the studying of mankind; and terms this knowledge of the town the knowledge of the world. Will ingenuously confesses that for half his life his head ached every morning with reading of men over-night; and at present comforts himself under certain pains which he endures from time to time, that without them he could not have been acquainted with the gallantries of the age. This Will looks upon as the learning of a gentleman, and regards all other kinds of science as the accomplishments of one whom he calls a scholar, a bookish man, or a philosopher.

For these reasons Will shines in mixed company, where he has the discretion not to go out of his depth, and has often a certain way of making his real ignorance appear a seeming one. Our club however has frequently caught him tripping, at which times they never spare him. For as Will often insults us with his knowledge of the town, we sometimes take our revenge upon him by our knowledge of books.

He was last week producing two or three letters
which he writ in his youth to a coquette lady. The
raillery of them was natural, and well enough for a
mere man of the town: but, very unluckily, several of
the words were wrong spelt. Will laughed this off
at first as well as he could; but finding himself pushed
on all sides, and especially by the Templar, he told us
with a little passion, that he never liked pedantry in
spelling, and that he spelt like a gentleman, and not
like a scholar: upon this Will had recourse to his old
topic of showing the narrow-spiritedness, the pride,
and ignorance of pedants; which he carried so far,
that upon my retiring to my lodgings, I could not forbear throwing together such reflections as occurred
to me upon that subject.

A man who has been brought up among books,
and is able to talk of nothing else, is a very indifferent
companion, and what we call a pedant. But, methinks,
we should enlarge the title, and give it to every one
that does not know how to think out of his profession
and particular way of life.

What is a greater pedant than a mere man of the
town? Bar him the play-houses, a catalogue of the
reigning beauties, and an account of a few fashionable
distempers that have befallen him, and you strike him
dumb. How many a pretty gentleman's knowledge
lies all within the verge of the court! He will tell you
the names of the principal favourites, repeat the
shrewd sayings of a man of quality, whisper an
intrigue that is not yet blown upon by common fame;
or, if the sphere of his observations is a little larger
than ordinary, will perhaps enter into all the incidents,
turns, and revolutions, in a game of *ombre*. When he
has gone thus far, he has shown you the whole circle
of his accomplishments; his parts are drained, and he
is disabled from any farther conversation. What are
these but rank pedants? and yet these are the men
who value themselves most on their exemption from
the pedantry of colleges.

I might here mention the military pedant, who

always talks in a camp—and is storming towns, making lodgments, and fighting battles, from one end of the year to the other. Every thing he speaks smells of gunpowder; if you take away his artillery from him, he has not a word to say for himself. I might likewise mention the law pedant, that is perpetually putting cases, repeating the transactions of Westminster Hall, wrangling with you upon the most indifferent circumstances of life, and not to be convinced of the distance of a place, or of the most trivial point in conversation, but by dint of argument. The state pedant is wrapped up in news, and lost in politics. If you mention either of the kings of Spain or Poland, he talks very notably; but if you go out of the Gazette, you drop him. In short, a mere courtier, a mere soldier, a mere scholar, a mere any thing, is an insipid pedantic character, and equally ridiculous.

Of all the species of pedants which I have mentioned, the book pedant is much the most supportable; he has at least an exercised understanding, a head which is full, though confused—so that a man who converses with him may often receive from him hints of things that are worth knowing, and what he may possibly turn to his own advantage, though they are of little use to the owner. The worst kind of pedants among learned men, are such as are naturally endued with a very small share of common sense, and have read a great number of books without taste or distinction.

The truth of it is, learning, like travelling, and all other methods of improvement, as it finishes good sense, so it makes a silly man ten thousand times more insufferable, by supplying variety of matter to his impertinence, and giving him an opportunity of abounding in absurdities.

Shallow pedants cry up one another much more than men of solid and useful learning. To read the titles they give an editor, or collator of a manuscript, you would take him for the glory of the commonwealth of letters, and the wonder of his age! when perhaps upon examination you find that he has only rectified a Greek particle, or laid out a whole sentence in proper commas.

They are obliged indeed to be thus lavish of their praises, that they may keep one another in countenance; and it is no wonder if a great deal of knowledge which is not capable of making a man wise, has a natural tendency to make him vain and arrogant.

SIR ROGER'S COUNTRY-HOUSE

Hinc tibi copia
Manabit ad plenum benigno
Ruris honorum opulenta cornu.
                    HOR. *Od.* i. xvii. 14.

Here plenty's liberal horn shall pour
Of fruits for thee a copious show'r
Rich honours of the quiet plain.

HAVING often received an invitation from my friend Sir Roger de Coverley, to pass away a month with him in the country, I last week accompanied him thither, and am settled with him for some time at his country-house, where I intend to form several of my ensuing speculations. Sir Roger, who is very well acquainted with my humour, lets me rise and go to bed when I please, dine at his own table or in my chamber as I think fit, sit still and say nothing without bidding me be merry. When the gentlemen of the country come to see him, he only shows me at a distance. As I have been walking in his fields I have observed them stealing a sight of me over a hedge, and have heard the knight desiring them not to let me see them, for that I hated to be stared at.

I am the more at ease in Sir Roger's family, because it consists of sober and staid persons; for as the knight is the best master in the world, he seldom changes his servants; and as he is beloved by all about him, his servants never care for leaving him;

by this means his domestics are all in years, and
grown old with their master. You would take his
valet-de-chambre for his brother, his butler is gray-
headed, his groom is one of the gravest men that I
have ever seen, and his coachman has the looks of a
privy-counsellor. You see the goodness of the master
even in his old house-dog, and in a gray pad that is
kept in the stable with great care and tenderness, out
of regard to his past services, though he has been
useless for several years.

I could not but observe with a great deal of pleasure,
the joy that appeared in the countenances of these
ancient domestics upon my friend's arrival at his
country seat. Some of them could not refrain from
tears at the sight of their old master; every one of
them pressed forward to do something for him, and
seemed discouraged if they were not employed. At
the same time the good old knight, with a mixture of
the father and the master of the family, tempered the
inquiries after his own affairs with several kind questions
relating to themselves. This humanity and good-
nature engages every body to him, so that when he is
pleasant upon any of them, all his family are in good
humour, and none so much as the person whom he
diverts himself with: on the contrary, if he coughs, or
betrays any infirmity of old age, it is easy for a stander-
by to observe a secret concern in the looks of all his
servants.

My worthy friend has put me under the particular
care of his butler, who is a very prudent man, and,
as well as the rest of his fellow-servants, wonderfully desirous of pleasing me, because they have often
heard their master talk of me as his particular friend.

My chief companion, when Sir Roger is diverting
himself in the woods or the fields, is a very venerable
man who is ever with Sir Roger, and has lived at
his house in the nature of a chaplain above thirty
years. This gentleman is a person of good sense and
some learning, of a very regular life and obliging
conversation: he heartily loves Sir Roger, and knows

that he is very much in the old knight's esteem, so
that he lives in the family rather as a relation than a
dependant.

I have observed in several of my papers, that my
friend Sir Roger, amidst all his good qualities, is
something of a humorist; and that his virtues, as
well as imperfections, are as it were tinged by a certain
extravagance, which makes them particularly his, and
distinguishes them from those of other men.   This
cast of mind, as it is generally very innocent in itself,
so it renders his conversation highly agreeable, and
more delightful than the same degree of sense and
virtue would appear in their common and ordinary
colours.   As I was walking with him last night, he
asked me how I liked the good man whom I have just
now mentioned? and without staying for my answer,
told me that he was afraid of being insulted with
Latin and Greek at his own table; for which reason
he desired a particular friend of his at the university
to find him out a clergyman rather of plain sense than
much learning, of a good aspect, a clear voice, a
sociable temper, and, if possible, a man that understood
a little of backgammon.   "My friend," says Sir Roger,
"found me out this gentleman, who, besides the
endowments required of him, is, they tell me, a good
scholar, though he does not show it.   I have given him
the patronage of the parish; and because I know his
value, have settled upon him a good annuity for life.
If he outlives me, he shall find that he was higher in
my esteem than perhaps he thinks he is.   He has now
been with me thirty years; and though he does not
know I have taken notice of it, has never in all that
time asked any thing of me for himself, though he is
every day soliciting me for something in behalf of one
or other of my tenants his parishioners.   There has
not been a lawsuit in the parish since he has lived
among them; if any dispute arises, they apply themselves to him for the decision; if they do not acquiesce
in his judgment, which I think never happened above
once or twice at most, they appeal to me.   At his

first settling with me, I made him a present of all the good sermons which have been printed in English, and only begged of him that every Sunday he woul pro-nounce one of them in the pulpit. Accordingly he has digested them into such a series, that they follow one another naturally, and make a continued system of practical divinity."

As Sir Roger was going on in his story, the gentle-man we were talking of came up to us; and upon the knight's asking him who preached to-morrow (for it was Saturday night,) told us, the bishop of St Asaph in the morning, and Dr South in the afternoon. He then showed us his list of preachers for the whole year, where I saw with a great deal of pleasure Archbishop Tillotson, Bishop Saunderson, Dr Barrow, Dr Calamy, with several living authors who have published discourses of practical divinity. I no sooner saw this venerable man in the pulpit, but I very much approved of my friend's insisting upon the qualifications of a good aspect and a clear voice; for I was so charmed with the gracefulness of his figure and delivery, as well as with the discourses he pronounced, that I think I never passed any time more to my satisfaction. A sermon repeated after this manner, is like the composition of a poet in the mouth of a graceful actor.

I could heartily wish that more of our country clergy would follow this example; and instead of wasting their spirits in laborious compositions of their own, would endeavour after a handsome elocution, and all those other talents that are proper to enforce what has been penned by great masters. This would not only be more easy to themselves, but more edifying to the people.

WILL WIMBLE

Gratis anhelans, multa agendo nihil agens.
PHÆDR. *Fab.* v. 2.

Out of breath to no purpose, and very busy about nothing.

As I was yesterday morning walking with Sir Roger before his house, a country fellow brought him a huge fish, which, he told him, Mr William Wimble had caught that very morning; and that he presented it with his service to him, and intended to come and dine with him. At the same time he delivered a letter, which my friend read to me as soon as the messenger left him.

"SIR ROGER,

"I desire you to accept of a jack, which is the best I have caught this season. I intend to come and stay with you a week, and see how the perch bite in the Black river. I observed with some concern, the last time I saw you upon the bowling-green, that your whip wanted a lash to it; I will bring half a dozen with me that I twisted last week, which I hope will serve you all the time you are in the country. I have not been out of the saddle for six days last past, having been at Eton with Sir John's eldest son. He takes to his learning hugely.

"I am, Sir, your humble servant,
"WILL WIMBLE."

This extraordinary letter, and message that accompanied it, made me very curious to know the character and quality of the gentleman who sent them; which I found to be as follow:—Will Wimble is younger brother to a baronet, and descended of the ancient family of the Wimbles. He is now between forty and fifty; but being bred to no business and born to no estate, he generally lives with his elder brother as superintendent of his game. He hunts a pack of dogs better than any man in the country, and is very famous for finding out a hare. He is extremely well versed in all the little handicrafts of an idle man. He makes a May-fly to a miracle: and furnishes the whole country with angle-rods. As he is a good-natured officious fellow, and very much esteemed upon account of his family, he is a welcome guest at every house, and keeps up a good correspondence among all the gentlemen about him. He carries a tulip root in his pocket from one to another, or exchanges a puppy between a couple of friends that live perhaps in the opposite sides of the country. Will is a particular favourite of all the young heirs, whom he frequently obliges with a net that he has weaved, or a setting-dog that he has made himself. He now and then presents a pair of garters of his own knitting to their mothers and sisters; and raises a great deal of mirth among them, by inquiring as often as he meets them "how they wear!" These gentleman-like manufactures and obliging little humours, make Will the darling of the country.

Sir Roger was proceeding in the character of him, when he saw him make up to us with two or three hazle twigs in his hand that he had cut in Sir Roger's woods, as he came through them in his way to the house. I was very much pleased to observe on one side the hearty and sincere welcome with which Sir Roger received him, and on the other, the secret joy which his guest discovered at the sight of the good old knight. After the first salutes were over, Will desired Sir Roger to lend him one of his servants to carry a set of shuttle-cocks he had with him in a little box, to a lady that lived about a mile off, to whom it seems he had promised such a present for above this half year. Sir Roger's back was no sooner turned, but honest Will began to tell me of a large cock pheasant that he had sprung in one of the neighbouring woods, with two or three other adventures of the same nature. Odd and uncommon characters are the game that I look for and most delight in; for which reason

I was as much pleased with the novelty of the person
that talked to me, as he could be for his life with the
springing of a pheasant, and therefore listened to him
with more than ordinary attention.

In the midst of his discourse the bell rang to
dinner, where the gentleman I have been speaking of
had the pleasure of seeing the huge jack he had caught
served up for the first dish in a most sumptuous
manner. Upon our sitting down to it he gave us
a long account how he had hooked it, played with it,
foiled it, and at length drew it out upon the bank—
with several other particulars that lasted all the first
course. A dish of wild fowl that came afterward
furnished conversation for the rest of the dinner,
which concluded with a late invention of Will's for
improving the quail-pipe.

Upon withdrawing into my room after dinner,
I was secretly touched with compassion towards the
honest gentleman that had dined with us; and could
not but consider with a great deal of concern, how
so good a heart and such busy hands were wholly
employed in trifles; that so much humanity should be
so little beneficial to others, and so much industry
so little advantageous to himself. The same temper
of mind and application to affairs, might have recommended him to the public esteem, and have raised
his fortune in another station of life. What good
to his country or himself might not a trader or a
merchant have done with such useful though ordinary
qualifications!

Will Wimble's is the case of many a younger
brother of a great family, who had rather see their
children starve like gentlemen, than thrive in a trade
or profession that is beneath their quality. This
humour fills several parts of Europe with pride and
beggary. It is the happiness of a trading nation like
ours, that the younger sons, though incapable of any
liberal art or profession, may be placed in such a way
of life, as may perhaps enable them to vie with the
best of their family. Accordingly we find several

citizens that were launched into the world with narrow fortunes, rising by an honest industry to greater estates than those of their elder brothers. It is not improbable but Will was formerly tried at divinity, law, or physic; and that, finding his genius did not lie that way, his parents gave him up at length to his own inventions. But certainly, however improper he might have been for studies of a higher nature, he was perfectly well turned for the occupations of trade and commerce. As I think this is a point which cannot be too much inculcated, I shall desire my reader to compare what I have here written with what I have said in my twenty-first speculation.

SIR ROGER IN CHURCH

'Αθανάτους μὲν πρῶτα θεοὺς, νόμῳ ὡς διάκειται,
Τίμα.   PYTHAG.
First, in obedience to thy country's rites,
Worship th' immortal gods.

I AM always very well pleased with a country Sunday, and think, if keeping holy the seventh day were only a human institution, it would be the best method that could have been thought of for polishing and civilizing of mankind. It is certain, the country people would soon degenerate into a kind of savages and barbarians, were there not such frequent returns of a stated time, in which the whole village meet together with their best faces, and in their cleanliest habits, to converse with one another upon different subjects, hear their duties explained to them, and join together in adoration of the Supreme Being. Sunday clears away the rust of the whole week, not only as it refreshes in their minds the notions of religion, but as it puts both the sexes upon appearing in their most agreeable forms, and exerting all such qualities as are apt to give them a figure in the eye of the village. A country fellow distinguishes himself as much in the churchyard, as a citizen does upon the

'Change, the whole parish-politics being generally
discussed in that place either after sermon or before
the bell rings.

My friend Sir Roger, being a good churchman,
has beautified the inside of his church with several
texts of his own choosing. He has likewise given a
handsome pulpit-cloth, and railed in the communion-
table at his own expense. He has often told me,
that at his coming to his estate he found his parishioners very irregular: and that in order to make them
kneel and join in the responses, he gave every one of
them a hassock and a common-prayer book: and at
the same time employed an itinerant singing-master,
who goes about the country for that purpose, to
instruct them rightly in the tunes of the Psalms; upon
which they now very much value themselves, and
indeed outdo most of the country churches that I have
ever heard.

As Sir Roger is landlord to the whole congregation,
he keeps them in very good order, and will suffer
nobody to sleep in it besides himself; for if by chance
he has been surprised into a short nap at sermon,
upon recovering out of it he stands up and looks about
him, and if he sees any body else nodding, either
wakes them himself or sends his servants to them.
Several other of the old knight's particularities break
out upon these occasions. Sometimes he will be
lengthening out a verse in the singing Psalms half
a minute after the rest of the congregation have done
with it; sometimes, when he is pleased with the
matter of his devotion, he pronounces amen three or
four times to the same prayer; and sometimes stands
up when every body else is upon their knees, to count
the congregation, or see if any of his tenants are
missing.

I was yesterday very much surprised to hear my
old friend, in the midst of the service, calling out to
one John Matthews to mind what he was about, and
not disturb the congregation. This John Matthews
it seems is remarkable for being an idle fellow, and

at that time was kicking his heels for his diversion. This authority of the knight, though exerted in that odd manner which accompanies him in all the circumstances of life, has a very good effect upon the parish, who are not polite enough to see any thing ridiculous in his behaviour; besides that the general good sense and worthiness of his character make his friends observe these little singularities as foils that rather set off than blemish his good qualities.

As soon as the sermon is finished, nobody presumes to stir till Sir Roger is gone out of the church. The knight walks down from his seat in the chancel between a double row of his tenants, that stand bowing to him on each side; and every now and then inquires how such a one's wife, or mother, or son, or father do, whom he does not see at church; which is understood as a secret reprimand to the person that is absent.

The chaplain has often told me that, upon a catechising day, when Sir Roger has been pleased with a boy that answers well, he has ordered a Bible to be given to him next day for his encouragement; and sometimes accompanies it with a flitch of bacon to his mother. Sir Roger has likewise added five pounds a year to the clerk's place; and that he may encourage the young fellows to make themselves perfect in the church service, has promised upon the death of the present incumbent, who is very old, to bestow it according to merit.

The fair understanding between Sir Roger and his chaplain, and their mutual concurrence in doing good, is the more remarkable, because the very next village is famous for the differences and contentions that arise between the parson and the squire, who live in a perpetual state of war. The parson is always preaching at the squire; and the squire, to be revenged on the parson, never comes to church. The squire has made all his tenants atheists and tithe-stealers; while the parson instructs them every Sunday in the dignity of his order, and insinuates to them, in almost every sermon, that he is a better man than his patron. In short, matters are come to such an extremity, that the squire has not said his prayers either in public or private this half year; and the parson threatens him, if he does not mend his manners, to pray for him in the face of the whole congregation.

Feuds of this nature, though too frequent in the country, are very fatal to the ordinary people, who are so used to be dazzled with riches, that they pay as much deference to the understanding of a man of an estate, as of a man of learning; and are very hardly brought to regard any truth, how important soever it may be, that is preached to them, when they know there are several men of five hundred a year who do not believe it.

THE VALUE OF EXERCISE

Ut sit mens sana in corpore sano.
JUV. *Sat.* x. 356.
Pray for a sound mind in a sound body.

BODILY labour is of two kinds,—either that which a man submits to for his livelihood, or that which he undergoes for his pleasure. The latter of them generally changes the name of labour for that of exercise, but differs only from ordinary labour as it rises from another motive.

A country life abounds in both these kinds of labour—and for that reason gives a man a greater stock of health, and consequently a more perfect enjoyment of himself, than any other way of life. I consider the body as a system of tubes and glands, or, to use a more rustic phrase, a bundle of pipes and strainers, fitted to one another after so wonderful a manner as to make a proper engine for the soul to work with. This description does not only comprehend the bowels, bones, tendons, veins, nerves, and arteries, but every muscle and every ligature, which is a composition of fibres, that are so many imperceptible tubes or pipes interwoven on all sides with invisible glands or strainers.

This general idea of a human body, without considering it in the niceties of anatomy, lets us see how absolutely necessary labour is for the right preservation of it. There must be frequent motions and agitations, to mix, digest, and separate the juices contained in it, as well as to clear and cleanse that infinitude of pipes and strainers of which it is composed, and to give their solid parts a more firm and lasting tone. Labour or exercise ferments the humours, casts them into their proper channels, throws off redundancies, and helps nature in those secret distributions, without which the body cannot subsist in its vigour, nor the soul act with cheerfulness.

I might here mention the effects which this has upon all the faculties of the mind, by keeping the understanding clear, the imagination untroubled, and refining those spirits which are necessary for the proper exertion of our intellectual faculties, during the present laws of union between soul and body. It is to a neglect in this particular that we must ascribe the spleen, which is so frequent in men of studious and sedentary tempers, as well as the vapours, to which those of the other sex are so often subject.

Had not exercise been absolutely necessary for our well-being, nature would not have made the body so proper for it, by giving such an activity to the limbs, and such a pliancy to every part as necessarily produce those compressions, extensions, contortions, dilations, and all other kinds of motions that are necessary for the preservation of such a system of tubes and glands as has been before mentioned. And that we might not want inducements to engage us in such an exercise of the body as is proper for its welfare, it is so ordered that nothing valuable can be procured without it. Not to mention riches and honour, even food and

raiment are not to be come at without the toil of the
hands and sweat of the brows. Providence furnishes
materials, but expects that we should work them up
ourselves. The earth must be laboured before it gives
its increase; and when it is forced into its several
products, how many hands must they pass through
before they are fit for use! Manufactures, trade, and
agriculture, naturally employ more than nineteen
parts of the species in twenty; and as for those who
are not obliged to labour, by the condition in which
they are born, they are more miserable than the rest
of mankind, unless they indulge themselves in that
voluntary labour which goes by the name of exercise.

My friend Sir Roger has been an indefatigable man
in business of this kind, and has hung several parts of
his house with the trophies of his former labours.
The walls of his great hall are covered with the horns
of several kinds of deer that he has killed in the chase,
which he thinks the most valuable furniture of his
house, as they afford him frequent topics of discourse,
and show that he has not been idle. At the lower end
of the hall is a large otter's skin stuffed with hay, which
his mother ordered to be hung up in that manner, and
the knight looks upon it with great satisfaction,
because it seems he was but nine years old when his
dog killed him. A little room adjoining to the hall
is a kind of arsenal filled with guns of several sizes
and inventions, with which the knight has made great
havoc in the woods, and destroyed many thousands of
pheasants, partridges, and woodcocks. His stable doors
are patched with noses that belonged to foxes of the
knight's own hunting down. Sir Roger showed me one of
them that for distinction sake has a brass nail struck
through it, which cost him about fifteen hours riding,
carried him through half a dozen counties, killed him
a brace of geldings, and lost above half his dogs.
This the knight looks upon as one of the greatest
exploits of his life. The perverse widow, whom I
have given some account of, was the death of several
foxes; for Sir Roger has told me, that in the course

of his amours he patched the western door of his stable. Whenever the widow was cruel, the foxes were sure to pay for it. In proportion as his passion for the widow abated and old age came on, he left off fox-hunting; but a hare is not yet safe that sits within ten miles of his house.

There is no kind of exercise which I would so recommend to my readers of both sexes as this of riding, as there is none which so much conduces to health, and is every way accommodated to the body, according to the idea which I have given of it. Doctor Sydenham is very lavish in its praises; and if the English reader would see the mechanical effects of it described at length, he may find them in a book published not many years since, under the title of *Medicina Gymnastica*. For my own part, when I am in town, for want of these opportunities, I exercise myself an hour every morning upon a dumb-bell that is placed in a corner of my room, and it pleases me the more because it does every thing that I require of it in the most profound silence. My landlady and her daughters are so well acquainted with my hours of exercise, that they never come into my room to disturb me whilst I am ringing.

When I was some years younger than I am at present, I used to employ myself in a more laborious diversion, which I learned from a Latin treatise of exercises that is written with great erudition: it is there called the fighting with a man's own shadow, and consists in the brandishing of two short sticks grasped in each hand, and loaden with plugs of lead at either end. This opens the chest, exercises the limbs, and gives a man all the pleasure of boxing, without the blows. I could wish that several learned men would lay out that time which they employ in controversies and disputes about nothing, in this method of fighting with their own shadows. It might conduce very much to evaporate the spleen, which makes them uneasy to the public as well as to themselves.

To conclude, as I am a compound of soul and body,

I consider myself as obliged to a double scheme of duties; and think I have not fulfilled the business of the day when I do not thus employ the one in labour and exercise, as well as the other in study and contemplation.

SIR ROGER AND WITCHCRAFT

Ipsi sibi somnia fingunt. VIRG.   *Ecl.* viii. 108.

With voluntary dreams they cheat their minds.

THERE are some opinions in which a man should stand neuter, without engaging his assent to one side or the other.   Such a hovering faith as this, which refuses to settle upon his determination, is absolutely necessary in a mind that is careful to avoid errors and prepossessions.   When the arguments press equally on both sides in matters that are indifferent to us, the safest method is to give up ourselves to neither.

It is with this temper of mind that I consider the subject of witchcraft.   When I hear the relations that are made from all parts of the world, not only from Norway and Lapland, from the East and West Indies, but from every particular nation in Europe, I cannot forbear thinking that there is such an intercourse and commerce with evil spirits, as that which we express by the name of witchcraft.   But when I consider that the ignorant and credulous parts of the world abound most in these relations, and the persons among us, who are supposed to engage in such an infernal commerce, are people of a weak understanding and crazed imagination—and at the same time reflect upon the many impostures and delusions of this nature that have been detected in all ages, I endeavour to suspend my belief till I hear more certain accounts than any which have yet come to my knowledge.   In

short, when I consider the question, whether there are
such persons in the world as those we call witches, my
mind is divided between two opposite opinions, or
rather (to speak my thoughts freely) I believe in general
that there is, and has been, such a thing as witchcraft;
but at the same time can give no credit to any
particular instance of it.

I am engaged in this speculation, by some
occurrences that I met with yesterday, which I shall
give my reader an account of at large. As I was
walking with my friend Sir Roger by the side of one
of his woods, an old woman applied herself to me for
my charity. Her dress and figure put me in mind of
the following description in Otway:

In a close lane, as I pursu'd my journey,
I spy'd a wrinkled hag, with age grown double,
Picking dry sticks, and mumbling to herself.
Her eyes with scalding rheum were gall'd and red
Cold palsy shook her head; her hands seem'd wither'd:
And on her crooked shoulders had she wrapt
The tatter'd remnant of an old striped hanging,
Which served to keep her carcass from the cold·
So there was nothing of a piece about her.
Her lower weeds were all o'er coarsely patch'd
With different colour'd rags, black, red, white, yellow
And seem'd to speak variety of wretchedness.

As I was musing on this description, and comparing
it with the object before me, the knight told me, that
this very old woman had the reputation of a witch all
over the country; that her lips were observed to be
always in motion; and that there was not a switch about
her house which her neighbours did not believe had
carried her several hundreds of miles. If she chanced
to stumble, they always found sticks or straws that lay
in the figure of a cross before her. If she made any
mistake at church, and cried amen in a wrong place,
they never failed to conclude that she was saying her
prayers backwards. There was not a maid in the
parish that would take a pin of her, though she should
offer a bag of money with it. She goes by the name

of Moll White, and has made the country ring with several imaginary exploits which are palmed upon her. If the dairy-maid does not make her butter come so soon as she would have it, Moll White is at the bottom of the churn. If a horse sweats in the stable, Moll White has been upon his back. If a hare makes an unexpected escape from the hounds, the huntsman curses Moll White. "Nay," says Sir Roger, "I have known the master of the pack, upon such an occasion, send one of his servants to see if Moll White had been out that morning."

This account raised my curiosity so far, that I begged my friend Sir Roger to go with me into her hovel, which stood in a solitary corner under the side of the wood. Upon our first entering, Sir Roger winked to me, and pointed to something that stood behind the door, which, upon looking that way, I found to be an old broom-staff. At the same time he whispered me in the ear to take notice of a tabby cat that sate in the chimney corner, which, as the old knight told me, lay under as bad a report as Moll White herself; for besides that Moll is said often to accompany her in the same shape, the cat is reported to have spoken twice or thrice in her life, and to have played several pranks above the capacity of an ordinary cat.

I was secretly concerned to see human nature in so much wretchedness and disgrace, but at the same time could not forbear smiling to hear Sir Roger who is a little puzzled about the old woman, advising her as a justice of peace to avoid all communication with the devil, and never to hurt any of her neighbour's cattle. We concluded our visit with a bounty which was very acceptable.

In our return home Sir Roger told me that old Moll had been often brought before him for making children spit pins, and giving maids the nightmare; and that the country-people would be tossing her into a pond and trying experiments with her every day, if it was not for him and his chaplain.

I have since found upon inquiry that Sir Roger
was several times staggered with the reports that had
been brought him concerning this old woman, and
would frequently have bound her over to the county
sessions, had not his chaplain with much ado persuaded
him to the contrary.

I have been the more particular in this account,
because I hear there is scarce a village in England
that has not a Moll White in it. When an old woman
begins to doat, and grow chargeable to a parish, she is
generally turned into a witch, and fills the whole country
with extravagant fancies, imaginary distempers, and
terrifying dreams. In the meantime, the poor wretch
that is the innocent occasion of so many evils, begins
to be frighted at herself, and sometimes confesses
secret commerces and familiarities that her imagination
forms in a delirious old age. This frequently cuts off
charity from the greatest objects of compassion, and
inspires people with a malevolence towards those poor
decrepid parts of our species, in whom human nature
is defaced by infirmity and dotage.

SIR ROGER ON THE BENCH

Comes jucundus in via pro vehiculo est.   PUBL. SYR. *Frag.*

An agreeable companion upon the road is as good as a
coach.

A MAN's first care should be to avoid the reproaches of his own heart; his next, to escape the
censures of the world. If the last interferes with the
former, it ought to be entirely neglected; but otherwise there cannot be a greater satisfaction to an
honest mind, than to see those approbations which
it gives itself, seconded by the applauses of the public.
A man is more sure of his conduct, when the verdict
which he passes upon his own behaviour is thus
warranted and confirmed by the opinion of all that
know him.

My worthy friend Sir Roger is one of those who is not only at peace within himself, but beloved and esteemed by all about him. He receives a suitable tribute for his universal benevolence to mankind, in the returns of affection and good-will which are paid him by every one that lives in his neighbourhood. I lately met with two or three odd instances of that general respect which is shown to the good old knight. He would needs carry Will Wimble and myself with him to the county assizes. As we were upon the road, Will Wimble joined a couple of plain men who rid before us, and conversed with them for some time; during which my friend Sir Roger acquainted me with their characters.

"The first of them," says he, "that has a spaniel by his side, is a yeoman of about a hundred pounds a year, an honest man. He is just within the game-act, and qualified to kill a hare or a pheasant. He knocks down a dinner with his gun twice or thrice a week; and by that means lives much cheaper than those who have not so good an estate as himself. He would be a good neighbour if he did not destroy so many partridges. In short, he is a very sensible man—shoots flying—and has been several times foreman of the petty-jury.

"The other that rides along with him is Tom Touchy, a fellow famous for taking 'the law' of everybody. There is not one in the town where he lives that he has not sued at a quarter-sessions. The rogue had once the impudence to go to law with the widow. His head is full of costs, damages, and ejectments. He plagued a couple of honest gentlemen so long for a trespass in breaking one of his hedges, till he was forced to sell the ground it enclosed to defray the charges of the prosecution. His father left him fourscore pounds a year; but he has cast and been cast so often, that he is not now worth thirty. I suppose he is going upon the old business of the willow-tree."

As Sir Roger was giving me this account of Tom

Touchy, Will Wimble and his two companions stopped short till we came up to them. After having paid their respects to Sir Roger, Will told him that Mr Touchy and he must appeal to him upon a dispute that arose between them. Will, it seems, had been giving his fellow-traveller an account of his angling one day in such a hole; when Tom Touchy, instead of hearing out his story, told him that Mr Such-a-one, if he pleased, might "take the law of him," for fishing in that part of the river. My friend Sir Roger heard them both upon a round trot; and after having paused some time, told them with the air of a man who would not give his judgment rashly, that "much might be said on both sides." They were neither of them dissatisfied with the knight's determination, because neither of them found himself in the wrong by it. Upon which we made the best of our way to the assizes.

The court was sat before Sir Roger came; but notwithstanding all the justices had taken their places upon the bench, they made room for the old knight at the head of them; who for his reputation in the country took occasion to whisper in the judge's ear, that he was glad his lordship had met with so much good weather in his circuit. I was listening to the proceedings of the court with much attention, and infinitely pleased with that great appearance of solemnity which so properly accompanies such a public administration of our laws; when, after about an hour's sitting, I observed, to my great surprise, in the midst of a trial, Sir Roger was getting up to speak. I was in some pain for him, until I found he had acquitted himself of two or three sentences with a look of much business and great intrepidity.

Upon his first rising the court was hushed, and a general whisper ran among the country people, that Sir Roger "was up." The speech he made was so little to the purpose, that I shall not trouble my readers with an account of it; and I believe was not so much designed by the knight himself to inform the court, as to give him a figure in my eye, and keep up his credit in the country.

I was highly delighted, when the court rose, to see the gentlemen of the country gathering about my old friend, and striving who should compliment him most; at the same time that the ordinary people gazed upon him at a distance, not a little admiring his courage, that he was not afraid to speak to the judge.

In our return home we met with a very odd accident; which I cannot forbear relating, because it shows how desirous all who know Sir Roger are of giving him marks of their esteem. When we were arrived upon the verge of his estate, we stopped at a little inn to rest ourselves and our horses. The man of the house had, it seems, been formerly a servant in the knight's family; and to do honour to his old master, had some time since, unknown to Sir Roger, put him up in a sign-post before the door; so that the knight's head hung out upon the road about a week before he himself knew any thing of the matter. As soon as Sir Roger was acquainted with it, finding that his servant's indiscretion proceeded wholly from affection and good-will, he only told him that he had made him too high a compliment; and when the fellow seemed to think that could hardly be, added with a more decisive look, that it was too great an honour for any man under a duke; but told him at the same time, that it might be altered with a very few touches, and that he himself would be at the charge of it. Accordingly they got a painter by the knight's directions to add a pair of whiskers to the face, and by a little aggravation to the features to change it to the Saracen's Head. I should not have known this story, had not the inn-keeper, upon Sir Roger's alighting, told him in my hearing that his honour's head was brought last night with the alterations that he had ordered to be made in it. Upon this, my friend, with his usual cheerfulness, related the particulars above-mentioned, and ordered the head to be brought into the room. I could not for-bear discovering greater expressions of mirth than ordinary upon the appearance of this monstrous face, under which, notwithstanding it was made to frown and stare in a most extraordinary manner, I could still discover a distant resemblance of my old friend. Sir Roger, upon seeing me laugh, desired me to tell him truly if I thought it possible for people to know him in that disguise. I at first kept my usual silence; but upon the knight's conjuring me to tell him whether it was not still more like himself than a Saracen, I composed my countenance in the best manner I could, and replied, "that much might be said on both sides."

These several adventures, with the knight's be-haviour in them, gave me as pleasant a day as ever I met with in any of my travels.

PERIODICAL ESSAYS

Μέγα βιβλίον, μέγα κακόν.

A great book is a great evil.

A MAN who publishes his works in a volume, has an infinite advantage over one who communicates his writings to the world in loose tracts and single pieces. We do not expect to meet with any thing in a bulky volume, till after some heavy preamble, and several words of course, to prepare the reader for what follows. Nay, authors have established it as a kind of rule, that a man ought to be dull sometimes; as the most severe reader makes allowances for many rests and nodding-places in a voluminous writer. This gave occasion to the famous Greek proverb which I have chosen for my motto, that, "a great book is a great evil."

On the contrary, those who publish their thoughts

in distinct sheets, and as it were by piece-meal, have none of these advantages. We must immediately fall into our subject, and treat every part of it in a lively manner, or our papers are thrown by as dull and insipid. Our matter must lie close together, and either be wholly new in itself, or in the turn it receives from our expressions. Were the books of our best authors thus to be retailed by the public, and every page submitted to the taste of forty or fifty thousand readers, I am afraid we should complain of many flat expressions, trivial observations, beaten topics, and common thoughts, which go off very well in the lump. At the same time, notwithstanding some papers may be made up of broken hints and irregular sketches, it is often expected that every sheet should have been a kind of treatise, and make out in thought what it wants in bulk: that a point of humour should be worked up in all its parts; and a subject touched upon in its most essential articles, without the repetitions, tautologies, and enlargements, that are indulged in longer labours. The ordinary writers of morality prescribe to their readers after the Galenic way; their medicines are made up in large quantities. An essay-writer must practise in the chemical method, and give the virtue of a full draught in a few drops. Were all books reduced thus to their quintessence, many a bulky author would make his appearance in a penny-paper. There would be scarce such a thing in nature as a folio; the works of an age would be contained on a few shelves; not to mention millions of volumes that would be utterly annihilated.

I cannot think that the difficulty of furnishing out separate papers of this nature has hindered authors from communicating their thoughts to the world after such a manner: though I must confess I am amazed that the press should be only made use of in this way by news-writers, and the zealots of parties; as if it were not more advantageous to mankind, to be instructed in wisdom and virtue, than in politics; and to be made good fathers, husbands and sons, than counsellors and statesmen. Had the philosophers and great men of antiquity who took so much pains in order to instruct mankind, and leave the world wiser and better than they found it; had they, I say, been possessed of the art of printing, there is no question but they would have made such an advantage of it, in dealing out their lectures to the public. Our common prints would be of great use were they thus calculated to diffuse good sense through the bulk of a people, to clear up their understandings, animate their minds with virtue, dissipate the sorrows of a heavy heart, or unbend the mind from its more severe employments, with innocent amusements. When knowledge, instead of being bound up in books, and kept in libraries and retirements, is thus obtruded upon the public; when it is canvassed in every assembly, and exposed upon every table, I cannot forbear reflecting upon that passage in the Proverbs: "Wisdom crieth without, she uttereth her voice in the streets; she crieth in the chief place of concourse, in the openings of the gates. In the city she uttereth her words, saying, How long, ye simple ones, will ye love simplicity? And the scorners delight in their scorning? And fools hate knowledge?"

The many letters which come to me from persons of the best sense in both sexes (for I may pronounce their characters from their way of writing) do not a little encourage me in the prosecution of this my undertaking: besides that my bookseller tells me, the demand for these my papers increases daily. It is at his instance that I shall continue my rural speculations to the end of this month; several having made up separate sets of them, as they have done of those relating to wit, to operas, to points of morality or subjects of humour.

I am not at all mortified, when sometimes I see my works thrown aside by men of no taste or learning. There is a kind of heaviness and ignorance that hangs upon the minds of ordinary men, which is too thick for knowledge to break through.   Their souls are not to be enlightened.

> Nox atra cava circumvolat umbra.
>
> VIRG. *Æn*. ii. 360.

Black night enwraps them in her gloomy shade.

To these I must apply the fable of the mole, that, after having consulted many oculists for the bettering of his sight, was at last provided with a good pair of spectacles; but upon his endeavouring to make use of them, his mother told him very prudently, "That spectacles, though they might help the eye of a man, could be of no use to a mole."   It is not therefore for the benefit of moles that I publish these my daily essays.

But besides such as are moles through ignorance, there are others who are moles through envy.   As it is said in the Latin proverb, "That one man is a wolf to another"; so, generally speaking, one author is a mole to another.   It is impossible for them to discover beauties in one another's works; they have eyes only for spots and blemishes: they can indeed see the light, as it is said of the animals which are their namesakes, but the idea of it is painful to them; they immediately shut their eyes upon it, and withdraw themselves into a wilful obscurity.   I have already caught two or three of these dark undermining vermin, and intend to make a string of them, in order to hang them up in one of my papers, as an example to all such voluntary moles.

SIR ROGER AND THE GIPSIES

Semperque recentes
Convectare juvat prædas, et vivere rapto.
VIRG. *Æn.* vii. 748.

A plundering race, still eager to invade,
On spoil they live, and make of theft a trade.

As I was yesterday riding out in the fields with
my friend Sir Roger, we saw at a little distance from
us a troop of gipsies. Upon the first discovery of
them, my friend was in some doubt whether he
should not exert the justice of the peace upon such
a band of lawless vagrants; but not having his clerk
with him, who is a necessary counsellor with him
on these occasions, and fearing that his poultry
might fare the worse for it, he let the thought drop—
but at the same time gave me a particular account of
the mischiefs they do in the country, in stealing
people's goods and spoiling their servants. "If a
stray piece of linen hangs upon a hedge," says Sir
Roger, "they are sure to have it; if the hog loses
his way in the fields, it is ten to one but he becomes
their prey: our geese cannot live in peace for them;
if a man prosecutes them with severity, his henroost
is sure to pay for it. They generally straggle into
these parts about this time of the year; and set
the heads of our servant-maids so agog for husbands,
that we do not expect to have any business done as
it should be whilst they are in the country. I have
an honest dairy-maid who crosses their hands with
a piece of silver every summer, and never fails being
promised the handsomest young fellow in the parish
for her pains. Your friend the butler has been fool
enough to be seduced by them; and though he is
sure to lose a knife, a fork, or a spoon every time
his fortune is told him, generally shuts himself up
in the pantry with an old gipsy for above half an
hour once in a twelvemonth. Sweethearts are the

things they live upon, which they bestow very plentifully upon all those that apply themselves to them.
You see now and then some handsome young jades
among them: the sluts have white teeth and black
eyes."

Sir Roger observing that I listened with great
attention to his account of a people who were so
entirely new to me, told me, that if I would, they
should tell us our fortunes. As I was very well
pleased with the knight's proposal, we rid up, and
communicated our hands to them. A Cassandra of
the crew, after having examined my lines very diligently, told me, that I loved a pretty maid in a
corner, that I was a good woman's man, with some
other particulars which I do not think proper to
relate. My friend Sir Roger alighted from his horse,
and exposing his palm to two or three that stood by
him, they crumpled it all shapes, and diligently
scanned every wrinkle that could be made in it;
when one of them, who was older and more sun-
burnt than the rest, told him, that he had a widow
in his line of life. Upon which the knight cried,
"Go, go, you are an idle baggage"; and at the
same time smiled upon me. The gipsy finding he
was not displeased in his heart, told him after a
farther inquiry into his hand, that his true-love was
constant, and that she should dream of him to-night.
My old friend cried pish, and bid her go on. The
gipsy told him that he was a bachelor, but would not
be so long; and that he was dearer to somebody
than he thought. The knight still repeated, " She
was an idle baggage," and bid her go on. "Ah,
master," says the gipsy, "that roguish leer of yours
makes a pretty woman's heart ache; you have not that
simper about the mouth for nothing."—The uncouth
gibberish with which all this was uttered, like the
darkness of an oracle, made us the more attentive to
it. To be short, the knight left the money with her
that he had crossed her hand with, and got up again
on his horse.

As we were riding away, Sir Roger told me, that he knew several sensible people who believed these gipsies now and then foretold very strange things; and for half an hour together appeared more jocund than ordinary. In the height of his good-humour, meeting a common beggar upon the road, who was no conjuror, as he went to relieve him he found his pocket was picked; that being a kind of palmistry at which this race of vermin are very dexterous.

I might here entertain my reader with historical remarks on this idle profligate people, who infest all the countries of Europe, and live in the midst of governments in a kind of commonwealth by themselves. But instead of entering into observations of this nature, I shall fill the remaining part of my paper with a story which is still fresh in Holland, and was printed in one of our monthly accounts about twenty years ago. "As the *trek-schuyt*, or hackney-boat which carries passengers from Leyden to Amsterdam, was putting off, a boy running along the side of the canal desired to be taken in: which the master of the boat refused, because the lad had not quite money enough to pay the usual fare. An eminent merchant being pleased with the looks of the boy, and secretly touched with compassion towards him, paid the money for him, and ordered him to be taken on board. Upon talking with him afterward, he found that he could speak readily in three or four languages, and learned upon farther examination that he had been stolen away when he was a child by a gipsy, and had rambled ever since with a gang of those strollers up and down several parts of Europe. It happened that the merchant, whose heart seems to have inclined towards the boy by a secret kind of instinct, had himself lost a child some years before. The parents, after a long search for him, gave him for drowned in one of the canals with which that country abounds; and the mother was so afflicted at the loss of a fine boy, who was her only son, that she died for grief of it. Upon laying together all particulars, and examining the several moles and marks by which the mother used to describe the child when he was first missing, the boy proved to be the son of the merchant whose heart had so unaccountably melted at the sight of him. The lad was very well pleased to find a father who was so rich and likely to leave him a good estate: the father on the other hand was not a little delighted to see a son return to him, whom he had given up for lost, with such a strength of constitution, sharpness of understanding, and skill in languages." Here the printed story leaves off; but if I may give credit to reports, our linguist having received such extraordinary rudiments towards a good education, was afterwards trained up in every thing that becomes a gentleman; wearing off by little and little all the vicious habits and practices that he had been used to in the course of his peregrinations. Nay, it is said, that he has since been employed in foreign courts upon national business, with great reputation to himself and honour to those who sent him, and that he has visited several countries as a public minister in which he formerly wandered as a gipsy.

TOWN AND COUNTRY

Ipsæ rursum concedite sylvæ.
VIRG. *Ecl.* x. 63.

Once more, ye woods, adieu.

IT is usual for a man who loves country sports to preserve the game in his own grounds, and divert himself upon those that belong to his neighbour. My friend Sir Roger generally goes two or three miles from his house, and gets into the frontiers of his estate, before he beats about in search of a hare or partridge, on purpose to spare his own fields, where he is always sure of finding diversion, when the worst comes to the worst. By this means the breed about his house has time to increase and multiply, besides that the sport is more agreeable where the game is harder to come at, and where it does not lie so thick as to produce any perplexity or confusion in the pursuit. For these reasons the country gentleman, like the fox, seldom preys near his own home.

In the same manner I have made a month's excursion out of the town, which is the great field of game for sportsmen of my species, to try my fortune in the country, where I have started several subjects, and hunted them down, with some pleasure to myself, and I hope to others. I am here forced to use a great deal of diligence before I can spring anything to my mind; whereas in town, whilst I am following one character, it is ten to one but I am crossed in my way by another, and put up such a variety of odd creatures in both sexes, that they foil the scent of one another, and puzzle the chase. My greatest difficulty in the country is to find sport, and in town to choose it. In the meantime, as I have given a whole month's rest to the cities of London and Westminster, I promise myself abundance of new game upon my return thither.

It is indeed high time for me to leave the country, since I find the whole neighbourhood begin to grow very inquisitive after my name and character; my love of solitude, taciturnity, and particular way of life, having raised a great curiosity in all these parts.

The notions which have been framed of me are various: some look upon me as very proud, some as very modest, and some as very melancholy. Will Wimble, as my friend the butler tells me, observing me very much alone, and extremely silent when I am in company, is afraid I have killed a man. The country people seem to suspect me for a conjuror; and some of them, hearing of the visit which I made to Moll White, will needs have it that Sir Roger has brought down a cunning man with him, to cure the old woman, and free the country from her charms. So that the character which I go under in part of the neighbourhood, is what they call here a White Witch.

A justice of peace, who lives about five miles off, and is not of Sir Roger's party, has, it seems, said twice or thrice at his table, that he wishes Sir Roger does not harbour a Jesuit in his house, and that he thinks the gentlemen of the country would do very well to make me give some account of myself.

On the other side, some of Sir Roger's friends are afraid the old knight is imposed upon by a designing fellow; and as they have heard that he converses very promiscuously when he is in town, do not know but he has brought down with him some discarded whig, that is sullen, and says nothing because he is out of place.

Such is the variety of opinions which are here entertained of me, so that I pass among some for a disaffected person, and among others for a popish priest; among some for a wizard, and among others for a murderer; and all this for no other reason that I can imagine, but because I do not hoot, and halloo, and make a noise. It is true, my friend Sir Roger tells them,—"That it is my way," and that I am only a philosopher;—but this will not satisfy them. They think there is more in me than he discovers, and that I do not hold my tongue for nothing.

For these and other reasons I shall set out for London to-morrow, having found by experience that the country is not a place for a person of my temper, who does not love jollity, and what they call good neighbourhood. A man that is out of humour when an unexpected guest breaks in upon him, and does not care for sacrificing an afternoon to every chance comer—that will be the master of his own time, and the pursuer of his own inclinations,—makes but a very unsociable figure in this kind of life. I shall therefore retire into the town, if I may make use of that phrase, and get into the crowd again as fast as I can, in order to be alone. I can there raise what speculations I please upon others without being observed myself, and at the same time enjoy all the advantages of company with all the privileges of solitude. In the mean while, to finish the month, and conclude these my rural speculations, I shall here insert a letter from my friend Will Honeycomb, who has not lived a month for these forty years out of the smoke of London, and rallies me after his way upon my country life.

"DEAR SPEC.

"I suppose this letter will find thee picking of daisies, or smelling to a lock of hay, or passing away thy time in some innocent country diversion of the like nature. I have however orders from the club to summon thee up to town, being all of us cursedly afraid thou wilt not be able to relish our company, after thy conversations with Moll White and Will Wimble. Pr'ythee do not send us up any more stories of a cock and a bull, nor frighten the town with spirits and witches. Thy speculations begin to smell confoundedly of woods and meadows. If thou dost not come up quickly, we shall conclude that thou art in love with one of Sir Roger's dairy-maids. Service to the knight. Sir Andrew is grown the cock of the club since he left us, and if he does not return quickly will make every mother's son of us commonwealth's-men.

Dear Spec.,

Thine eternally,

"WILL HONEYCOMB."

THE GENIUS OF THE ENGLISH LANGUAGE

Est brevitate opus, ut currat sententia.
HOR. *Sat.* i. x. 9.

Let brevity dispatch the rapid thought.

I HAVE somewhere read of an eminent person, who used in his private offices of devotion to give thanks to Heaven that he was born a Frenchman: for my own part, I look upon it as a peculiar blessing that I was born an Englishman. Among many other reasons, I think myself very happy in my country, as the language of it is wonderfully adapted to a man who is sparing of his words, and an enemy to loquacity.

As I have frequently reflected on my good fortune in this particular, I shall communicate to the public my speculations on the English tongue, not doubting but they will be acceptable to all my curious readers.

The English delight in silence more than any other European nation, if the remarks which are made on us by foreigners are true. Our discourse is not kept up in conversation, but falls into more pauses and intervals than in our neighbouring countries; as it is observed, that the matter of our writings is thrown much closer together, and lies in a narrower compass than is usual in the works of foreign authors; for, to favour our natural taciturnity, when we are obliged to utter our thoughts, we do it in the shortest way we are able, and give as quick a birth to our conceptions as possible.

This humour shows itself in several remarks that we may make upon the English language. As first of all by its abounding in monosyllables, which gives us an opportunity of delivering our thoughts in few sounds. This indeed takes off from the elegance of our tongue, but at the same time expresses our ideas in the readiest manner, and consequently answers the first design of speech better than the multitude of syllables, which makes the words of other languages more tuneable and sonorous. The sounds of our English words are commonly like those of string-music, short and transient, which rise and perish upon a single touch; those of other languages are like the notes of wind-instruments, sweet and swelling, and lengthened out into a variety of modulation.

In the next place we may observe, that where the words are not monosyllables, we often make them so, so much as lies in our power, by our rapidity of pronunciation; as it generally happens in most of our long words which are derived from the Latin, where we contract the length of the syllables that gives them a grave and solemn air in their own language, to make them more proper for dispatch, and more conformable to the genius of our tongue. This we may find in a multitude of words, as "liberty, conspiracy, theatre, orator," &c.

The same natural aversion to loquacity has of late years made a very considerable alteration in our language, by closing in one syllable the termination of our preterperfect tense, as in these words, "drown'd, walk'd, arriv'd," for "drowned, walked, arrived," which has very much disfigured the tongue, and turned a tenth part of our smoothest words into so many clusters of consonants. This is the more remarkable, because the want of vowels in our language has been the general complaint of our politest authors, who nevertheless are the men that have made these retrenchments, and consequently very much increased our former scarcity.

This reflection on the words that end in ED, I have heard in conversation from one of the greatest geniuses this age has produced. I think we may add to the foregoing observation, the change which has happened in our language, by the abbreviation of several words that are terminated in "eth," by substituting an s in the room of the last syllable, as in "drowns, walks, arrives," and innumerable other words, which in the pronunciation of our forefathers were "drowneth, walketh, arriveth." This has wonderfully multiplied a letter which was before too frequent in the English tongue, and added to that hissing in our language, which is taken so much notice of by foreigners; but at the same time humours our taciturnity, and eases us of many superfluous syllables.

I might here observe, that the same single letter on many occasions does the office of a whole word, and represents the "his" and "her" of our forefathers. There is no doubt but the ear of a foreigner, which is the best judge in this case, would very much disapprove of such innovations, which indeed we do ourselves in some measure, by retaining the old termination in writing, and in all solemn offices of our religion.

As in the instances I have given we have epitomized many of our particular words to the detriment of our tongue, so on other occasions we have drawn two words into one, which has likewise very much untuned our language, and clogged it with consonants—as "mayn't, can't, shan't, won't," and the like, for "may not, cannot, shall not, will not," &c.

It is perhaps this humour of speaking no more than we needs must, which has so miserably curtailed some of our words, that in familiar writings and conversations they often lose all but their first syllables, as in "mob, rep. pos. incog." and the like; and as all ridiculous words make their first entry into a language by familiar phrases, I dare not answer for these, that they will not in time be looked upon as a part of our tongue. We see some of our poets have been so indiscreet as to imitate Hudibras's doggrel expressions in their serious compositions, by throwing out the signs of our substantives which are essential to the English language. Nay, this humour of shortening our language had once run so far, that some of our celebrated authors, among whom we may reckon Sir Roger L'Estrange in particular, began to prune their words of all superfluous letters, as they termed them, in order to adjust the spelling to the pronunciation; which would have confounded all our etymologies, and have quite destroyed our tongue.

We may here likewise observe, that our proper names, when familiarized in English, generally dwindle to monosyllables, whereas in other modern languages they receive a softer turn on this occasion, by the addition of a new syllable.—Nick in Italian is Nicolini: Jack in French Jeannot; and so of the rest.

There is another particular in our language which is a great instance of our frugality of words, and that is, the suppressing of several particles which must be produced in other tongues to make a sentence intelligible. This perplexes the best writers, when they find the relatives "whom," "which," or "they," at their mercy, whether they may have admission or not; and will never be decided until we have something like an academy, that by the best authorities and rules drawn from the analogy of languages shall settle all controversies between grammar and idiom.

I have only considered our language as it shows the genius and natural temper of the English, which is modest, thoughtful, and sincere, and which, perhaps, may recommend the people, though it has spoiled the tongue. We might, perhaps, carry the same thought into other languages, and deduce a great part of what is peculiar to them from the genius of the people who speak them. It is certain, the light talkative humour of the French has not a little infected their tongue, which might be shown by many instances; as the genius of the Italians, which is so much addicted to music and ceremony, has moulded all their words and phrases to those particular uses. The stateliness and gravity of the Spaniards shows itself to perfection in the solemnity of their language; and the blunt honest humour of the German sounds better in the roughness of the High-Dutch, than it would in a politer tongue.

THE VISION OF MIRZAH

Omnem, quæ nunc obducta tuenti
Mortales hebetat visus tibi, et humida circum
Caligat, nubem eripiam.   VIRG. *Æn.* ii. 604.

The cloud, which, intercepting the clear light,
Hangs o'er thy eyes, and blunts thy mortal sight,
I will remove.

WHEN I was at Grand Cairo, I picked up several oriental manuscripts, which I have still by me.— Among others I met with one entitled, The Visions of Mirzah, which I have read over with great pleasure. I intend to give it to the public when I ha ve no other entertainment for them; and shall begin with the first vision, which I have translated word for word as follows:

"On the fifth day of the moon, which according to the custom of my forefathers I always keep holy after having washed myself, and offered up my morning devotions, I ascended the high hills of Bagdat, in order to pass the rest of the day in meditation and prayer. As I was here airing myself on the tops of the mountains, I fell into a profound contemplation on the vanity of human life; and passing from one thought to another, 'Surely,' said I, 'man is but a shadow, and life a dream.' Whilst I was thus musing, I cast my eyes towards the summit of a rock that was not far from me, where I discovered one in the habit of a shepherd, with a little musical instrument in his hand. As I looked upon him he applied it to his lips, and began to play upon it. The sound of it was exceeding sweet, and wrought into a variety of tunes that were inexpressibly melodious, and altogether different from any thing I had ever heard. They put me in mind of those heavenly airs that are played to the departed souls of good men upon their first arrival in Paradise, to wear out the impressions of the last agonies, and qualify them for the pleasures of that happy place. My heart melted away in secret raptures.

"I had been often told that the rock before me was
the haunt of a genius; and that several had been
entertained with music who had passed by it, but never
heard that the musician had before made himself
visible. When he had raised my thoughts by those
transporting airs which he played, to taste the pleasures
of his conversation, as I looked upon him like one
astonished, he beckoned to me, and by the waving of
his hand directed me to approach the place where he
sat. I drew near with that reverence which is due to
a superior nature; and as my heart was entirely
subdued by the captivating strains I had heard, I fell
down at his feet and wept. The genius smiled upon
me with a look of compassion and affability that
familiarized him to my imagination, and at once dis-
pelled all the fears and apprehensions with which I
approached him. He lifted me from the ground, and
taking me by the hand, ' Mirzah,' said he, ' I have heard
thee in thy soliloquies; follow me.'

" He then led me to the highest pinnacle of the rock,
and placing me on the top of it—' Cast thy eyes east-
ward,' said he, ' and tell me what thou seest.'—' I see,'
said I, ' a huge valley, and a prodigious tide of water
rolling through it.'—' The valley that thou seest,' said
he, ' is the Vale of Misery, and the tide of water that
thou seest is part of the great tide of eternity.'—
' What is the reason,' said I, ' that the tide I see rises
out of a thick mist at one end, and again loses itself
in a thick mist at the other?'—' What thou seest,' said
he, ' is that portion of eternity which is called time,
measured out by the sun, and reaching from the
beginning of the world to its consummation.'—' Examine
now,' said he, ' this sea that is bounded with darkness
at both ends, and tell me what thou discoverest in
it.'—' I see a bridge,' said I, ' standing in the midst of
the tide.'—' The bridge thou seest,' said he, ' is human
life; consider it attentively.' Upon a more leisurely
survey of it, I found that it consisted of threescore
and ten entire arches, with several broken arches,
which, added to those that were entire, made up

L. E. A.   8

the number about a hundred. As I was counting the arches, the genius told me that this bridge consisted at first of a thousand arches: but that a great flood swept away the rest, and left the bridge in the ruinous condition I now beheld it. 'But tell me farther,' said he, 'what thou discoverest on it.'—'I see multitudes of people passing over it,' said I, 'and a black cloud hanging on each end of it.' As I looked more attentively, I saw several of the passengers dropping through the bridge into the great tide that flowed underneath it: and, upon farther examination, perceived there were innumerable trap-doors that lay concealed in the bridge, which the passengers no sooner trod upon, but they fell through them into the tide, and immediately disappeared. These hidden pit-falls were set very thick at the entrance of the bridge, so that throngs of people no sooner broke through the cloud, but many of them fell into them. They grew thinner towards the middle, but multiplied and lay closer together towards the end of the arches that were entire.

"There were indeed some persons, but their number was very small, that continued a kind of hobbling march on the broken arches, but fell through one after another, being quite tired and spent with so long a walk.

"I passed some time in the contemplation of this wonderful structure, and the great variety of objects which it presented. My heart was filled with a deep melancholy to see several dropping unexpectedly in the midst of mirth and jollity, and catching at every thing that stood by them to save themselves. Some were looking up towards heaven in a thoughtful posture, and in the midst of a speculation stumbled and fell out of sight. Multitudes were very busy in the pursuit of bubbles that glittered in their eyes and danced before them; but often when they thought themselves within the reach of them, their footing failed, and down they sank. In this confusion of objects, I observed some with scimitars in their hands, and others with pestles, who ran to and fro upon the bridge, thrusting several persons on trap-doors which did not seem to lie in their way, and which they might have escaped had they not been thus forced upon them.

"The genius seeing me indulge myself on this melancholy prospect, told me I had dwelt long enough upon it. 'Take thine eyes off the bridge,' said he, 'and tell me if thou yet seest any thing thou dost not comprehend.' Upon looking up, 'What mean,' said I, 'those great flights of birds that are perpetually hovering about the bridge, and settling upon it from time to time? I see vultures, harpies, ravens, cormorants, and among many other feathered creatures several little winged boys, that perch in great numbers upon the middle arches.'—'These,' said the genius, 'are Envy, Avarice, Superstition, Despair, Love, with the like cares and passions that infest human life.'

"I here fetched a deep sigh. 'Alas,' said I, 'man was made in vain! how is he given away to misery and mortality! tortured in life, and swallowed up in death!' The genius, being moved with compassion towards me, bid me quit so uncomfortable a prospect. 'Look no more,' said he, 'on man in the first stage of his existence, in his setting out for eternity; but cast thine eye on that thick mist into which the tide bears the several generations of mortals that fall into it.' I directed my sight as I was ordered, and (whether or no the good genius strengthened it with any supernatural force, or dissipated part of the mist that was before too thick for the eye to penetrate) I saw the valley opening at the farther end, and spreading forth into an immense ocean, that had a huge rock of adamant running through the midst of it, and dividing it into two equal parts. The clouds still rested on one half of it, insomuch that I could discover nothing in it: but the other appeared to me a vast ocean planted with innumerable islands, that were covered with fruits and flowers, and interwoven with a thousand little shining seas that ran among them. I could see persons dressed in glorious habits with garlands upon their heads, passing among the trees, lying down by the sides of fountains, or resting on beds of flowers; and could hear a confused harmony of singing-birds, falling waters, human voices, and musical instruments. Gladness grew in me upon the discovery of so delightful a scene. I wished for the wings of an eagle, that I might fly away to those happy seats: but the genius told me there was no passage to them, except through the gates of death that I saw opening every moment upon the bridge. 'The islands,' said he, 'that lie so fresh and green before thee, and with which the whole face of the ocean appears spotted as far as thou canst see, are more in number than the sands on the sea-shore; there are myriads of islands behind those which thou here discoverest, reaching farther than thine eye, or even thine imagination can extend itself. These are the mansions of good men after death, who, according to the degree and kinds of virtue in which they excelled, are distributed among these several islands; which abound with pleasures of different kinds and degrees, suitable to the relishes and perfections of those who are settled in them; every island is a paradise accommodated to its respective inhabitants. Are not these, O Mirzah, habitations worth contending for? Does life appear miserable, that gives thee opportunities of earning such a reward? Is death to be feared, that will convey thee to so happy an existence? Think not man was made in vain, who has such an eternity reserved for him.' I gazed with inexpressible pleasure on these happy islands. 'At length,' said I, 'show me now, I beseech thee, the secrets that lie hid under those dark clouds which cover the ocean on the other side of the rock of adamant.' The genius making me no answer, I turned about to address myself to him a second time, but I found that he had left me: I then turned again to the vision which I had been so long contemplating; but instead of the rolling tide, the arched bridge, and the happy islands, I saw nothing but the long hollow valley of Bagdat, with oxen, sheep, and camels, grazing upon the sides of it."

INCONSTANCY

Servetur ad imum,
Qualis ab incepto processerit, et sibi constet.
HOR. *Ars Poet.* v. 126.

Keep one consistent plan from end to end.

NOTHING that is not a real crime makes a man appear so contemptible and little in the eyes of the world as inconstancy, especially when it regards religion or party. In either of these cases, though a man perhaps does but his duty in changing his side, he not only makes himself hated by those he left, but is seldom heartily esteemed by those he comes over to.

In these great articles of life, therefore, a man's conviction ought to be very strong, and if possible so well timed, that worldly advantages may seem to have no share in it, or mankind will be ill-natured enough to think he does not change sides out of principle, but either out of levity of temper, or prospects of interest. Converts and renegadoes of all kinds should take particular care to let the world see they act upon honourable motives: or, whatever approbations they may receive from themselves, and applauses from those they converse with, they may be very well assured that they are the scorn of all good men, and the public marks of infamy and derision.

Irresolution on the schemes of life which offer themselves to our choice, and inconstancy in pursuing them, are the greatest and most universal causes of all our disquiet and unhappiness. When ambition pulls one way, interest another, inclination a third, and perhaps reason contrary to all, a man is likely to pass his time but ill who has so many different parties to please. When the mind hovers among such a variety of allurements, one had better settle on a way of life that is not the very best we might have chosen, than grow old without determining our choice, and go out of the world as the greatest part of mankind do, before we have resolved how to live in it. There is but one method of setting ourselves at rest in this particular, and that is by adhering steadfastly to one great end as the chief and ultimate aim of all our pursuits. If we are firmly resolved to live up to the dictates of reason, without any regard to wealth, reputation, or the like considerations, any more than as they fall in with our principal design, we may go through life with steadiness and pleasure; but if we act by several broken views, and will not only be virtuous, but wealthy, popular, and every thing that has a value set upon it by the world, we shall live and die in misery and repentance.

One would take more than ordinary care to guard one's self against this particular imperfection, because it is that which our nature very strongly inclines us to; for if we examine ourselves thoroughly, we shall find that we are the most changeable beings in the universe. In respect of our understanding, we often embrace and reject the very same opinions; whereas beings above and beneath us have probably no opinions at all, or, at least, no wavering and uncertainties in those they have. Our superiors are guided by intuition, and our inferiors by instinct. In respect of our wills, we fall into crimes and recover out of them, are amiable or odious in the eyes of our great Judge, and pass our whole life in offending and asking pardon. On the contrary, the beings underneath us are not capable of sinning, nor those above us of repenting. The one is out of the possibilities of duty, and the other fixed in an eternal course of sin, or an eternal course of virtue.

There is scarce a state of life, or stage in it, which does not produce changes and revolutions in the mind of man. Our schemes of thought in infancy are lost in those of youth; these too take a different turn in manhood, until old age often leads us back into our former infancy. A new title or an unexpected success throws us out of ourselves, and in a manner destroys our identity. A cloudy day, or a little sunshine, have as

great an influence on many constitutions, as the most
real blessing or misfortunes. A dream varies our being,
and changes our condition while it lasts; and every
passion, not to mention health and sickness, and
the greater alterations in body and mind, makes us
appear almost different creatures. If a man is so
distinguished among other beings by this infirmity,
what can we think of such as make themselves
remarkable for it even among their own species? It
is a very trifling character to be one of the most
variable beings of the most variable kind, especially if
we consider that he who is the great standard of
perfection has in him no shadow of change, but " is
the same yesterday, to-day, and for ever."

As this mutability of temper and inconsistency
with ourselves is the greatest weakness of human
nature, so it makes the person who is remarkable for
it in a very particular manner, more ridiculous than
any other infirmity whatsoever, as it sets him in
a greater variety of foolish lights, and distinguishes
him from himself by an opposition of party-coloured
characters. The most humorous character in Horace
is founded upon this unevenness of temper, and
irregularity of conduct:

Sardus habebat

Ille Tigellius hoc : Cæsar, qui cogere posset,
Si peteret per amicitiam patris, atque suam, non
Quidquam proficeret : si collibuisset, ab ovo
Usque ad mala citaret, Io Bacche, modo summa
Voce, modo hac, resonat quæ chordis quatuor ima,
Nil æquale homini fuit illi : sæpe velut qui
Currebat fugiens hostem : persæpe velut qui
Junonis sacra ferret : habebat sæpe ducentos,
Sæpe decem servos : modo reges atque tetrarchas,
Omnia magna loquens : modo sit mihi mensa tripes, et
Concha salis puri, et toga, quæ defendere frigus,
Quamvis crassa, queat. Decies centena dedisses
Huic parco, paucis contento, quinque diebus
Nil erat in loculis. Noctes vigilabat ad ipsum
Mane : diem totum stertebat. Nil fuit unquam
Sic impar sibi.   HOR. *Sat.* I. iiL

Instead of translating this passage in Horace, I shall entertain my English reader with the description of a parallel character that is wonderfully well finished by Mr Dryden, and raised upon the same foundation :

> In the first rank of these did Zimri stand :
> A man so various, that he seemed to be
> Not one, but all mankind's epitome.
> Stiff in opinions, always in the wrong,
> Was every thing by starts and nothing long ;
> But in the course of one revolving moon,
> Was chemist, fiddler, statesman, and buffoon :
> Then all for women, painting, rhyming, drinking,
> Besides ten thousand freaks that died in thinking.
> Blest madman who could every hour employ,
> With something new to wish, or to enjoy !

A GRINNING MATCH

> Remove fera monstra, tuæque
> Saxificos vultus, quæcunque ea, tolle Medusæ.
> OVID, *Met.* v. 215.

Hence with those monstrous features, and, O ! spare
That Gorgon's look and petrifying stare. P.

In a late paper I mentioned the project of an ingenious author for the erecting of several handicraft prizes to be contended for by our British artisans, and the influence they might have towards the improvement of our several manufactures. I have since that been very much surprised by the following advertisement, which I find in the *Post-Boy* of the 11th instant, and again repeated in the *Post-Boy* of the 15th :—

"On the 9th of October next will be run for upon Coleshill-heath, in Warwickshire, a plate of six guineas value, three heats, by any horse, mare, or gelding, that hath not won above the value of 5*l.* ; the winning horse to be sold for 10*l.* to carry ten stone weight, if fourteen hands high ; if above or under to carry or be allowed weight for inches, and to be entered Friday

the 5th at the Swan in Coleshill, before six in the
evening.   Also a plate of less value to be run for by
asses.   The same day a gold ring to be grinned for by
men."

The first of these diversions that is to be exhibited
by the 10*l.* race-horses, may probably have its use;
but the two last in which the asses and men are
concerned, seem to me altogether extraordinary and
unaccountable.   Why they should keep running asses
at Coleshill, or how making mouths turns to account
in Warwickshire, more than in any other parts of
England, I cannot comprehend.   I have looked over
all the Olympic games, and do not find any thing
in them like an ass-race, or a match at grinning.
However it be, I am informed that several asses are
now kept in body-clothes, and sweated every morning
upon the heath; and that all the country fellows
within ten miles of the Swan grin an hour or two
in their glasses every morning, in order to qualify
themselves for the 9th of October.   The prize which
is proposed to be grinned for has raised such an
ambition among the common people of out-grinning
one another, that many very discerning persons are
afraid it should spoil most of the faces in the county;
and that a Warwickshire man will be known by his
grin, as Roman Catholics imagine a Kentish man is
by his tail.   The gold ring, which is made the prize of
deformity, is just the reverse of the golden apple that
was formerly made the prize of beauty, and should
carry for its posy the old motto inverted:

" *Detur tetriori.*"

Or, to accommodate it to the capacity of the com-
batants,

> The frightfull'st grinner
> Be the winner.

In the meanwhile I would advise a Dutch painter
to be present at this great controversy of faces, in
order to make a collection of the most remarkable
grins that shall be there exhibited.

l must not here omit an account which l lately
received of one of these grinning matches from a
gentleman, who, upon reading the above-mentioned
advertisement, entertained a coffee-house with the
following narrative:—Upon the taking of Namur,
amidst other public rejoicings made on that occasion,
there was a gold ring given by a whig justice of peace
to be grinned for. The first competitor that entered
the lists was a black swarthy Frenchman, who acci-
dently passed that way; and being a man naturally of
a withered look, and hard features, promised himself
good success. He was placed upon a table in the great
point of view, and looking upon the company like
Milton's Death,

> Grinn'd horribly a ghastly smile :—

His muscles were so drawn together on each side
of his face, that he showed twenty teeth at a grin, and
put the country in some pain, lest a foreigner should
carry away the honour of the day; but upon a farther
trial they found he was master only of the merry
grin.

The next that mounted the table was a malecontent
in those days, and a great master in the whole art of
grinning, but particularly excelled in the angry grin.
He did his part well, but the justice being apprised by
one who stood near him, that the fellow who grinned
in his face was a Jacobite, and being unwilling that a
disaffected person should win the gold ring, and be
looked upon as the best grinner in the country, he
ordered the oaths to be tendered unto him upon his
quitting the table, which the grinner refusing, he was
set aside as an unqualified person. There were several
other grotesque figures that presented themselves,
which it would be too tedious to describe. I must not
however omit a ploughman, who lived in the further
part of the country, and being very lucky in a pair of
long lantern-jaws, wrung his face into such a hideous
grimace, that every feature of it appeared under a different distortion. The whole company stood astonished

at such a complicated grin, and were ready to assign the prize to him, had it not been proved by one of his antagonists, that he had practised with verjuice for some days before, and had a crab found upon him at the very time of grinning; upon which the best judges of grinning declared it as their opinion, that he was not to be looked upon as a fair grinner, and therefore ordered him to be set aside as a cheat.

The prize, it seems, at length fell upon a cobbler, Giles Gorgon by name, who produced several new grins of his own invention, having been used to cut faces for many years together over his last. At the very first grin he cast every human feature out of his countenance, at the second he became the face of a spout, at the third a baboon, at the fourth the head of a bass viol, and at the fifth a pair of nut-crackers. The whole assembly wondered at his accomplishments, and bestowed the ring on him unanimously; but, what he esteemed more than all the rest, a country wench, whom he had wooed in vain for above five years before, was so charmed with his grins, and the applauses which he received on all sides, that she married him the week following, and to this day wears the prize upon her finger, the cobbler having made use of it as his wedding ring.

This paper might perhaps seem very impertinent, if it grew serious in the conclusion. It would nevertheless leave to the consideration of those who are the patrons of this monstrous trial of skill, whether or no they are not guilty, in some measure, of an affront to their species, in treating after this manner the " human face divine," and turning that part of us, which has so great an image impressed upon it, into the image of a monkey; whether the raising such silly competitions among the ignorant, proposing prizes for such useless accomplishments, filling the common people's heads with such senseless ambitions, and inspiring them with such absurd ideas of superiority and pre-eminence, has not in it something immoral, as well as ridiculous.

ON CHARITY

Quis enim bonus, aut face dignus
Arcana, qualem Cereris vult esse sacerdos,
Ulla aliena sibi credat mala?

JUV. *Sat.* xv. 140.

Who can all sense of others' ills escape,
Is but a brute, at best, in human shape. TATE.

IN one of my last week's papers I treated of good-nature, as it is the effect of constitution; I shall now speak of it as a moral virtue. The first may make a man easy in himself and agreeable to others, but implies no merit in him that is possessed of it. A man is no more to be praised upon this account, than because he has a regular pulse, or a good digestion. This good-nature however in the constitution, which Mr Dryden somewhere calls a " milkiness of blood," is an admirable groundwork for the other. In order, therefore, to try our good-nature, whether it arises from the body or the mind, whether it be founded in the animal or rational part of our nature: in a word, whether it be such as is entitled to any other reward, besides that secret satisfaction and contentment of mind which is essential to it, and the kind reception it procures us in the world, we must examine it by the following rules:

First, whether it acts with steadiness and uniformity in sickness and in health, in prosperity and in adversity; if otherwise, it is to be looked upon as nothing else but an irradiation of the mind from some new supply of spirits, or a more kindly circulation of the blood. Sir Francis Bacon mentions a cunning solicitor, who would never ask a favour of a great man before dinner; but took care to prefer his petition at a time when the party petitioned had his mind free from care, and his appetites in good humour. Such a transient temporary good-nature as this, is not that philanthropy, that love of mankind, which deserves the title of a moral virtue.

The next way of a man's bringing his good-nature to the test, is, to consider whether it operates according to the rules of reason and duty: for if, notwithstanding its general benevolence to mankind, it makes no distinction between its objects, if it exerts itself promiscuously towards the deserving and the undeserving, if it relieves alike the idle and the indigent, if it gives itself up to the first petitioner and lights upon any one rather by accident than choice, it may pass for an amiable instinct, but must not assume the name of a moral virtue.

The third trial of good-nature will be the examining ourselves, whether or no we are able to exert it to our own disadvantage, and employ it on proper objects, notwithstanding any little pain, want, or inconvenience which may arise to ourselves from it. In a word, whether we are willing to risk any part of our fortune, our reputation, or health, or ease, for the benefit of mankind. Among all these expressions of good-nature, I shall single out that which goes under the general name of charity, as it consists in relieving the indigent; that being a trial of this kind which offers itself to us almost at all times, and in every place.

I should propose it as a rule, to every one who is provided with any competency of fortune more than sufficient for the necessaries of life, to lay aside a certain portion of his income for the use of the poor. This I would look upon as an offering to Him who has a right to the whole, for the use of those whom, in the passage hereafter mentioned, he has described as his own representatives upon earth. At the same time we should manage our charity with such prudence and caution, that we may not hurt our own friends or relations, whilst we are doing good to those who are strangers to us.

This may possibly be explained better by example than by a rule.

Eugenius is a man of a universal good-nature, and generous beyond the extent of his fortune; but withal so prudent in the economy of his affairs, that

what goes out in charity is made up by good management. Eugenius has what the world calls 200*l.* a
year; but never values himself above nine-score, as
not thinking he has a right to the tenth part, which
he always appropriates to charitable uses. To this
sum he frequently makes other voluntary additions,
insomuch that in a good year, for such he accounts
those in which he has been able to make greater
bounties than ordinary, he has given above twice that
sum to the sickly and indigent. Eugenius prescribes
to himself many particular days of fasting and abstinence, in order to increase his private bank of charity,
and sets aside what would be the current expenses of
those times for the use of the poor. He often goes
afoot where his business calls him, and at the end of his
walk has given a shilling, which in his ordinary methods
of expense would have gone for coach-hire, to the
first necessitous person that has fallen in his way. I
have known him, when he has been going to a play or
an opera, divert the money, which was designed for
that purpose, upon an object of charity whom he has
met with in the street; and afterward pass his evening
in a coffee-house, or at a friend's fire-side, with much
greater satisfaction to himself, than he could have
received from the most exquisite entertainments of
the theatre. By these means, he is generous without impoverishing himself, and enjoys his estate by
making it the property of others.

There are few men so cramped in their private
affairs, who may not be charitable after this manner,
without any disadvantage to themselves, or prejudice
to their families. It is but sometimes sacrificing a
diversion or convenience to the poor, and turning the
usual course of our expenses into a better channel.
This is, I think, not only the most prudent and
convenient, but the most meritorious piece of charity,
which we can put in practice. By this method, we
in some measure share the necessities of the poor
at the same time that we relieve them, and make
ourselves not only their patrons, but their fellow-
sufferers.

Sir Thomas Brown, in the last part of his Religio Medici, in which he describes his charity in several heroic instances, and with a noble heat of sentiment, mentions that verse in the Proverbs of Solomon, "He that giveth to the poor, lendeth to the Lord." There is more rhetoric in that one sentence, says he, than in a library of sermons; and, indeed, if those sentences were understood by the reader, with the same emphasis as they are delivered by the author, we needed not those volumes of instructions, but might be honest by an epitome.

This passage of Scripture is, indeed, wonderfully persuasive; but I think the same thought is carried much farther in the New Testament, where our Saviour tells us, in a most pathetic manner that he shall hereafter regard the clothing of the naked, the feeding of the hungry, and the visiting of the imprisoned, as offices done to himself, and reward them accordingly. Pursuant to those passages in Holy Scripture, I have somewhere met with the epitaph of a charitable man, which has very much pleased me. I cannot recollect the words, but the sense of it is to this purpose: What I spent I lost; what I possessed is left to others; what I gave away remains with me.

Since I am thus insensibly engaged in sacred writ, I cannot forbear making an extract of several passages which I have always read with great delight in the Book of Job. It is the account which that holy man gives of his behaviour in the days of his prosperity, and if considered only as a human composition, is a finer picture of a charitable and good-natured man than is to be met with in any other author.

"Oh that I were as in months past, as in the days when God preserved me: when his candle shined upon my head, and when by his light I walked through darkness; when the Almighty was yet with me; when my children were about me; when I washed my steps with butter, and the rock poured me out rivers of oil.

"When the ear heard me, then it blessed me; and when the eye saw me, it gave witness to me. Because I delivered the poor that cried, and the fatherless, and him that had none to help him. The blessing of him that was ready to perish came upon me, and I caused the widow's heart to sing for joy. I was eyes to the blind, and feet was I to the lame; I was a father to the poor, and the cause which I knew not I searched out. Did not I weep for him that was in trouble? was not my soul grieved for the poor? Let me be weighed in an even balance, that God may know mine integrity. If I did despise the cause of my man-servant or of my maid-servant when they contended with me; what then shall I do when God riseth up? and when he visiteth, what shall I answer him? Did not he that made me in the womb, make him? and did not one fashion us in the womb? If I have withheld the poor from their desire, or have caused the eyes of the widow to fail: Or have eaten my morsel myself alone, and the fatherless hath not eaten thereof: If I have seen any perish for want of clothing, or any poor without covering: If his loins have not blessed me, and if he were not warmed with the fleece of my sheep: If I have lifted up my hand against the fatherless, when I saw my help in the gate; then let mine arm fall from my shoulder-blade, and mine arm be broken from the bone. If I have rejoiced at the destruction of him that hated me, or lifted up myself when evil found him: (neither have I suffered my mouth to sin, by wishing a curse to his soul.) The stranger did not lodge in the street; but I opened my doors to the traveller. If my land cry against me, or that the furrows likewise therefore complain: If I have eaten the fruits thereof without money, or have caused the owners thereof to lose their life: let thistles grow instead of wheat, and cockle instead of barley."

WIT AND WISDOM

Centuriæ seniorum agitant expertia frugis:
Celsi prætereunt austera poemata Rhamnes,
Omne tulit punctum qui miscuit utile dulci,
Lectorem delectando, pariterque monendo.

HOR. *Ars Poet.* 341.

Old age is only fond of moral truth,
Lectures too grave disgust aspiring youth;
But he who blends instruction with delight,
Wins every reader, nor in vain shall write.   P.

I MAY cast my readers under two general divisions, the mercurial and the saturnine. The first are the gay part of my disciples, who require speculations of wit and humour; the others are those of a more solemn and sober turn, who find no pleasure but in papers of morality and sound sense. The former call every thing that is serious, stupid; the latter look upon every thing as impertinent that is ludicrous. Were I always grave, one half of my readers would fall off from me; were I always merry, I should lose the other. I make it, therefore, my endeavour to find out entertainments for both kinds, and by that means, perhaps, consult the good of both, more than I should do, did I always write to the particular taste of either. As they neither of them know what I proceed upon, the sprightly reader, who takes up my paper in order to be diverted, very often finds himself engaged unawares in a serious and profitable course of thinking; as, on the contrary, the thoughtful man who perhaps may hope to find something solid, and full of deep reflection, is very often insensibly betrayed into a fit of mirth. In a word, the reader sits down to my entertainment without knowing his bill of fare, and has therefore at least the pleasure of hoping there may be a dish to his palate.

I must confess, were I left to myself, I would rather aim at instructing than diverting; but if we will be useful to the world, we must take it as we find it. Authors of professed severity discourage the looser part of mankind from having any thing to do with their writings. A man must have virtue in him, before he will enter upon the reading of a Seneca or an Epictetus. The very title of a moral treatise has something in it austere and shocking to the careless and inconsiderate.

For this reason several unthinking persons fall in my way who would give no attention to lectures delivered with a religious seriousness or a philosophic gravity. They are insnared into sentiments of wisdom and virtue when they do not think of it; and if by that means they arrive only at such a degree of consideration as may dispose them to listen to more studied and elaborate discourses, I shall not think my speculations useless. I might likewise observe, that the gloominess in which sometimes the minds of the best men are involved, very often stands in need of such little incitements to mirth and laughter, as are apt to disperse melancholy, and put our faculties in good humour. To which some will add, that the British climate, more than any other, makes entertainments of this nature in a manner necessary.

If what I have here said does not recommend, it will at least excuse, the variety of my speculations. I would not willingly laugh but in order to instruct, or if I sometimes fail in this point, when my mirth ceases to be instructive, it shall never cease to be innocent. A scrupulous conduct in this particular has, perhaps, more merit in it than the generality of readers imagine; did they know how many thoughts occur in a point of humour, which a discreet author in modesty suppresses; how many strokes of raillery present themselves, which could not fail to please the ordinary taste of mankind, but are stifled in their birth by reason of some remote tendency which they carry in them to corrupt the minds of those who read them: did they know how many glances of ill-nature are industriously avoided for fear of doing injury to the reputation of another, they would be apt to think kindly of those writers who endeavour to make themselves diverting, without being immoral. One may apply to these authors that passage in Waller:

> Poets lose half the praise they would have got,
> Were it but known what they discreetly blot.

As nothing is more easy than to be a wit, with all the above-mentioned liberties, it requires some genius and invention to appear such without them.

What I have here said is not only in regard to the public, but with an eye to my particular correspondent, who has sent me the following letter, which I have castrated in some places upon these considerations:

"Sir,

"Having lately seen your discourse upon a match of grinning, I cannot forbear giving you an account of a whistling match, which, with many others, I was entertained with about three years since at the Bath. The prize was a guinea, to be conferred upon the ablest Whistler, that is, on him who could whistle clearest, and go through his time without laughing, to which at the same time he was provoked by the antic postures of a merry-andrew, who was to stand upon the stage and play his tricks in the eye of the performer. There were three competitors for the guinea. The first was a ploughman of a very promising aspect; his features were steady, and his muscles composed in so inflexible stupidity, that upon his first appearance every one gave the guinea for lost. The pickled-herring however found the way to shake him; for upon his whistling a country jig, this unlucky wag danced to it with such a variety of distortions and grimace, that the countryman could not forbear smiling upon him, and by that means spoiled his whistle, and lost the prize.

"The next that mounted the stage was an under-citizen of the Bath, a person remarkable among the inferior people of that place for his great wisdom, and his broad band. He contracted his mouth with much gravity, and, that he might dispose his mind to be more serious than ordinary, began the tune of the Children in the Wood. He went through part of it with good success, when on a sudden the wit at his elbow, who had appeared wonderfully grave and attentive for some time, gave him a touch upon the left shoulder, and stared him in the face with so bewitching a grin, that the whistler relaxed his fibres into a kind of simper, and at length burst out into an open laugh. The third who entered the lists was a footman, who in defiance of the merry-andrew and all his arts, whistled a Scotch tune, and an Italian sonata, with so settled a countenance that he bore away the prize, to the great admiration of some hundreds of persons, who, as well as myself, were present at this trial of skill. Now, Sir, I humbly conceive, whatever you have determined of the grinners, the whistlers ought to be encouraged, not only as their art is practised without distortion, but as it improves country-music, promotes gravity, and teaches ordinary people to keep their countenances, if they see any thing ridiculous in their betters; besides that it seems an entertainment very particularly adapted to the Bath, as it is usual for a rider to whistle to his horse when he would rub him down.

"I am, Sir," &c.

POSTSCRIPT

"After having dispatched these two important points of grinning and whistling, I hope you will oblige the world with some reflections upon yawning, as I have seen it practised on a twelfth-night among other Christmas gambols at the house of a very worthy gentleman, who always entertains his tenants at that time of the year. They yawn for a Cheshire cheese, and begin about midnight, when the whole company is disposed to be drowsy. He that yawns widest, and

at the same time so naturally as to produce the most
yawns among the spectators, carries home the cheese.
If you handle this subject as you ought, I question not
but your paper will set half the kingdom a yawning,
though I dare promise you it will never make any
body fall asleep."

THE TRUNK-MAKER

Populares
Vincentem strepitus.

HOR. *Ars Poet.* 81.

Awes the tumultuous noises of the pit. ROSCOMMON.

THERE is nothing which lies more within the
province of a Spectator than public shows and
diversions: and as among these there are none
which can pretend to vie with those elegant entertainments that are exhibited in our theatres, I think
it particularly incumbent on me to take notice of
every thing that is remarkable in such numerous
and refined assemblies.

It is observed, that of late years there has been a
certain person in the upper gallery of the playhouse,
who, when he is pleased with any thing that is acted
upon the stage, expresses his approbation by a loud
knock upon the benches or the wainscot, which may
be heard over the whole theatre. This person is
commonly known by the name of the "Trunk-maker
in the upper gallery." Whether it be that the blow
he gives on these occasions resembles that which is
often heard in the shops of such artisans, or that he
was supposed to have been a real trunk-maker, who,
after the finishing of his day's work, used to unbend
his mind at these public diversions with his hammer
in his hand, I cannot certainly tell. There are some,
I know, who have been foolish enough to imagine it is
a spirit which haunts the upper gallery, and from time
to time makes those strange noises; and the rather,

because he is observed to be louder than ordinary every time the ghost of Hamlet appears. Others have reported, that it is a dumb man, who has chosen this way of uttering himself when he is transported with any thing he sees or hears. Others will have it to be the playhouse thunderer, that exerts himself after this manner in the upper gallery, when he has nothing to do upon the roof.

But having made it my business to get the best information I could in a matter of this moment, I find that the trunk-maker, as he is commonly called, is a large black man whom nobody knows. He generally leans forward on a huge oaken plank with great attention to every thing that passes upon the stage. He is never seen to smile; but upon hearing any thing that pleases him, he takes up his staff with both hands, and lays it upon the next piece of timber that stands in his way with exceeding vehemence: after which, he composes himself in his former posture, till such time as something new sets him again at work.

It has been observed, his blow is so well-timed, that the most judicious critic could never except against it. As soon as any shining thought is expressed in the poet, or any uncommon grace appears in the actor, he smites the bench or wainscot. If the audience does not concur with him, he smites a second time; and if the audience is not yet awakened, looks round him with great wrath, and repeats the blow a third time, which never fails to produce the clap. He sometimes lets the audience begin the clap of themselves, and at the conclusion of their applause ratifies it with a single thwack.

He is of so great use to the playhouse, that it is said a former director of it, upon his not being able to pay his attendance by reason of sickness, kept one in pay to officiate for him until such time as he recovered; but the person so employed, though he laid about him with incredible violence, did it in such wrong places, that the audience soon found out that it was not their old friend the trunk-maker.

It has been remarked, that he has not yet exerted himself with vigour this season. He sometimes plies at the opera; and upon Nicolini's first appearance was said to have demolished three benches in the fury of his applause. He has broken half a dozen oaken planks upon Dogget, and seldom goes away from a tragedy of Shakspeare without leaving the wainscot extremely shattered.

The players do not only connive at his obstreperous approbation, but very cheerfully repair at their own cost whatever damages he makes. They once had a thought of erecting a kind of wooden anvil for his use, that should be made of a very sounding plank, in order to render his strokes more deep and mellow; but as this might not have been distinguished from the music of a kettle-drum, the project was laid aside.

In the meanwhile, I cannot but take notice of the great use it is to an audience, that a person should thus preside over their heads like the director of a concert, in order to awaken their attention, and beat time to their applauses; or, to raise my simile, I have sometimes fancied the trunk-maker in the upper gallery to be like Virgil's ruler of the winds, seated upon the top of a mountain, who, when he struck his sceptre upon the side of it, roused a hurricane, and set the whole cavern in an uproar.

It is certain the trunk-maker has saved many a good play, and brought many a graceful actor into reputation, who would not otherwise have been taken notice of. It is very visible, as the audience is not a little abashed, if they find themselves betrayed into a clap, when their friend in the upper gallery does not come into it; so the actors do not value themselves upon the clap, but regard it as a mere *brutum fulmen*, or empty noise, when it has not the sound of the oaken plant in it. I know it has been given out by those who are enemies to the trunk-maker, that he has sometimes been bribed to be in the interest of a bad poet, or a vicious player; but this is a surmise which has no foundation : his strokes are always just, and his admonitions seasonable: he does not deal about his blows at random, but always hits the right nail upon the head. The inexpressible force where-with he lays them on sufficiently shows the evidence and strength of his conviction. His zeal for a good author is indeed outrageous, and breaks down every fence and partition, every board and plank, that stands within the expression of his applause.

As I do not care for terminating my thoughts in barren speculations, or in reports of pure matter of fact, without drawing something from them for the advantage of my countrymen, I shall take the liberty to make a humble proposal, that whenever the trunk-maker shall depart this life, or whenever he shall have lost the spring of his arm by sickness, old age, infirmity, or the like, some able-bodied critic should be advanced to this post, and have a competent salary settled on him for life, to be furnished with bamboos for operas, crab-tree cudgels for comedies, and oaken plants for tragedy, at the public expense. And to the end that this place should be always disposed of according to merit, I would have none preferred to it, who has not given convincing proofs both of a sound judgment, and a strong arm; and who could not, upon occasion, either knock down an ox, or write a comment upon Horace's Art of Poetry. In short, I would have him a due composition of Hercules and Apollo, and so rightly qualified for this important office, that the trunk-maker may not be missed by our posterity.

FEMALE ORATORS

Τῶν δ' ἀκάματος ῥέει αὐδὴ
Ἐκ στομάτων ἡδεία.   HESIOD.

Their untir'd lips a wordy torrent pour.

WE are told by some ancient authors, that Socrates was instructed in eloquence by a woman,
whose name, if I am not mistaken, was Aspasia. I
have indeed very often looked upon that art as the
most proper for the female sex, and I think the
universities would do well to consider whether they
should not fill the rhetoric chairs with she-professors.

It has been said in the praise of some men, that
they could talk whole hours together upon any thing;
but it must be owned to the honour of the other sex,
that there are many among them who can talk whole
hours together upon nothing. I have known a woman
branch out into a long extempore dissertation upon
the edging of a petticoat, and chide her servant for
breaking a china cup, in all the figures of rhetoric.

Were women permitted to plead in courts of judi-
cature, I am persuaded they would carry the eloquence
of the bar to greater heights than it has yet arrived
at. If any one doubt this, let him but be present at
those debates which frequently arise among the ladies
of the British fishery.

The first kind, therefore, of female orators which
I shall take notice of, are those who are employed in
stirring up the passions; a part of rhetoric in which
Socrates' wife had perhaps made a greater proficiency
than his above-mentioned teacher.

The second kind of female orators are those who
deal in invectives, and who are commonly known by
the name of the censorious. The imagination and
elocution of this set of rhetoricians is wonderful.
With what a fluency of invention, and copiousness of
expression, will they enlarge upon every little slip in
the behaviour of another! With how many different
circumstances, and with what variety of phrases, will

they tell over the same story! I have known an old lady make an unhappy marriage the subject of a month's conversation. She blamed the bride in one place; pitied her in another; laughed at her in a third; wondered at her in a fourth; was angry with her in a fifth; and, in short, wore out a pair of coach-horses in expressing her concern for her. At length, after having quite exhausted the subject on this side, she made a visit to the new-married pair, praised the wife for the prudent choice she had made, told her the unreasonable reflections which some malicious people had cast upon her, and desired that they might be better acquainted. The censure and appro-bation of this kind of women are therefore only to be considered as helps to discourse.

A third kind of female orators may be compre-hended under the word gossips. Mrs Fiddle-Faddle is perfectly accomplished in this sort of eloquence; she launches out into descriptions of christenings, runs divisions upon a head-dress, knows every dish of meat that is served up in our neighbourhood, and entertains her company a whole afternoon together with the wit of her little boy, before he is able to speak.

The coquette may be looked upon as a fourth kind of female orator. To give herself the larger field for discourse, she hates and loves in the same breath, talks to her lap-dog or parrot, is uneasy in all kinds of weather, and in every part of the room. She has false quarrels and feigned obligations to all the men of her acquaintance; sighs when she is not sad, and laughs when she is not merry. The coquette is in particular a great mistress of that part of oratory which is called action, and indeed seems to speak for no other purpose, but as it gives her an opportunity of stirring a limb, or varying a feature, of glancing her eyes, or playing with her fan.

As for newsmongers, politicians, mimics, story-tellers, with other characters of that nature which gave birth to loquacity, they are as commonly found among the men as the women: for which reason I shall pass them over in silence.

I have often been puzzled to assign a cause why women should have this talent of a ready utterance in so much greater perfection than men. I have sometimes fancied that they have not a retentive power, or the faculty of suppressing their thoughts, as men have, but that they are necessitated to speak every thing they think; and if so, it would perhaps furnish a very strong argument to the Cartesians for the supporting of their doctrine that the soul always thinks. But as several are of opinion that the fair sex are not altogether strangers to the art of dissembling and concealing their thoughts, I have been forced to relinquish that opinion, and have therefore endeavoured to seek after some better reason. In order to it, a friend of mine, who is an excellent anatomist, has promised me by the first opportunity to dissect a woman's tongue, and to examine whether there may not be in it certain juices which render it so wonderfully voluble or flippant, or whether the fibres of it may not be made up of a finer or more pliant thread; or whether there are not in it some particular muscles which dart it up and down by such sudden glances and vibrations; or whether, in the last place, there may not be certain undiscovered channels running from the head and the heart to this little instrument of loquacity, and conveying into it a perpetual affluency of animal spirits. Nor must I omit the reason which Hudibras has given, why those who can talk on trifles speak with the greatest fluency; namely, that the tongue is like a race-horse, which runs the faster the lesser weight it carries.

Which of these reasons soever may be looked upon as the most probable, I think the Irishman's thought was very natural, who, after some hours' conversation with a female orator, told her, that he believed her tongue was very glad when she was asleep, for that it had not a moment's rest all the while she was awake.

That excellent old ballad of The Wanton Wife of
Bath has the following remarkable lines:

> I think, quoth Thomas, women's tongues
> Of aspen leaves are made.

And Ovid, though in the description of a very
barbarous circumstance, tells us, that when the
tongue of a beautiful female was cut out, and thrown
upon the ground, it could not forbear muttering
even in that posture:

> Comprensam forcipe linguam
> Abstulit ense fero, radix micat ultima linguæ.
> Ipsa jacet, terræque tremens immurmurat atræ;
> Utque salire solet mutitalæ cauda colubræ
> Palpitat   *Met.* vi. 556.

> The blade had cut
> Her tongue sheer off, close to the trembling root,
> The mangled part still quiver'd on the ground,
> Murmuring with a faint imperfect sound;
> And as a serpent writhes his wounded train,
> Uneasy, panting, and possessed with pain.
>   CROXALL.

If a tongue would be talking without a mouth,
what could it have done when it had all its organs of
speech, and accomplices of sound about it? I might
here mention the story of the Pippin Woman, had I
not some reason to look upon it as fabulous.

I must confess I am so wonderfully charmed with
the music of this little instrument, that I would by
no means discourage it. All that I aim at, by this
dissertation, is, to cure it of several disagreeable
notes, and in particular of those little jarrings and
dissonances which arise from anger, censoriousness,
gossiping and coquetry. In short, I would always
have it tuned by good-nature, truth, discretion, and
sincerity.

ON RIDICULE

Γέλως ἄκαιρος ἐν βροτοῖς δεινὸν κακόν.

Frag. Vet. Poet.

Mirth out of season is a grievous ill.

WHEN I make choice of a subject that has not
been treated on by others, I throw together my reflections on it without any order or method, so that
they may appear rather in the looseness and freedom
of an essay, than in the regularity of a set discourse.
It is after this manner that I shall consider laughter
and ridicule in my present paper.

Man is the merriest species of the creation; all
above and below him are serious. He sees things
in a different light from other beings, and finds his
mirth arising from objects that perhaps cause something like pity or displeasure in higher natures.
Laughter is indeed a very good counterpoise to the
spleen; and it seems but reasonable that we should
be capable of receiving joy from what is no real
good to us, since we can receive grief from what is
no real evil.

I have in my forty-seventh paper raised a speculation on the notion of a modern philosopher, who
describes the first motive of laughter to be a secret
comparison which we make between ourselves and
the persons we laugh at; or, in other words, that
satisfaction which we receive from the opinion of
some pre-eminence in ourselves, when we see the
absurdities of another, or when we reflect on any
past absurdities of our own. This seems to hold in
most cases, and we may observe that the vainest
part of mankind are the most addicted to this
passion.

I have read a sermon of a conventual in the
church of Rome, on those words of the wise man,
"I said of Laughter, it is mad; and of mirth, what
does it?" Upon which he laid it down as a point
of doctrine, that laughter was the effect of original
sin, and that Adam could not laugh before the fall.

Laughter, while it lasts, slackens and unbraces the mind, weakens the faculties, and causes a kind of remissness and dissolution in all the powers of the soul; and thus far it may be looked upon as a weakness in the composition of human nature. But if we consider the frequent reliefs we receive from it, and how often it breaks the gloom which is apt to depress the mind and damp our spirits, with transient unexpected gleams of joy, one would take care not to grow too wise for so great a pleasure of life.

The talent of turning men into ridicule, and exposing to laughter those one converses with, is the qualification of little ungenerous tempers. A young man with this cast of mind cuts himself off from all manner of improvement. Every one has his flaws and weaknesses; nay, the greatest blemishes are often found in the most shining characters; but what an absurd thing is it to pass over all the valuable parts of a man, and fix our attention on his infirmities? to observe his imperfections more than his virtues? and to make use of him for the sport of others, rather than for our own improvement?

We therefore very often find, that persons the most accomplished in ridicule are those that are very shrewd at hitting a blot, without exerting any thing masterly in themselves. As there are many eminent critics who never *writ* a good line, there are many admirable buffoons that animadvert upon every single defect in another, without ever discovering the least beauty of their own. By this means, these unlucky little wits often gain reputation in the esteem of vulgar minds, and raise themselves above persons of much more laudable characters.

If the talent of ridicule were employed to laugh men out of vice and folly, it might be of some use to the world; but instead of this, we find that it is generally made use of to laugh men out of virtue and good sense, by attacking every thing that is solemn and serious, decent and praiseworthy in human life.

We may observe that in the first ages of the world, when the great souls and master-pieces of human nature were produced, men shined by a noble simplicity of behaviour, and were strangers to those little embellishments which are so fashionable in our present conversation. And it is very remarkable, that notwithstanding we fall short at present of the ancients in poetry, painting, oratory, history, architecture, and all the noble arts and sciences which depend more upon genius than experience, we exceed them as much in doggrel humour, burlesque, and all the trivial arts of ridicule. We meet with more raillery among the moderns, but more good sense among the ancients.

The two great branches of ridicule in writing are comedy and burlesque. The first ridicules persons by drawing them in their proper characters, the other by drawing them quite unlike themselves. Burlesque is therefore of two kinds; the first represents mean persons in the accoutrements of heroes; the other describes great persons acting and speaking like the basest among the people. Don Quixote is an instance of the first, and Lucian's gods of the second. It is a dispute among the critics, whether burlesque poetry runs best in heroic verse, like that of the Dispensary; or in doggrel, like that of Hudibras. I think where the low character is to be raised, the heroic is the proper measure; but when a hero is to be pulled down and degraded, it is done best in doggrel.

If Hudibras had been set out with as much wit and humour in heroic verse as he is in doggrel, he would have made a much more agreeable figure than he does; though the generality of his readers are so wonderfully pleased with the double rhymes, that I do not expect many will be of my opinion in this particular.

I shall conclude this essay upon laughter with

observing that the metaphor of laughing, applied to fields and meadows when they are in flower, or to trees when they are in blossom, runs through all languages; which I have not observed of any other metaphor, excepting that of fire and burning when they are applied to love. This shows that we naturally regard laughter, as what is in itself both amiable and beautiful. For this reason likewise Venus has gained the title of *Philomydes* "the laughter-loving dame," as Waller has translated it, and is represented by Horace as the goddess who delights in laughter. Milton, in a joyous assembly of imaginary persons, has given us a very poetical figure of Laughter. His whole band of mirth is so finely described, that I shall set down the passage at length:

> But come, thou goddess fair and free,
> In heaven yclep'd Euphrosyne,
> And by men, heart-easing mirth,
> Whom lovely Venus at a birth
> With two sister Graces more,
> To ivy-crowned Bacchus bore.
> Haste thee, nymph, and bring with thee
> Jest and youthful jollity,
> Quips, and cranks, and wanton wiles,
> Nods, and becks, and wreathed smiles,
> Such as hang on Hebe's cheek,
> And love to live in dimple sleek;
> Sport that wrinkled Care derides,
> And Laughter holding both his sides.
> Come, and trip it as you go,
> On the light fantastic toe:
> And in thy right hand lead with thee
> The mountain nymph, sweet Liberty;
> And if I give thee honour due,
> Mirth, admit me of thy crew,
> To live with her, and live with thee,
> In unreproved pleasures free.

THE CRIES OF LONDON

Linguæ centum sunt, oraque centum,
Ferrea vox.   VIR. *Æn.* vi. 625.

A hundred mouths, a hundred tongues,
And throats of brass inspir'd with iron lungs.
                                      DRYDEN.

THERE is nothing which more astonishes a foreigner, and frights a country squire, than the
Cries of London. My good friend Sir Roger often
declares that he cannot get them out of his head
or go to sleep for them, the first week that he is in
town. On the contrary, Will Honeycomb calls
them the *Ramage de la Ville*, and prefers them to
the sound of larks and nightingales, with all the
music of fields and woods. I have lately received
a letter from some very odd fellow upon this subject, which I shall leave with my reader, without
saying any thing further of it.

" SIR,
" I am a man out of all business, and would willingly turn my head to any thing for an honest livelihood. I have invented several projects for raising
many millions of money without burdening the subject, but I cannot get the parliament to listen to me
who look upon me, forsooth, as a crack, and a pro-
jector; so that despairing to enrich either myself
or my country by this public-spiritedness, I would
make some proposals to you relating to a design
which I have very much at heart, and which may
procure me a handsome subsistence, if you will be
pleased to recommend it to the cities of London and
Westminster.
" The post I would aim at, is to be comptroller-
general of the London Cries, which are at present
under no manner of rules or discipline. I think I
am pretty well qualified for this place, as being a
man of very strong lungs, of great insight into all

the branches of our British trades and manufactures, and of a competent skill in music.

"The Cries of London may be divided into vocal and instrumental. As for the latter, they are at present under a very great disorder. A freeman of London has the privilege of disturbing a whole street for an hour together, with a twanking of a brass kettle or frying-pan. The watchman's thump at midnight startles us in our beds as much as the breaking in of a thief. The sowgelder's horn has indeed something musical in it, but this is seldom heard within the liberties. I would therefore propose, that no instrument of this nature should be made use of, which I have not tuned and licensed, after having carefully examined in what manner it may affect the ears of her majesty's liege subjects.

"Vocal cries are of a much larger extent, and indeed so full of incongruities and barbarisms, that we appear a distracted city to foreigners, who do not comprehend the meaning of such enormous outcries. Milk is generally sold in a note above E-la, and in sounds so exceedingly shrill, that it often sets our teeth on edge. The chimney-sweeper is confined to no certain pitch; he sometimes utters himself in the deepest bass, and sometimes in the sharpest treble; sometimes in the highest, and sometimes in the lowest, note of the gamut. The same observation might be made on the retailers of small-coal, not to mention broken glasses, or brick-dust. In these, therefore, and the like cases, it should be my care to sweeten and mellow the voices of these itinerant tradesmen, before they make their appearance in our streets, as also to accommodate their cries to their respective wares; and to take care in particular, that those may not make the most noise, who have the least to sell, which is very observable in the venders of card-matches, to whom I cannot but apply that old proverb of 'Much cry, but little wool.'

"Some of these last-mentioned musicians are so very loud in the sale of these trifling manufactures, that an honest splenetic gentleman of my acquaint-

ance bargained with one of them never to come into
the street where he lived. But what was the effect
of this contract? Why the whole tribe of card-
matchmakers which frequent that quarter passed by
his door the very next day, in hopes of being bought
off after the same manner.

"It is another great imperfection in our London
Cries, that there is no just time nor measure observed
in them. Our news should indeed be published in a
very quick time, because it is a commodity that will
not keep cold. It should not, however, be cried with
the same precipitation as fire. Yet this is generally
the case. A bloody battle alarms the town from one
end to another in an instant. Every motion of the
French is published in so great a hurry, that one
would think the enemy were at our gates. This likewise I would take upon me to regulate in such a
manner, that there should be some distinction made
between the spreading of a victory, a march, or an
encampment, a Dutch, a Portugal, or a Spanish mail.
Nor must I omit under this head those excessive
alarms with which several boisterous rustics infest
our streets in turnip season; and which are more
inexcusable, because they are wares which are in no
danger of cooling upon their hands.

"There are others who affect a very slow time,
and are in my opinion much more tuneable than the
former. The cooper in particular swells his last note
in a hollow voice, that is not without its harmony;
nor can I forbear being inspired with a most agreeable
melancholy, when I hear that sad and solemn air
with which the public are very often asked, if they
have any chairs to mend? Your own memory may
suggest to you many other lamentable ditties of the
same nature, in which the music is wonderfully
languishing and melodious.

"I am always pleased with that particular time of
the year which is proper for the pickling of dill and
cucumbers; but alas! this cry, like the song of the
nightingale, is not heard above two months. It would

therefore be worth while to consider, whether the
same air might not in some cases be adapted to other
words.

" It might likewise deserve our most serious consideration, how far, in a well-regulated city, those
humourists are to be tolerated, who, not contented
with the traditional cries of their forefathers, have
invented particular songs and tunes of their own :
such as was, not many years since, the pastry-man,
commonly known by the name of the Colly-Molly-
Puff : and such as is at this day the vender of powder
and wash-balls, who, if I am rightly informed, goes
under the name of Powder-Wat.

" I must not here omit one particular absurdity
which runs through this whole vociferous generation,
and which renders their cries very often not only
incommodious, but altogether useless to the public.
I mean, that idle accomplishment which they all of
them aim at, of crying so as not to be understood.
Whether or no they have learned this from several of
our affected singers, I will not take upon me to say ;
but most certain it is, that people know the wares
they deal in rather by their tunes than by their words ;
insomuch that I have sometimes seen a country boy
run out to buy apples of a bellows-mender, and ginger-
bread from a grinder of knives and scissors. Nay, so
strangely infatuated are some very eminent artists of
this particular grace in a cry, that none but their
acquaintance are able to guess at their profession ;
for who else can know, that 'work if I had it' should
be the signification of a corn-cutter ?

" Forasmuch, therefore, as persons of this rank
are seldom men of genius or capacity I think it would
be very proper that some men of good sense and
sound judgment should preside over these public cries,
who should permit none to lift up their voices in our
streets, that have not tuneable throats, and are not
only able to overcome the noise of the crowd, and the
rattling of coaches, but also to vend their respective
merchandises in apt phrases, and in the most distinct

and agreeable sounds.   I do therefore humbly recommend myself as a person rightly qualified for this post;
and if I meet with fitting encouragement, shall communicate some other projects which I have by me,
that may no less conduce to the emolument of the
public.

"I am, Sir, &c.

"RALPH CROTCHET."

THE PHILOSOPHY OF HOODS

Dixerit e multis aliquis, quid virus in angues
Adjicis? et rabidæ tradis ovile lupæ.
                    OVID, *de Art. Am.* ill. 7.

But some exclaim ; What frenzy rules your mind?
Would you increase the craft of womankind?
Teach them new wiles and arts?   As well you may
Instruct a snake to bite, or wolf to prey.   CONGREVE.

ONE of the fathers, if I am rightly informed, has
defined a woman to be ζῷον φιλόκοσμον, an animal that
delights in finery.   I have already treated of the sex in
two or three papers, conformably to this definition;
and have in particular observed, that in all ages they
have been more careful than the men to adorn that part
of the head which we generally call the outside.

This observation is so very notorious, that when
in ordinary discourse we say a man has a fine head,
a long head, or a good head, we express ourselves
metaphorically, and speak in relation to his understanding; whereas when we say of a woman, she has
a fine, a long, or a good head, we speak only in relation
to her commode.

It is observed among birds, that nature has lavished
all her ornaments upon the male, who very often
appears in a most beautiful head-dress: whether it be
a crest, a comb, a tuft of feathers, or a natural little

plume, erected like a kind of pinnacle on the very top
of the head.   As Nature on the contrary has poured
out her charms in the greatest abundance upon the
female part of our species, so they are very assiduous
in bestowing upon themselves the finest garnitures of
art.   The peacock, in all his pride, does not display
half the colours that appear in the garments of a
British lady, when she is dressed either for a ball or
a birth-day.

But to return to our female heads.   The ladies
have been for some time in a kind of moulting season
with regard to that part of their dress, having cast
great quantities of riband, lace, and cambric, and in
some measure reduced that part of the human figure
to the beautiful globular form, which is natural to it.
We have for a great while expected what kind of
ornament would be substituted in the place of those
antiquated commodes.   Our female projectors were
all the last summer so taken up with the improvement
of their petticoats, that they had not time to attend
to any thing else; but having at length sufficiently
adorned their lower parts, they now begin to turn
their thoughts upon the other extremity, as well
remembering the old kitchen proverb, "that if you
light the fire at both ends, the middle will shift for
itself."

I am engaged in this speculation by a sight which
I lately met with at the opera.   As I was standing in
the hinder part of a box, I took notice of a little
cluster of women sitting together in the prettiest
coloured hoods that I ever saw.   One of them was
blue, another yellow, and another philomot; the
fourth was of a pink colour, and the fifth of a pale
green.   I looked with as much pleasure upon this
little party-coloured assembly, as upon a bed of tulips,
and did not know at first whether it might not be an
embassy of Indian queens; but upon my going about
into the pit, and taking them in front, I was immediately undeceived, and saw so much beauty in every
face, that I found them all to be English.   Such eyes

and lips, cheeks and foreheads, could be the growth of no other country. The complexion of their faces hindered me from observing any further the colour of their hoods, though I could easily perceive, by that unspeakable satisfaction which appeared in their looks, that their own thoughts were wholly taken up on those pretty ornaments they wore upon their heads.

I am informed that this fashion spreads daily, insomuch that the Whig and Tory ladies begin already to hang out different colours, and to show their principles in their head-dress. Nay, if I may believe my friend Will Honeycomb, there is a certain old coquette of his acquaintance, who intends to appear very suddenly in a rainbow hood, like the Iris in Dryden's Virgil, not questioning but that among such a variety of colours she shall have a charm for every heart.

My friend Will, who very much values himself upon his great insight into gallantry, tells me, that he can already guess at the humour a lady is in by her hood, as the courtiers of Morocco know the disposition of their present emperor by the colour of the dress which he puts on. When Melesinda wraps her head in flame colour, her heart is set upon execution. When she covers it with purple, I would not, says he, advise her lover to approach her; but if she appears in white, it is peace, and he may hand her out of her box with safety.

Will informs me likewise, that these hoods may be used as signals. Why else, says he, does Cornelia always put on a black hood when her husband is gone into the country?

Such are my friend Honeycomb's dreams of gallantry. For my own part, I impute this diversity of colours in the hoods to the diversity of complexion in the faces of my pretty countrywomen. Ovid, in his *Art of Love*, has given some precepts as to this particular, though I find they are different from those which prevail among the moderns. He recommends a red striped silk to the pale complexion; white to the brown, and dark to the fair. On the contrary, my

friend Will, who pretends to be a greater master in
this art than Ovid, tells me, that the palest features
look the most agreeable in white sarcenet; that a
face which is over-flushed appears to advantage in
the deepest scarlet; and that the darkest complexion
is not a little alleviated by a black hood. In short,
he is for losing the colour of the face in that of the
hood, as a fire burns dimly, and a candle goes half
out in the light of the sun. "This," says he, "your
Ovid himself has hinted, where he treats of these
matters, when he tells us that the blue-water nymphs
are dressed in sky-coloured garments; and that
Aurora, who always appears in the light of the rising
sun, is robed in saffron."

Whether these his observations are justly grounded
I cannot tell; but I have often known him, as we
have stood together behind the ladies, praise or dis-
praise the complexion of a face which he never saw,
from observing the colour of her hood, and [he] has
been very seldom out in these his guesses.

As I have nothing more at heart than the honour
and improvement of the fair sex, I cannot conclude
this paper without an exhortation to the British ladies,
that they would excel the women of all other nations
as much in virtue and good sense as they do in
beauty; which they may certainly do, if they will be
as industrious to cultivate their minds as they are to
adorn their bodies. In the meanwhile I shall recommend to their most serious consideration the saying
of an old Greek poet:

Γυναικὶ κόσμος ὁ τρόπος, κ' οὐ χρυσία.

SIR ROGER COMES TO TOWN

Ævo rarissima nostro
Simplicitas.   OVID, *Ars Am.* i. 241.

Most rare is now our old simplicity.   DRYDEN.

I WAS this morning surprised with a great knocking
at the door, when my landlady's daughter came up to
me, and told me that there was a man below desired
to speak with me. Upon my asking her who it was,
she told me it was a very grave elderly person, but
that she did not know his name I immediately went
down to him, and found him to be the coachman of
my worthy friend, Sir Roger de Coverley. He told
me that his master came to town last night, and
would be glad to take a turn with me in Gray's-inn
walks. As I was wondering with myself what had
brought Sir Roger to town, not having lately received
any letter from him, he told me that his master was
come up to get a sight of Prince Eugene, and that he
desired I would immediately meet him.

I was not a little pleased with the curiosity of the
old knight, though I did not much wonder at it,
having heard him say more than once in private
discourse, that he looked upon Prince Eugenio (for
so the knight always calls him) to be a greater man
than Scanderbeg.

I was no sooner come into Gray's-inn walks, but
I heard my friend hemming twice or thrice to himself
with great vigour, for he loves to clear his pipes in
good air (to make use of his own phrase), and is
not a little pleased with any one who takes notice of
the strength which he still exerts in his morning
hems.

I was touched with a secret joy at the sight of the
good old man, who, before he saw me, was engaged
in conversation with a beggar-man that had asked
an alms of him. I could hear my friend chide him

for not finding out some work; but at the same time
saw him put his hand in his pocket and give him six-
pence.

Our salutations were very hearty on both sides,
consisting of many kind shakes of the hand, and
several affectionate looks which we cast upon one
another. After which the knight told me my good
friend his chaplain was very well, and much at my
service, and that the Sunday before he had made a
most incomparable sermon out of Dr Barrow. "I
have left," says he, "all my affairs in his hands, and
being willing to lay an obligation upon him, have
deposited with him thirty marks, to be distributed
among his poor parishioners."

He then proceeded to acquaint me with the welfare of Will Wimble. Upon which he put his hand
into his fob and presented me in his name with a
tobacco-stopper, telling me that Will had been busy
all the beginning of the winter in turning great
quantities of them; and that he made a present of
one to every gentleman in the country who has good
principles, and smokes. He added, that poor Will
was at present under great tribulation, for that Tom
Touchy had taken the law of him for cutting some
hazel sticks out of one of his hedges.

Among other pieces of news which the knight
brought from his country-seat, he informed me that
Moll White was dead, and that about a month after
her death the wind was so very high that it blew down
the end of one of his barns. "But for my own part,"
says Sir Roger, "I do not think that the old woman
had any hand in it."

He afterwards fell into an account of the diversions which had passed in his house during the
holidays: for Sir Roger, after the laudable custom
of his ancestors, always keeps open house at
Christmas.

I learned from him that he had killed eight fat
hogs, for this season, that he had dealt about his
chines very liberally amongst his neighbours, and

that in particular he had sent a string of hogs' puddings with a pack of cards to every poor family in
the parish. "I have often thought," says Sir Roger,
"it happens very well that Christmas should fall out
in the middle of winter. It is the most dead uncomfortable time of the year, when the poor people would
suffer very much from their poverty and cold, if they
had not good cheer, warm fires, and Christmas
gambols to support them. I love to rejoice their poor
hearts at this season, and to see the whole village
merry in my great hall. I allow a double quantity of
malt to my small-beer, and set it a running for twelve
days to every one that calls for it. I have always a
piece of cold beef and a mince-pie upon the table,
and am wonderfully pleased to see my tenants pass
away a whole evening in playing their innocent tricks,
and smutting one another. Our friend Will Wimble
is as merry as any of them, and shows a thousand
roguish tricks upon these occasions."

I was very much delighted with the reflection of
my old friend, which carried so much goodness in it.
He then launched out into the praise of the late act
of parliament for securing the Church of England,
and told me with great satisfaction, that he believed
it already began to take effect, for that a rigid dis-
senter, who chanced to dine at his house on Christmas-
day, had been observed to eat very plentifully of his
plum-porridge.

After having dispatched all our country matters,
Sir Roger made several inquiries concerning the
club, and particularly of his old antagonist Sir
Andrew Freeport. He asked me with a kind of smile
whether Sir Andrew had not taken advantage of his
absence, to vent among them some of his republican
doctrines; but soon after gathering up his countenance
into a more than ordinary seriousness, "Tell me truly,"
says he, "don't you think Sir Andrew had a hand in
the Pope's procession?" But without giving me time
to answer him, "Well, well," says he, "I know you
are a wary man, and do not care to talk of public
matters."

The knight then asked me if I had seen Prince Eugenio, and made me promise to get him a stand in some convenient place where he might have a full sight of that extraordinary man, whose presence did so much honour to the British nation. He dwelt very long on the praises of this great general, and I have found that since I was with him in the country, he had drawn many observations together out of his reading in *Baker's Chronicle* and other authors, who always lie in his hall-window, which very much redound to the honour of this prince.

Having passed away the greatest part of the morning in hearing the knight's reflections, which were partly private and partly political, he asked me if I would smoke a pipe with him over a dish of coffee at Squire's? As I love the old man, I take delight in complying with every thing that is agreeable to him, and accordingly waited on him to the coffee-house, where his venerable figure drew upon us the eyes of the whole room. He had no sooner seated himself at the upper end of the high table, but he called for a clean pipe, a paper of tobacco, a dish of coffee, a wax-candle, and the *Supplement*, with such an air of cheerfulness and good-humour, that all the boys in the coffee-room (who seemed to take pleasure in serving him) were at once employed on his several errands, insomuch that nobody else could come at a dish of tea, until the knight had got all his conveniences about him.

MILTON (I)

Reddere personæ scit convenientia cuique.
              HOR. *Ars Poet.* v. 316.

He knows what best befits each character.

WE have already taken a general survey of the fable and characters in Milton's Paradise Lost. The parts which remain to be considered, according to Aristotle's method, are the sentiments and the

language. Before I enter upon the first of these, I
must advertise my reader, that it is my design, as
soon as I have finished my general reflections on
these four several heads, to give particular instances
out of the poem which is now before us of beauties
and imperfections which may be observed under each
of them, as also of such other particulars as may not
properly fall under any of them. This I thought fit
to premise, that the reader may not judge too hastily
of this piece of criticism, or look upon it as imperfect,
before he has seen the whole extent of it.

The sentiments in an epic poem are the thoughts
and behaviour which the author ascribes to the persons
whom he introduces, and are just when they are
conformable to the characters of the several persons.
The sentiments have likewise a relation to things as
well as persons, and are then perfect when they are
such as are adapted to the subject. If in either of
these cases the poet endeavours to argue or explain,
to magnify or diminish, to raise love or hatred, pity or
terror, or any other passion, we ought to consider
whether the sentiments he makes use of are proper
for those ends. Homer is censured by the critics for
his defect as to this particular in several parts of the
Iliad and Odyssey, though at the same time those who
have treated this great poet with candour, have
attributed this defect to the times in which he lived.
It was the fault of the age and not of Homer, if there
wants that delicacy in some of his sentiments, which
now appears in the works of men of a much inferior
genius. Besides, if there are blemishes in any particular thoughts, there is an infinite beauty in the
greatest part of them. In short, if there are many
poets who would not have fallen into the meanness
of some of his sentiments, there are none who could
have risen up to the greatness of others. Virgil has
excelled all others in the propriety of his sentiments.
Milton shines likewise very much in this particular:
nor must we omit one consideration which adds to his
honour and reputation. Homer and Virgil introduced

persons whose characters are commonly known
among men, and such as are to be met with either
in history or in ordinary conversation.   Milton's
characters, most of them, lie out of nature, and were
to be formed purely by his own invention.   It shows
a greater genius in Shakspeare to have drawn his
Caliban, than his Hotspur, or Julius Cæsar: the one
was to be supplied out of his own imagination, whereas the other might have been formed upon tradition,
history, and observation.   It was much easier therefore for Homer to find proper sentiments for an
assembly of Grecian generals, than for Milton to
diversify his infernal council with proper characters,
and inspire them with a variety of sentiments.   The
loves of Dido and Æneas are only copies of what has
passed between other persons.   Adam and Eve, before
the Fall, are a different species from that of mankind,
who are descended from them; and none but a poet
of the most unbounded invention, and the most
exquisite judgment, could have filled their conversation and behaviour with so many apt circumstances
during their state of innocence.

Nor is it sufficient for an epic poem to be filled
with such thoughts as are natural, unless it abound
also with such as are sublime.   Virgil in this particular falls short of Homer.   He has not indeed so
many thoughts that are low and vulgar; but at the
same time has not so many thoughts that are sublime and noble.   The truth of it is, Virgil seldom
rises into very astonishing sentiments, where he is
not fired by the Iliad.   He everywhere charms and
pleases us by the force of his own genius; but
seldom elevates and transports us where he does
not fetch his hints from Homer.

Milton's chief talent, and indeed his distinguishing excellence, lies in the sublimity of his thoughts.
There are others of the moderns who rival him in
every other part of poetry; but in the greatness of
his sentiments he triumphs over all the poets both
modern and ancient, Homer only excepted.   It is

impossible for the imagination of man to distend itself with greater ideas, than those which he has laid together in his first, second, and sixth books. The seventh, which describes the creation of the world, is likewise wonderfully sublime, though not so apt to stir up emotion in the mind of the reader, nor consequently so perfect in the epic way of writing, because it is filled with less action. Let the judicious reader compare what Longinus has observed on several passages in Homer, and he will find parallels for most of them in the Paradise Lost.

From what has been said we may infer, that as there are two kinds of sentiments, the natural and the sublime, which are always to be pursued in a heroic poem, there are also two kinds of thoughts which are carefully to be avoided. The first are such as are affected and unnatural; the second such as are mean and vulgar. As for the first kind of thoughts, we meet with little or nothing that is like them in Virgil. He has none of those trifling points and puerilities that are so often to be met with in Ovid, none of the epigrammatic turns of Lucan, none of those swelling sentiments which are so frequent in Statius and Claudian, none of those mixed embellishments of Tasso. Every thing is just and natural. His sentiments show that he had a perfect insight into human nature, and that he knew every thing which was the most proper to affect it.

Mr Dryden has in some places, which I may hereafter take notice of, misrepresented Virgil's way of thinking as to this particular, in the translation he has given us of the Æneid. I do not remember that Homer anywhere falls into the faults above mentioned, which were indeed the false refinements of latter ages. Milton, it must be confessed, has sometimes erred in this respect, as I shall show more at large in another paper; though considering how all the poets of the age in which

he writ were infected with this wrong way of thinking, he is rather to be admired that he did not give
more into it, than that he did sometimes comply
with the vicious taste which still prevails so much
among modern writers.

But since several thoughts may be natural which
are low and grovelling an epic poet should not only
avoid such sentiments as are unnatural or affected,
but also such as are mean and vulgar. Homer has
opened a great field of raillery to men of more delicacy than greatness of genius, by the homeliness
of some of his sentiments. But as I have before
said these are rather to be imputed to the simplicity of the age in which he lived, to which I may
also add, of that which he described, than to any
imperfection in that divine poet. Zoilus among
the ancients, and Monsieur Perrault among the
moderns, pushed their ridicule very far upon him
on account of some such sentiments. There is no
blemish to be observed in Virgil under this head,
and but a very few in Milton.

I shall give but one instance of this impropriety
of thought in Homer, and at the same time compare
it with an instance of the same nature, both in
Virgil and Milton. Sentiments which raise laughter
can very seldom be admitted with any decency into
a heroic poem, whose business it is to excite passions of a much nobler nature. Homer, however,
in his characters of Vulcan and Thersites, in his
story of Mars and Venus, in his behaviour of Irus,
and in other passages, has been observed to have
lapsed into the burlesque character, and to have departed from that serious air which seems essential
to the magnificence of an epic poem. I remember
but one laugh in the whole Æneid, which rises in
the fifth book, upon Monœtes, where he is represented as thrown overboard, and drying himself upon
a rock. But this piece of mirth is so well-timed
that the severest critic can have nothing to say
against it; for it is the book of games and diver-

sions, where the reader's mind may be supposed
sufficiently relaxed for such an entertainment. The
only piece of pleasantry in Paradise Lost, is where
the evil spirits are described as rallying the angels
upon the success of their new-invented artillery.
This passage I look upon to be the most exception-
able in the whole poem, as being nothing else but a
string of puns, and those, too, very indifferent ones:

> Satan beheld their plight,
> And to his mates thus in derision call'd:
> "O friends, why come not on those victors proud?
> Ere while they fierce were coming; and when we,
> To entertain them fair with open front
> And breast (what could we more?) propounded terms
> Of composition, straight they chang'd their minds,
> Flew off, and into strange vagaries fell
> As they would dance; yet for a dance they seem'd
> Somewhat extravagant, and wild; perhaps
> For joy of offer'd peace; but I suppose
> If our proposals once again were heard,
> We should compel them to a quick result."
> To whom thus Belial in like gamesome mood:
> "Leader, the terms we sent were terms of weight,
> Of hard contents, and full of force urg'd home:
> Such as we might perceive amus'd them all,
> And stumbled many; who receives them right,
> Had need from head to foot well understand;
> Not understood, this gift they have besides,
> They show us when our foes walk not upright."
> Thus they among themselves in pleasant vein
> Stood scoffing.

MILTON'S *Par. Lost*, b. vi. l. 609, &c.

MILTON (II)

Volet hæc sub luce videri,
Judicis argutum quæ non formidat acumen.
HOR. *Ars Poet.* 363.

Some choose the clearest light,
And boldly challenge the most piercing eye.
ROSCOMMON.

I HAVE seen, in the works of a modern philosopher, a map of the spots in the sun. My last paper
of the faults and blemishes in Milton's Paradise
Lost may be considered as a piece of the same
nature. To pursue the illusion: as it is observed,
that among the bright parts of the luminous body
above mentioned, there are some which glow more
intensely, and dart a stronger light than others; so,
notwithstanding I have already shown Milton's poem
to be very beautiful in general, I shall now proceed
to take notice of such beauties as appear to me more
exquisite than the rest. Milton has proposed the
subject of his poem in the following verses:

> Of man's first disobedience, and the fruit
> Of that forbidden tree, whose mortal taste
> Brought death into the world and all our woe,
> With loss of Eden, till one greater man
> Restore us, and regain the blissful seat,
> Sing, heavenly Muse!

These lines are, perhaps, as plain, simple, and
unadorned, as any of the whole poem, in which particular the author has conformed himself to the
example of Homer, and the precept of Horace.

His invocation to a work which turns in a great
measure upon the creation of the world, is very
properly made to the Muse who inspired Moses in
those books from whence our author drew his subject,
and to the Holy Spirit, who is therein represented as
operating after a particular manner in the first pro-

duction of nature. This whole exordium rises very happily into noble language and sentiments, as I think the transition to the fable is exquisitely beautiful and natural.

The nine days' astonishment, in which the angels lay entranced after their dreadful overthrow and fall from heaven, before they could recover either the use of thought or speech, is a noble circumstance, and very finely imagined. The division of hell into seas of fire, and into firm ground impregnated with the same furious element, with that particular circumstance of the exclusion of Hope from those infernal regions, are instances of the same great and fruitful invention.

The thoughts in the first speech and description of Satan, who is one of the principal actors in this poem, are wonderfully proper to give us a full idea of him. His pride, envy, and revenge, obstinacy, despair, and impenitence, are all of them very artfully interwoven. In short, his first speech is a complication of all those passions which discover themselves separately in several other of his speeches in the poem. The whole part of this great enemy of mankind is filled with such incidents, as are very apt to raise and terrify the reader's imagination. Of this nature, in the book now before us, is his being the first that awakens out of the general trance, with his posture on the burning lake, his rising from it, and the description of his shield and spear:

> Thus Satan talking to his nearest mate,
> With head up-lift above the wave, and eyes
> That sparkling blaz'd, his other parts beside
> Prone on the flood extended long and large,
> Lay floating many a rood——
> Forthwith upright he rears from off the pool
> His mighty stature; on each hand the flames
> Driv'n backward slope their pointing spires, and, roll'd
> In billows, leave i' th' midst a horrid vale.
> Then with expanded wings he steers his flight
> Aloft, incumbent on the dusky air
> That felt unusual weight——

11—2

> ——His pond'rous shield,
> Ethereal temper, massy, large, and round,
> Behind him cast; the broad circumference
> Hung on his shoulders like the moon, whose orb
> Through optic glass the Tuscan artists view
> At ev'ning from the top of Fesole,
> Or in Valdarno, to descry new lands,
> Rivers, or mountains, on her spotty globe.
> His spear (to equal which the tallest pine
> Hewn on Norwegian hills to be the mast
> Of some great ammiral, were but a wand)
> He walk'd with, to support uneasy steps
> Over the burning marl.

To which we may add his call to the fallen angels
that lay plunged and stupified in the sea of fire:

> He call'd so loud, that all the hollow deep
> Of hell resounded.

But there is no single passage in the whole poem
worked up to a greater sublimity, than that wherein
his person is described in those celebrated lines:

> He, above the rest
> In shape and gesture proudly eminent,
> Stood like a tower, &c.

His sentiments are every way answerable to his
character, and suitable to a created being of the
most exalted and most depraved nature. Such is
that in which he takes possession of his place of
torments:

> Hail, horrors! hail,
> Infernal world! and thou, profoundest hell,
> Receive thy new possessor, one who brings
> A mind not to be chang'd by place or time.

And afterward:

> Here at least
> We shall be free! th' Almighty hath not built
> Here for his envy; will not drive us hence:
> Here we may reign secure; and in my choice
> To reign is worth ambition, though in hell:
> Better to reign in hell, than serve in heavn.

Amidst those impieties which this enraged spirit utters in other places of the poem, the author has taken care to introduce none that is not big with absurdity, and incapable of shocking a religious reader; his words, as the poet himself describes them, bearing only a "semblance of worth, not substance." He is likewise with great art described as owning his adversary to be Almighty. Whatever perverse interpretation he puts on the justice, mercy, and other attributes of the Supreme Being, he frequently confesses his omnipotence, that being the perfection he was forced to allow him, and the only consideration which could support his pride under the shame of his defeat.

Nor must I here omit that beautiful circumstance of his bursting out into tears, upon his survey of those innumerable spirits whom he had involved in the same guilt and ruin with himself:

> He now prepar'd
> To speak : whereat their doubled ranks they bend
> From wing to wing, and half inclose him round
> With all his peers ; Attention held them mute.
> Thrice he assay'd, and thrice, in spite of scorn,
> Tears, such as angels weep, burst forth.

The catalogue of evil spirits has abundance of learning in it, and a very agreeable turn of poetry, which rises in a great measure from its describing the places where they were worshipped, by those beautiful marks of rivers so frequent among the ancient poets. The author had doubtless in this place Homer's catalogue of ships, and Virgil's list of warriors, in his view. The characters of Moloch and Belial prepare the reader's mind for their respective speeches and behaviour in the second and sixth books. The account of Thammuz is finely romantic, and suitable to what we read among the ancients of the worship which was paid to that idol;

> Thammuz came next behind,
> Whose annual wound in Lebanon allur'd

> The Syrian damsels to lament his fate
> In am'rous ditties all a summer's day,
> While smooth Adonis from his native rock
> Ran purple to the sea, suppos'd with blood
> Of Thammuz yearly wounded : the love-tale
> Infected Sion's daughters with like heat,
> Whose wanton passions in the sacred porch
> Ezekiel saw, when, by the vision led,
> His eye survey'd the dark idolatries
> Of alienated Judah.

The reader will pardon me if I insert as a note on this beautiful passage, the account given us by the late ingenious Mr Maundrell of this ancient piece of worship, and probably the first occasion of such a superstition. "We came to a fair large river; doubtless the ancient river Adonis, as famous for the idolatrous rites performed here in lamentation of Adonis. We had the fortune to see what may be supposed to be the occasion of that opinion which Lucian relates concerning this river, viz. That this stream, at certain seasons of the year, especially about the feast of Adonis, is of a bloody colour; which the heathens looked upon as proceeding from a kind of sympathy in the river for the death of Adonis, who was killed by a wild boar in the mountains, out of which this stream rises. Something like this we saw actually come to pass; for the water was stained to a surprising redness: and, as we observed in travelling, had discoloured the sea a great way into a reddish hue, occasioned doubtless by a sort of minium, or red earth, washed into the river by the violence of the rain, and not by any stain from Adonis's blood."

The passage in the catalogue, explaining the manner how spirits transform themselves by contraction or enlargement of their dimensions, is introduced with great judgment, to make way for several surprising accidents in the sequel of the poem. There follows one at the very end of the first book, which is what the French critics call marvellous, but at the same time probable, by reason of the passage last mentioned. As soon as the infernal palace is finished, we are told the multitude and rabble of spirits immediately shrunk themselves into a small compass, that there might be room for such a number-less assembly in this capacious hall. But it is the poet's refinement upon this thought which I most admire, and which indeed is very noble in itself. For he tells us, that notwithstanding the vulgar among the fallen spirits contracted their forms, those of the first rank and dignity still preserved their natural dimensions:

> Thus incorporeal spirits to smallest forms
> Reduc'd their shapes immense, and were at large,
> Though without number, still amidst the hall
> Of that infernal court. But far within,
> And in their own dimensions like themselves,
> The great seraphic lords and cherubim
> In close recess and secret conclave sat,
> A thousand demi-gods on golden seats,
> Frequent and full.

The character of Mammon, and the description of the Pandæmonium, are full of beauties.

There are several other strokes in the first book wonderfully poetical, and instances of that sublime genius so peculiar to the author. Such is the de-scription of Azazel's stature, and the infernal standard which he unfurls; as also of that ghastly light by which the fiends appear to one another in their place of torments:

> The seat of desolation, void of light,
> Save what the glimm'ring of those livid flames
> Casts pale and dreadful.

The shout of the whole host of fallen angels when drawn up in battle array:

> The universal host up sent
> A shout that tore hell's concave, and beyond
> Frighted the reign of Chaos and old Night.

The review, which the leader makes of his infernal army:

> He through the armed files
> Darts his experienc'd eye, and soon traverse
> The whole battalion views, their order due,
> Their visages and stature as of gods,
> Their number last he sums ; and now his heart
> Distends with pride, and hard'ning in his strength
> Glories.

The flash of light which appeared upon the drawing of their swords:

> He spake ; and to confirm his words out flew
> Millions of flaming swords, drawn from the thighs
> Of mighty cherubim ; the sudden blaze
> Far round illumin'd hell.

The sudden production of the Pandæmonium:

> Anon out of the earth a fabric huge
> Rose like an exhalation, with the sound
> Of dulcet symphonies and voices sweet.

The artificial illuminations made in it:

> From the arched roof
> Pendent by subtle magic, many a row
> Of starry lamps and blazing cressets, fed
> With Naphtha and Asphaltus, yielded light
> As from a sky.

There are also several noble similes and allusions in the first book of Paradise Lost. And here I must observe, that when Milton alludes either to things or persons, he never quits his simile until it rises to some very great idea, which is often foreign to the occasion that gave birth to it. The resemblance does not, perhaps, last above a line or two, but the poet runs on with the hint until he has raised out of it some glorious image or sentiment, proper to inflame the mind of the reader, and to give it that sublime kind of entertainment which is suitable to the nature of an heroic poem. Those who are acquainted with Homer's and Virgil's way of writing, cannot but be pleased with this kind of structure in Milton's similitudes. I am the more particular on this head, because ignorant readers, who have formed their taste upon the quaint similes and little turns of wit, which are so much in vogue among modern poets, cannot relish these beauties, which are of a much higher nature, and are therefore apt to censure Milton's comparisons, in which they do not see any surprising points of likeness. Monsieur Perrault was a man of this vitiated relish, and for that very reason has endeavoured to turn into ridicule several of Homer's similitudes, which he calls "*comparaisons à longue queue*," "long-tailed comparisons." I shall conclude this paper on the first book of Milton with the answer which Monsieur Boileau makes to Perrault on this occasion: "Comparisons," says he, "in odes and epic poems, are not introduced only to illustrate and embellish the discourse, but to amuse and relax the mind of the reader, by frequently disengaging him from too painful an attention to the principal subject, and by leading him into other agreeable images. Homer," says he, "excelled in this particular, whose comparisons abound with such images of nature as are proper to relieve and diversify his subjects. He continually instructs the reader, and makes him take notice, even in objects which are every day before his eyes, of such circumstances as he should not otherwise have observed." To this he adds, as a maxim universally acknowledged, "that it is not necessary in poetry for the points of the comparison to correspond with one another exactly, but that a general resemblance is sufficient, and that too much nicety in this particular savours of the rhetorician and epigrammatist."

In short, if we look into the conduct of Homer, Virgil, and Milton, as the great fable is the soul of each poem, so to give their works an agreeable variety, their episodes are so many short fables, and their similes so many short episodes; to which you may add, if you please, that their metaphors are so many short similes. If the reader considers the comparisons

In the first book of Milton, of the sun in an eclipse, of the sleeping leviathan, of the bees swarming about their hive, of the fairy dance, in the view wherein I have here placed them, he will easily discover the great beauties that are in each of those passages.

SIR ROGER VISITS THE ABBEY

Ire tamen restat, Numa quo devenit et Ancus.
                              HOR. *Ep.* I. vi. 27.

With Ancus, and with Numa, kings of Rome,
We must descend into the silent tomb.

My friend Sir Roger de Coverley told me t'other night, that he had been reading my paper upon Westminster Abbey, in which, says he, there are a great many ingenious fancies. He told me at the same time, that he observed, I had promised another paper upon the tombs, and that he should be glad to go and see them with me, not having visited them since he had read history. I could not imagine at first how this came into the knight's head, till I recollected that he had been busy all last summer upon Baker's *Chronicle*, which he has quoted several times in his disputes with Sir Andrew Freeport since his last coming to town. Accordingly I promised to call upon him the next morning, that we might go together to the abbey.

I found the knight under the butler's hands, who always shaves him. He was no sooner dressed, than he called for a glass of the widow Truby's water, which he told me he always drank before he went abroad. He recommended me a dram of it at the same time, with so much heartiness, that I could not forbear drinking it. As soon as I had got it down, I found it very unpalatable; upon which the knight, observing that I had made several wry faces, told me that he knew I should not like it at first, but that it

was the best thing in the world against the stone or
gravel.

I could have wished indeed that he had acquainted
me with the virtues of it sooner; but it was too late to
complain, and I knew what he had done was out of
good-will. Sir Roger told me further, that he looked
upon it to be very good for a man whilst he stayed in
town, to keep off infection, and that he got together
a quantity of it upon the first news of the sickness
being at Dantzick: when of a sudden turning short
to one of his servants, who stood behind him, he bid
him call a hackney-coach, and take care it was an
elderly man that drove it.

He then resumed his discourse upon Mrs Truby's
water, telling me that the widow Truby was one who
did more good than all the doctors and apothecaries
in the country; that she distilled every poppy that
grew within five miles of her; that she distributed
her water gratis among all sorts of people: to which
the knight added, that she had a very great jointure,
and that the whole country would fain have it a
match between him and her; "and truly," says Sir
Roger, "if I had not been engaged, perhaps I could
not have done better."

His discourse was broken off by his man's telling
him he had called a coach. Upon our going to it,
after having cast his eye upon the wheels, he asked
the coachman if his axle-tree was good; upon the
fellow's telling him he would warrant it, the knight
turned to me, told me he looked like an honest man,
and went in without further ceremony.

We had not gone far, when Sir Roger, popping
out his head, called the coachman down from his box,
and, upon presenting himself at the window, asked
him if he smoked. As I was considering what this
would end in, he bid him stop by the way at any good
tobacconist's, and take in a roll of their best Virginia.
Nothing material happened in the remaining part of
our journey, till we were set down at the west end of
the abbey.

As we went up the body of the church, the knight pointed at the trophies upon one of the new monuments, and cried out, " A brave man, I warrant him ! " Passing afterward by Sir Cloudesly Shovel, he flung his hand that way, and cried, " Sir Cloudesly Shovel ! a very gallant man." As we stood before Busby's tomb, the knight uttered himself again after the same manner : " Dr Busby ! a great man ! he whipped my grandfather ; a very great man ! I should have gone to him myself, if I had not been a blockhead : a very great man ! "

We were immediately conducted into the little chapel on the right hand. Sir Roger planting himself at our historian's elbow, was very attentive to every thing he said, particularly to the account he gave us of the lord who had cut off the king of Morocco's head. Among several other figures, he was very well pleased to see the statesman Cecil upon his knees ; and concluding them all to be great men, was conducted to the figure which represents that martyr to good housewifery who died by the prick of a needle. Upon our interpreter's telling us that she was a maid of honour to Queen Elizabeth, the knight was very inquisitive into her name and family ; and, after having regarded her finger for some time, " I wonder," says he, " that Sir Richard Baker has said nothing of her in his Chronicle."

We were then conveyed to the two coronation chairs, where my old friend, after having heard that the stone under the most ancient of them, which was brought from Scotland, was called Jacob's pillar, sat himself down in the chair, and, looking like the figure of an old Gothic king, asked our interpreter, what authority they had to say that Jacob had ever been in Scotland ? The fellow, instead of returning him an answer, told him, that he hoped his honour would pay his forfeit. I could observe Sir Roger a little ruffled upon being thus trepanned ; but our guide not insisting upon his demand, the knight soon recovered his good humour, and whispered in my ear, that if

Will Wimble were with us, and saw those chairs, it would go hard but he would get a tobacco-stopper out of one or t'other of them.

Sir Roger in the next place laid his hand upon Edward the Third's sword, and leaning upon the pommel of it, gave us the whole history of the Black Prince: concluding, that in Sir Richard Baker's opinion, Edward the Third was one of the greatest princes that ever sat upon the English throne.

We were then shown Edward the Confessor's tomb; upon which Sir Roger acquainted us, that he was the first who touched for the evil: and afterward Henry the Fourth's; upon which he shook his head, and told us there was fine reading in the casualties of that reign.

Our conductor then pointed to that monument where there is the figure of one of our English kings without a head; and upon giving us to know, that the head, which was of beaten silver, had been stolen away several years since; "Some whig, I'll warrant you," says Sir Roger; "you ought to lock up your kings better; they will carry off the body too, if you don't take care."

The glorious names of Henry the Fifth and Queen Elizabeth gave the knight great opportunities of shining, and of doing justice to Sir Richard Baker, who, as our knight observed with some surprise, had a great many kings in him, whose monuments he had not seen in the abbey.

For my own part, I could not but be pleased to see the knight show such an honest passion for the glory of his country, and such a respectful gratitude to the memory of its princes.

I must not omit, that the benevolence of my good old friend, which flows out towards every one he converses with, made him very kind to our interpreter, whom he looked upon as an extraordinary man: for which reason he shook him by the hand at parting, telling him, that he should be very glad to see him at his lodgings in Norfolk-buildings, and talk over these matters with him more at leisure.

SIR ROGER AT THE PLAY

Respicere exemplar vitæ morumque jubebo
Doctum imitatorem, et veras hinc ducere voces.
                                    HOR. *Ars Poet.* 317.

Keep Nature's great original in view,
And thence the living images pursue. FRANCIS.

My friend Sir Roger de Coverley, when we last
met together at the club, told me that he had a great
mind to see the new tragedy with me, assuring me at
the same time, that he had not been at a play these
twenty years. "The last I saw," said Sir Roger,
"was the Committee, which I should not have gone to
neither, had not I been told beforehand that it was
a good church of England comedy." He then proceeded to inquire of me who this distrest mother
was; and upon hearing that she was Hector's widow,
he told me that her husband was a brave man, and
that when he was a school-boy he had read his life
at the end of the dictionary. My friend asked me in
the next place, if there would not be some danger in
coming home late, in case the Mohocks should be
abroad. "I assure you," says he, "I thought I had
fallen into their hands last night; for I observed two
or three lusty black men that followed me half way
up Fleet-street, and mended their pace behind me,
in proportion as I put on to get away from them.
You must know," continued the knight with a smile,
"I fancied they had a mind to hunt me; for I remember an honest gentleman in my neighbourhood,
who was served such a trick in King Charles the
Second's time, for which reason he has not ventured
himself in town ever since. I might have shown
them very good sport, had this been their design;
for, as I am an old fox-hunter, I should have turned
and dodged, and have played them a thousand tricks
they had never seen in their lives before." Sir Roger

added, that "if these gentlemen had any such intention, they did not succeed very well in it; for I
threw them out," says he, "at the end of Norfolk-
street, where I doubled the corner, and got shelter in
my lodgings before they could imagine what was
become of me. However," says the knight, "if Captain
Sentry will make one with us to-morrow night, and
you will both of you call upon me about four o'clock,
that we may be at the house before it is full, I will
have my own coach in readiness to attend you, for
John tells me he has got the fore-wheels mended."

The captain, who did not fail to meet me there at
the appointed hour, bid Sir Roger fear nothing, for
that he had put on the same sword which he made
use of at the battle of Steenkirk. Sir Roger's
servants, and among the rest my old friend the butler,
had, I found, provided themselves with good oaken
plants, to attend their master upon this occasion.
When we had placed him in his coach, with myself at
his left hand, the captain before him, and his butler
at the head of his footmen in the rear, we convoyed
him in safety to the playhouse, where, after having
marched up the entry in good order, the captain and
I went in with him, and seated him betwixt us in the
pit. As soon as the house was full, and the candles
lighted, my old friend stood up, and looked about him
with that pleasure which a mind seasoned with
humanity naturally feels in itself, at the sight of a
multitude of people who seem pleased with one
another, and partake of the same common entertainment. I could not but fancy to myself, as the old
man stood up in the middle of the pit, that he made
a very proper centre to a tragic audience. Upon the
entering of Pyrrhus, the knight told me, that he did
not believe the king of France himself had a better
strut. I was indeed very attentive to my old friend's
remarks, because I looked upon them as a piece of
natural criticism, and was well pleased to hear him,
at the conclusion of almost every scene, telling me
that he could not imagine how the play would end.

One while he appeared much concerned for Andro-mache ; and a little while after as much for Hermione; and was extremely puzzled to think what would become of Pyrrhus.

When Sir Roger saw Andromache's obstinate refusal to her lover's importunities, he whispered me in the ear, that he was sure she would never have him; to which he added, with a more than ordinary vehemence, "You can't imagine, Sir, what it is to have to do with a widow." Upon Pyrrhus his threatening to leave her, the knight shook his head and muttered to himself, "Ay, do if you can." This part dwelt so much upon my friend's imagination, that at the close of the third act, as I was thinking on something else, he whispered me in my ear, "These widows, Sir, are the most perverse creatures in the world. But pray," says he, "you that are a critic, is the play according to your dramatic rules, as you call them ? Should your people in tragedy always talk to be understood ? Why, there is not a single sentence in this play that I do not know the meaning of."

The fourth act very luckily began before I had time to give the old gentleman an answer. "Well," says the knight, sitting down with great satisfaction, "I suppose we are now to see Hector's ghost." He then renewed his attention, and, from time to time, fell a-praising the widow. He made, indeed, a little mis-take as to one of her pages, whom at his first entering he took for Astyanax; but quickly set himself right in that particular, though, at the same time, he owned he should have been very glad to have seen the little boy, who, says he, must needs be a very fine child by the account that is given of him. Upon Hermione's going off with a menace to Pyrrhus, the audience gave a loud clap, to which Sir Roger added, "On my word, a notable young baggage !"

As there was a very remarkable silence and still-ness in the audience during the whole action, it was natural for them to take the opportunity of the intervals between the acts to express their opinion of the players, and of their respective parts. Sir Roger, hearing a cluster of them praise Orestes, struck in with them, and told them that he thought his friend Pylades was a very sensible man. As they were afterward applauding Pyrrhus, Sir Roger put in a second time: "And let me tell you," says he, "though he speaks but little, I like the old fellow in whiskers as well as any of them." Captain Sentry, seeing two or three wags who sat near us lean with an attentive ear towards Sir Roger, and fearing lest they should smoke the knight, plucked him by the elbow, and whispered something in his ear, that lasted till the opening of the fifth act. The knight was wonderfully attentive to the account which Orestes gives of Pyrrhus's death, and, at the conclusion of it, told me it was such a bloody piece of work, that he was glad it was not done upon the stage. Seeing afterward Orestes in his raving fit, he grew more than ordinarily serious, and took occasion to moralize (in his way) upon an evil conscience, adding, that Orestes, in his madness, looked as if he saw something.

As we were the first that came into the house, so we were the last that went out of it: being resolved to have a clear passage for our old friend, whom we did not care to venture among the justling of the crowd. Sir Roger went out fully satisfied with his entertainment, and we guarded him to his lodging in the same manner that we brought him to the playhouse, being highly pleased for my own part, not only with the performance of the excellent piece which had been presented, but with the satisfaction which it had given to the good old man.

ON CHEERFULNESS

Æquam memento rebus in arduis
Servare mentem, non secus in bonis
  Ab insolenti temperatam
  Lætitia, moriture Delli.

HOR. Od. II. iii. 1.

Be calm, my Dellius, and serene,
However fortune change the scene,
In thy most dejected state,
Sink not underneath the weight;
Nor yet, when happy days begin,
And the full tide comes rolling in
Let a fierce, unruly, joy
The settled quiet of thy mind destroy. ANON.

I HAVE always preferred cheerfulness to mirth. The latter I consider as an act, the former as a habit of the mind. Mirth is short and transient, cheerfulness fixed and permanent. Those are often raised into the greatest transports of mirth who are subject to the greatest depressions of melancholy. On the contrary, cheerfulness, though it does not give the mind such an exquisite gladness, prevents us from falling into any depths of sorrow. Mirth is like a flash of lightning, that breaks through a gloom of clouds, and glitters for a moment; cheerfulness keeps up a kind of day-light in the mind, and fills it with a steady and perpetual serenity.

Men of austere principles look upon mirth as too wanton and dissolute for a state of probation, and as filled with a certain triumph and insolence of heart that is inconsistent with a life which is every moment obnoxious to the greatest dangers. Writers of this complexion have observed, that the Sacred Person who was the great pattern of perfection was never seen to laugh.

Cheerfulness of mind is not liable to any of these exceptions; it is of a serious and composed nature; it does not throw the mind into a condition improper for the present state of humanity, and is very conspicuous in the characters of those who are looked upon as the greatest philosophers among the heathens, as well as among those who have been deservedly esteemed as saints and holy men among Christians.

If we consider cheerfulness in three lights, with regard to ourselves, to those we converse with, and to the great Author of our being, it will not a little recommend itself on each of these accounts. The man who is possessed of this excellent frame of mind, is not only easy in his thoughts, but a perfect master of all the powers and faculties of his soul. His imagination is always clear, and his judgment undisturbed; his temper is even and unruffled, whether in action or in solitude. He comes with relish to all those goods which nature has provided for him, tastes all the pleasures of the creation which are poured about him, and does not feel the full weight of those accidental evils which may befall him.

If we consider him in relation to the persons whom he converses with, it naturally produces love and good-will towards him. A cheerful mind is not only disposed to be affable and obliging; but raises the same good humour in those who come within its influence. A man finds himself pleased, he does not know why, with the cheerfulness of his companion. It is like a sudden sunshine that awakens a secret delight in the mind, without her attending to it. The heart rejoices of its own accord, and naturally flows out into friendship and benevolence towards the person who has so kindly an effect upon it.

When I consider this cheerful state of mind in its third relation, I cannot but look upon it as a constant habitual gratitude to the great Author of nature. An inward cheerfulness is an implicit praise and thanksgiving to Providence under all its dispensations. It is a kind of acquiescence in the state wherein we are placed, and a secret approbation of the Divine Will in his conduct towards man.

There are but two things which, in my opinion, can reasonably deprive us of this cheerfulness of heart. The first of these is the sense of guilt. A man who lives in a state of vice and impenitence, can have no title to that evenness and tranquillity of mind which is the health of the soul, and the natural effect of virtue and innocence. Cheerfulness in an ill man deserves a harder name than language can furnish us with, and is many degrees beyond what we commonly call folly or madness.

Atheism, by which I mean a disbelief of a Supreme Being, and consequently of a future state, under whatsoever titles it shelter itself, may likewise very reasonably deprive a man of this cheerfulness of temper. There is something so particularly gloomy and offensive to human nature in the prospect of non-existence, that I cannot but wonder, with many excellent writers, how it is possible for a man to outlive the expectation of it. For my own part, I think the being of a God is so little to be doubted, that it is almost the only truth we are sure of; and such a truth as we meet with in every object, in every occurrence, and in every thought. If we look into the characters of this tribe of infidels, we generally find they are made up of pride, spleen, and cavil. It is indeed no wonder, that men who are uneasy to themselves should be so to the rest of the world; and how is it possible for a man to be otherwise than uneasy in himself, who is in danger every moment of losing his entire existence, and dropping into nothing?

The vicious man and Atheist have therefore no pretence to cheerfulness, and would act very unreasonably should they endeavour after it. It is impossible for any one to live in good-humour, and enjoy his present existence, who is apprehensive either of torment or of annihilation; of being miserable, or of not being at all.

After having mentioned these two great principles, which are destructive of cheerfulness in their own nature, as well as in right reason, I cannot think of any other that ought to banish this happy temper from a virtuous mind. Pain and sickness, shame and reproach, poverty and old age, nay death itself, considering the shortness of their duration, and the advantage we may reap from them, do not deserve the name of evils. A good mind may bear up under them with fortitude, with indolence, and with cheerfulness of heart. The tossing of a tempest does not discompose him, which he is sure will bring him to a joyful harbour.

A man who uses his best endeavours to live according to the dictates of virtue and right reason, has two perpetual sources of cheerfulness, in the consideration of his own nature, and of that Being on whom he has a dependance. If he looks into himself, he cannot but rejoice in that existence which is so lately bestowed upon him, and which, after millions of ages, will be still new, and still in its beginning. How many self-congratulations naturally arise in the mind, when it reflects on this its entrance into eternity, when it takes a view of those improvable faculties, which in a few years, and even at its first setting out, have made so considerable a progress, and which will still be receiving an increase of perfection, and consequently an increase of happiness! The consciousness of such a being spreads a perpetual diffusion of joy through the soul of a virtuous man, and makes him look upon himself every moment as more happy than he knows how to conceive.

The second source of cheerfulness to a good mind is the consideration of that Being on whom we have our dependance, and in whom, though we behold him as yet but in the first faint discoveries of his perfections, we see every thing that we can imagine as great, glorious, or amiable. We find ourselves every where upheld by his goodness, and surrounded with an immensity of love and mercy. In short, we depend upon a Being, whose power qualifies him to make us happy by an infinity of means, whose goodness and truth engage him to make those happy who desire it of him, and whose unchangeableness will secure us in this happiness to all eternity.

Such considerations, which every one should perpetually cherish in his thoughts, will banish from us all that secret heaviness of heart which unthinking men are subject to when they lie under no real affliction; all that anguish which we may feel from any evil that actually oppresses us, to which I may likewise add those little cracklings of mirth and folly that are apter to betray virtue than support it; and establish in us such an even and cheerful temper, as makes us pleasing to ourselves, to those with whom we converse, and to Him whom we were made to please.

COFFEE-HOUSE POLITICIANS

Qui mores hominum multorum vidit.
HOR. *Ars Poet.* 142.

Of many men he saw the manners.

WHEN I consider this great city in its several quarters and divisions, I look upon it as an aggregate of various nations distinguished from each other by their respective customs, manners, and interests. The courts of two countries do not so much differ from one another, as the court and city, in their peculiar ways of life and conversation. In short, the inhabitants of St James's, notwithstanding they live under the same laws, and speak the same language, are a distinct people from those of Cheapside, who are likewise removed from those of the Temple on one side, and those of Smithfield on the other, by several climates and degrees in their ways of thinking and conversing together.

For this reason, when any public affair is upon the anvil, I love to hear the reflections that arise upon it in the several districts and parishes of London and Westminster, and to ramble up and down a whole day together, in order to make myself acquainted with the opinions of my ingenious countrymen. By this means I know the faces of all the principal politicians within the bills of mortality; and as every coffee-house has some particular statesman belonging to it, who is the mouth of the street where he lives, I always take care to place myself near him, in order to know his judgment on the present posture of affairs. The last progress that I made with this intention, was about three months ago, when we had a current report of the king of France's death. As I foresaw this would produce a new face of things in Europe, and many curious speculations in our British coffee-houses, I was very desirous to learn the thoughts of our most eminent politicians on that occasion.

That I might begin as near the fountain-head as possible, I first of all called in at St James's, where I found the whole outward room in a buzz of politics. The speculations were but very indifferent towards the door, but grew finer as you advanced to the upper end of the room, and were so very much improved by a knot of theorists, who sat in the inner room, within the steams of the coffee-pot, that I there heard the whole Spanish monarchy disposed of, and all the line of Bourbon provided for in less than a quarter of an hour.

I afterwards called in at Giles's, where I saw a board of French gentlemen sitting upon the life and death of their grand monarque. Those among them who had espoused the whig interest, very positively affirmed, that he departed this life about a week since, and therefore proceeded without any further delay to the release of their friends in the galleys, and to their own re-establishment; but finding they could not agree among themselves, I proceeded on my intended progress.

Upon my arrival at Jenny Man's I saw an *alerte* young fellow that cocked his hat upon a friend of his who entered just at the same time with myself, and accosted him after the following manner: "Well, Jack, the old prig is dead at last. Sharp's the word. Now or never, boy. Up to the walls of Paris directly." With several other deep reflections of the same nature.

I met with very little variation in the politics between Charing-cross and Covent-garden. And upon my going into Will's, I found their discourse was gone off from the death of the French king to that of Monsieur Boileau, Racine, Corneille, and several other poets, whom they regretted on this occasion, as persons who would have obliged the world with very noble elegies on the death of so great a prince, and so eminent a patron of learning.

At a coffee-house near the Temple, I found a couple of young gentlemen engaged very smartly in a dispute on the succession to the Spanish monarchy. One of them seemed to have been retained as advocate for the Duke of Anjou, the other for his imperial majesty. They were both for regulating the title to that kingdom by the statute laws of England; but finding them going out of my depth, I passed forward to St Paul's churchyard, where I listened with great attention to a learned man, who gave the company an account of the deplorable state of France during the minority of the deceased king.

I then turned on my right hand into Fish-street, where the chief politician of that quarter, upon hearing the news (after having taken a pipe of tobacco, and ruminated for some time), " If," says he, "the king of France is certainly dead, we shall have plenty of mackerel this season: our fishery will not be disturbed by privateers, as it has been for these ten years past." He afterwards considered how the death of this great man would affect our pilchards, and by several other remarks infused a general joy into his whole audience.

I afterward entered a by-coffee-house that stood at the upper end of a narrow lane, where I met with a non-juror, engaged very warmly with a lace-man who was the great support of a neighbouring conventicle. The matter in debate was, whether the late French king was most like Augustus Cæsar or Nero. The controversy was carried on with great heat on both sides; and as each of them looked upon me very frequently during the course of their debate, I was under some apprehension that they would appeal to me, and therefore laid down my penny at the bar, and made the best of my way to Cheapside.

I here gazed upon the signs for some time, before I found one to my purpose. The first object I met in the coffee-room was a person who expressed great grief for the death of the French king; but, upon his explaining himself, I found his sorrow did not arise from the loss of the monarch, but for his having sold out of the bank about three days before he heard the news of it. Upon which, a haberdasher, who was the oracle of the coffee-house, and had his circle of admirers about him, called several to witness that he had declared his opinion above a week before, that the French king was certainly dead; to which he added, that, considering the late advices we had received from France, it was impossible that it could be otherwise. As he was laying these together, and dictating to his hearers with great authority, there came in a gentleman from Garraway's who told us that there were several letters from France just come in, with advice that the king was gone out a-hunting the very morning the post came away: upon which, the haberdasher stole off his hat that hung upon a wooden peg by him, and retired to his shop with great confusion. This intelligence put a stop to my travels, which I had prosecuted with much satisfaction, not being a little pleased to hear so many different opinions upon so great an event, and to observe how naturally upon such a piece of news every one is apt to consider it with regard to his own particular interest and advantage.

ON FINE TASTE

Musæo contingens cuncta lepore. LUCR. l. 933.

To grace each subject with enliv'ning wit.

GRATIAN very often recommends fine taste as the utmost perfection of an accomplished man.

As this word arises very often in conversation, I shall endeavour to give some account of it, and to lay down rules how we may know whether we are possessed of it, and how we may acquire that fine taste of writing which is so much talked of among the polite world.

Most languages make use of this metaphor, to express that faculty of the mind which distinguishes all the most concealed faults and nicest perfections in writing. We may be sure this metaphor would not have been so general in all tongues, had there not been a very great conformity between that mental taste, which is the subject of this paper, and that sensitive taste, which gives us a relish of every different flavour that affects the palate. Accordingly we find there are as many degrees of refinement in the intellectual faculty as in the sense which is marked out by this common denomination.

I knew a person who possessed the one in so great a perfection, that, after having tasted ten different kinds of tea, he would distinguish, without seeing the colour of it, the particular sort which was offered him; and not only so, but any two sorts of them that were mixed together in an equal proportion; nay, he has carried the experiment so far, as, upon tasting the composition of three different sorts, to name the parcels from whence the three several ingredients were taken. A man of a fine taste in writing will discern, after the same manner, not only the general beauties and imperfections of an author, but discover the several ways of thinking and expressing himself, which diversify him from all other authors, with the several foreign infusions of thought and language, and the particular authors from whom they were borrowed.

After having thus far explained what is generally meant by a fine taste in writing, and shown the propriety of the metaphor which is used on this occasion, I think I may define it to be "that faculty of the soul, which discerns the beauties of an author with pleasure, and the imperfections with dislike." If a man would know whether he is possessed of this faculty, I would have him read over the celebrated works of antiquity, which have stood the test of so many different ages and countries, or those works among the moderns which have the sanction of the politer part of our contemporaries. If, upon the perusal of such writings, he does not find himself delighted in an extraordinary manner, or if, upon reading the admired passages in such authors, he finds a coldness and indifference in his thoughts, he ought to conclude, not (as is too usual among taste-less readers) that the author wants those perfections which have been admired in him, but that he himself wants the faculty of discovering them.

He should, in the second place, be very careful to observe, whether he tastes the distinguishing perfections, or, if I may be allowed to call them so, the specific qualities of the author whom he peruses; whether he is particularly pleased with Livy for his manner of telling a story, with Sallust for his entering into those internal principles of action which arise from the characters and manners of the persons he describes, or with Tacitus for displaying those outward motives of safety and interest which gave birth to the whole series of transactions which he relates.

He may likewise consider, how differently he is affected by the same thought which presents itself in a great writer, from what he is when he finds it delivered by a person of an ordinary genius; for there is as much difference in apprehending a thought clothed in Cicero's language, and that of a common author, as in seeing an object by the light of a taper, or by the light of the sun.

It is very difficult to lay down rules for the acquirement of such a taste as that I am here speaking of. The faculty must in some degree be born with us; and it very often happens, that those who have other qualities in perfection, are wholly void of this. One of the most eminent mathematicians of the age has assured me, that the greatest pleasure he took in reading Virgil was in examining Æneas's voyage by the map; as I question not but many a modern compiler of history would be delighted with little more in that divine author than the bare matters of fact.

But, notwithstanding this faculty must in some measure be born with us, there are several methods for cultivating and improving it, and without which it will be very uncertain, and of little use to the person that possesses it. The most natural method for this purpose is to be conversant among the writings of the most polite authors. A man who has any relish for fine writing, either discovers new beauties, or receives stronger impressions, from the masterly strokes of a great author, every time he peruses him; besides that he naturally wears himself into the same manner of speaking and thinking.

Conversation with men of a polite genius is another method for improving our natural taste. It is impossible for a man of the greatest parts to consider any thing in its whole extent, and in all its variety of lights. Every man, besides those general observations which are to be made upon an author, forms several reflections that are peculiar to his own manner of thinking; so that conversation will naturally furnish us with hints which we did not attend to, and make us enjoy other men's parts and reflections as well as our own. This is the best reason I can give for the observation which several have made, that men of great genius in the same way of writing seldom rise up

singly, but at certain periods of time appear together,
and in a body; as they did at Rome in the reign of
Augustus, and in Greece about the age of Socrates.
I cannot think that Corneille, Racine, Moliere, Boileau,
La Fontaine, Bruyere, Bossu, or the Daciers, would
have written so well as they have done, had they not
been friends and contemporaries.

It is likewise necessary for a man who would form
to himself a finished taste of good writing, to be well
versed in the works of the best critics, both ancient
and modern. I must confess that I could wish there
were authors of this kind, who, besides the mechanical
rules, which a man of very little taste may discourse
upon, would enter into the very spirit and soul of fine
writing, and show us the several sources of that
pleasure which rises in the mind upon the perusal of
a noble work. Thus, although in poetry it be absolutely necessary that the unities of time, place, and
action, with other points of the same nature, should
be thoroughly explained and understood, there is still
something more essential to the art, something that
elevates and astonishes the fancy, and gives a greatness of mind to the reader, which few of the critics
besides Longinus have considered.

Our general taste in England is for epigram, turns
of wit, and forced conceits, which have no manner of
influence either for the bettering or enlarging the
mind of him who reads them, and have been carefully avoided by the greatest writers, both among the
ancients and moderns. I have endeavoured, in several
of my speculations, to banish this Gothic taste which
has taken possession among us. I entertained the
town for a week together with an essay upon wit, in
which I endeavoured to detect several of those false
kinds which have been admired in the different ages
of the world, and at the same time to show wherein
the nature of true wit consists. I afterward gave an
instance of the great force which lies in a natural
simplicity of thought to affect the mind of the reader,
from such vulgar pieces as have little else besides this

single qualification to recommend them. I have likewise examined the works of the greatest poet which
our nation, or perhaps any other, has produced, and
particularized most of those rational and manly
beauties which give a value to that divine work. I
shall next Saturday enter upon an essay on "The
Pleasures of the Imagination," which, though it shall
consider that subject at large, will perhaps suggest to
the reader what it is that gives a beauty to many
passages of the finest writers both in prose and verse.
As an undertaking of this nature is entirely new, I
question not but it will be received with candour.

WEALTH AND POVERTY

Auream quisquis mediocritatem
Diligit, tutus caret obsoleti
Sordibus tecti, caret invidenda
      Sobrius aula.   HOR. *Od.* II. x. 5.

The golden mean, as she's too nice to dwell
Among the ruins of a filthy cell,
So is her modesty withal as great,
To baulk the envy of a princely seat. NORRIS.

I AM wonderfully pleased when I meet with any
passage in an old Greek and Latin author, that is not
blown upon, and which I have never met with in a
quotation. Of this kind is a beautiful saying in
Theognis: "Vice is covered by wealth, and virtue by
poverty"; or, to give it in the verbal translation,
"Among men there are some who have their vices
concealed by wealth, and others who have their virtues
concealed by poverty." Every man's observation will
supply him with instances of rich men, who have
several faults and defects that are overlooked, if not
entirely hidden, by means of their riches; and, I
think, we cannot find a more natural description of a
poor man, whose merits are lost in his poverty, than

that in the words of the wise man : " There was a little city, and, few men within it, and there came a great king against it, and besieged it, and built great bulwarks against it. Now there was found in it a poor wise man, and he, by his wisdom, delivered the city ; yet no man remembered that same poor man. Then said I, wisdom is better than strength ; nevertheless, the poor man's wisdom is despised, and his words are not heard."

The middle condition seems to be the most advantageously situated for the gaining of wisdom. Poverty turns our thoughts too much upon the supplying of our wants, and riches upon enjoying our superfluities ; and, as Cowley has said in another case, " It is hard for a man to keep a steady eye upon truth, who is always in a battle or a triumph."

If we regard poverty and wealth, as they are apt to produce virtues or vices in the mind of man, one may observe that there is a set of each of these growing out of poverty, quite different from that which rises out of wealth. Humility and patience, industry and temperance, are very often the good qualities of a poor man. Humanity and good-nature, magnanimity and a sense of honour, are as often the qualifications of the rich. On the contrary, poverty is apt to betray a man into envy, riches into arrogance. Poverty is too often attended with fraud, vicious compliance, repining, murmur, and discontent ; riches expose a man to pride and luxury, a foolish elation of heart and too great a fondness for the present world. In short, the middle condition is most eligible to the man who would improve himself in virtue ; as I have before shown, it is the most advantageous for the gaining of knowledge. It was upon this consideration that Agur founded his prayer, which, for the wisdom of it, is recorded in holy writ. " Two things have I required of thee : deny me them not before I die. Remove far from me vanity and lies ; give me neither poverty nor riches ; feed me with food convenient for me ; lest I be full and deny thee, and say, Who is the

Lord? or lest I be poor and steal, and take the name
of my God in vain."

I shall fill the remaining part of my paper with a
very pretty allegory, which is wrought into a play
by Aristophanes, the Greek comedian. It seems
originally designed as a satire upon the rich, though,
in some parts of it, it is, like the foregoing discourse,
a kind of comparison between wealth and poverty.

Chremylus, who was an old and a good man, and
withal exceeding poor, being desirous to leave some
riches to his son, consults the oracle of Apollo upon
the subject. The oracle bids him follow the first
man he should see upon his going out of the temple.
The person he chanced to see was to appearance an
old blind sordid man, but, upon his following him
from place to place, he at last found, by his own
confession, that he was Plutus the god of riches, and
that he was just come out of the house of a miser.
Plutus further told him, that when he was a boy, he
used to declare, that as soon as he came to age he
would distribute wealth to no one but virtuous and
just men; upon which Jupiter, considering the pernicious consequences of such a resolution, took his
sight away from him, and left him to stroll about the
world in the blind condition wherein Chremylus beheld
him. With much ado Chremylus prevailed upon him
to go to his house, where he met an old woman in a
tattered raiment, who had been his guest for many
years, and whose name was Poverty. The old woman
refusing to turn out so easily as he would have her,
he threatened to banish her not only from his own house,
but out of all Greece, if she made any more words
upon the matter. Poverty on this occasion pleads
her cause very notably, and represents to her old
landlord, that, should she be driven out of the country,
all their trades, arts, and sciences, would be driven
out with her; and that, if every one was rich, they
would never be supplied with those pomps, ornaments,
and conveniences of life, which made riches desirable.
She likewise represented to him the several advantages

which she bestowed upon her votaries in regard to
their shape, their health, and their activity, by pre-
serving them from gouts, dropsies, unwieldiness, and
intemperance. But whatever she had to say for
herself, she was at last forced to troop off. Chremylus
immediately considered how he might restore Plutus
to his sight; and, in order to it, conveyed him to
the temple of Æsculapius, who was famous for cures
and miracles of this nature. By this means, the deity
recovered his eyes, and began to make a right use of
them, by enriching every one that was distinguished
by piety towards the gods, and justice towards men;
and at the same time by taking away his gifts from
the impious and undeserving. This produces several
merry incidents, till in the last act Mercury descends
with great complaints from the gods, that since the
good men were grown rich, they had received no
sacrifices; which is confirmed by a priest of Jupiter,
who enters with a remonstrance, that since this late
innovation he was reduced to a starving condition,
and could not live upon his office. Chremylus, who
in the beginning of the play was religious in his
poverty, concludes it with a proposal, which was
relished by all the good men who were now grown rich
as well as himself, that they should carry Plutus in a
solemn procession to the temple, and instal him in
the place of Jupiter. This allegory instructed the
Athenians in two points; first, as it vindicated the
conduct of Providence in its ordinary distributions of
wealth; and, in the next place, as it showed the great
tendency of riches to corrupt the morals of those who
possessed them.

QUALIFICATIONS FOR OFFICE

Detrahere aliquid alteri, et hominem hominis incommodo
   suum augere commodum, magis est contra naturam
   quam mors, quam paupertas, quam dolor, quam cætera
   quæ possunt aut corpori accidere, aut rebus externis.
                                                   TULL.

To detract any thing from another, and for one man to
   multiply his own conveniences by the inconveniences
   of another, is more against nature than death, than
   poverty, than pain, and the other things which can
   befal the body, or external circumstances.

I AM persuaded there are few men, of generous
principles, who would seek after great places, were
it not rather to have an opportunity in their hands
of obliging their particular friends, or those whom
they look upon as men of worth, than to procure
wealth and honour for themselves. To an honest
mind, the best perquisites of a place are the advantages it gives a man of doing good.

Those who are under the great officers of state,
and are the instruments by which they act, have
more frequent opportunities for the exercise of compassion and benevolence, than their superiors themselves. These men know every little case that is to
come before the great man, and, if they are possessed
with honest minds, will consider poverty as a recom-
mendation in the person who applies himself to them,
and make the justice of his cause the most powerful
solicitor in his behalf. A man of this temper, when
he is in a post of business, becomes a blessing to the
public. He patronizes the orphan and the widow,
assists the friendless, and guides the ignorant. He
does not reject the person's pretensions, who does
not know how to explain them, or refuse doing a good
office for a man because he cannot pay the fee of it.
In short, though he regulates himself in all his proceedings by justice and equity, he finds a thousand

occasions for all the good-natured offices of generosity and compassion.

A man is unfit for such a place of trust, who is of a sour untractable nature, or has any other passion that makes him uneasy to those who approach him. Roughness of temper is apt to discountenance the timorous or modest. The proud man discourages those from approaching him, who are of a mean condition, and who most want his assistance. The impatient man will not give himself time to be informed of the matter that lies before him. An officer, with one or more of these unbecoming qualities, is sometimes looked upon as a proper person to keep off impertinence and solicitation from his superior; but this is a kind of merit that can never atone for injustice which may very often arise from it.

There are two other vicious qualities which render a man very unfit for such a place of trust. The first of these is a dilatory temper, which commits innumerable cruelties without design. The maxim which several have laid down for a man's conduct in ordinary life, should be inviolable with a man in office, never to think of doing that to-morrow which may be done to-day. A man who defers doing what ought to be done, is guilty of injustice so long as he defers it. The dispatch of a good office is very often as beneficial to the solicitor as the good office itself. In short, if a man compared the inconveniences which another suffers by his delays, with the trifling motives and advantages which he himself may reap by such a delay, he would never be guilty of a fault which very often does an irreparable prejudice to the person who depends upon him, and which might be remedied with little trouble to himself.

But in the last place there is no man so improper to be employed in business, as he who is in any degree capable of corruption; and such a one is the man who, upon any pretence whatsoever, receives more than what is the stated and unquestioned fee of his office. Gratifications, tokens of thankfulness, dispatch-money, and the like spacious terms, are the pretences under which corruption very frequently shelters itself. An honest man will, however, look on all these methods as unjustifiable, and will enjoy himself better in a moderate fortune that is gained with honour and reputation, than in an overgrown state that is cankered with the acquisitions of rapine and exaction. Were all our offices discharged with such an inflexible integrity, we should not see men in all ages, who grow up to exorbitant wealth, with the abilities which are to be met with in an ordinary mechanic. I cannot but think that such a corruption proceeds chiefly from men's employing the first that offer themselves, or those who have the character of shrewd worldly men, instead of searching out such as have had a liberal education, and have been trained up in the studies of knowledge and virtue.

It has been observed, that men of learning who take to business, discharge it generally with greater honesty than men of the world. The chief reason for it I take to be as follows: A man that has spent his youth in reading, has been used to find virtue extolled, and vice stigmatized. A man that has passed his time in the world, has often seen vice triumphant, and virtue discountenanced. Extortion, rapine, and injustice, which are branded with infamy in books, often give a man a figure in the world; while several qualities, which are celebrated in authors, as generosity, ingenuity, and good-nature, impoverish and ruin him. This cannot but have a proportionable effect on men whose tempers and principles are equally good and vicious.

There would be at least this advantage in employing men of learning and parts in business; that their prosperity would sit more gracefully on them, and that we should not see many worthless persons shot up into the greatest figures of life.

GARDENS

An me ludit amabilis
Insania? Audire, et videor pios
  Errare per lucos, amoenæ
    Quos et aquæ subeunt et auræ.
HOR. Od. III. iv. 5.

Does airy fancy cheat
My mind well pleas'd with the deceit?
I seem to hear, I seem to move,
And wander through the happy grove,
Where smooth springs flow, and murm'ring breeze
Wantons through the waving trees. CREECH.

" SIR,

" HAVING lately read your essay on The Pleasures
of the Imagination, I was so taken with your thoughts
upon some of our English gardens, that I cannot forbear troubling you with a letter upon that subject.
I am one, you must know, who am looked upon as a
humourist in gardening. I have several acres about
my house, which I call my garden, and which a skilful
gardener would not know what to call. It is a
confusion of kitchen and parterre, orchard and
flower-garden, which lie so mixt and interwoven with
one another, that if a foreigner who had seen nothing
of our country, should be conveyed into my garden at
his first landing, he would look upon it as a natural
wilderness, and one of the uncultivated parts of our
country. My flowers grow up in several parts of the
garden in the greatest luxuriancy and profusion. I
am so far from being fond of any particular one, by
reason of its rarity, that if I meet with any one in a
field which pleases me, I give it a place in my garden.
By this means, when a stranger walks with me, he is
surprised to see several large spots of ground covered
with ten thousand different colours, and has often
singled out flowers that he might have met with under
a common hedge, in a field, or in a meadow, as some

of the greatest beauties of the place. The only method
I observe in this particular, is to range in the same
quarter the products of the same season, that they
may make their appearance together, and compose
a picture of the greatest variety. There is the same
irregularity in my plantations, which run into as great
a wilderness as their natures will permit. I take in
none that do not naturally rejoice in the soil; and am
pleased, when I am walking in a labyrinth of my own
raising, not to know whether the next tree I shall
meet with is an apple or an oak, an elm or a pear-
tree. My kitchen has likewise its particular quarters
assigned it; for besides the wholesome luxury which
that place abounds with, I have always thought a
kitchen-garden a more pleasant sight than the finest
orangery, or artificial green-house. I love to see
every thing in its perfection; and am more pleased to
survey my rows of coleworts and cabbages, with a
thousand nameless pot-herbs, springing up in their
full fragrancy and verdure, than to see the tender
plants of foreign countries kept alive by artificial
heats, or withering in an air and soil that are not
adapted to them. I must not omit, that there is a
fountain rising in the upper part of my garden, which
forms a little wandering rill, and administers to the
pleasure as well as the plenty of the place. I have so
conducted it, that it visits most of my plantations:
and have taken particular care to let it run in the
same manner as it would do in an open field, so that
it generally passes through banks of violets and
primroses, plats of willow, or other plants, that seem
to be of its own producing. There is another circumstance in which I am very particular, or, as my
neighbours call me, very whimsical: as my garden
invites into it all the birds of the country, by offering
them the conveniency of springs and shades, solitude
and shelter, I do not suffer any one to destroy their
nests in the spring, or drive them from their usual
haunts in fruit-time; I value my garden more for
being full of blackbirds than cherries, and very frankly

give them fruit for their songs. By this means, I
have always the music of the season in its perfection,
and am highly delighted to see the jay or the thrush
hopping about my walks, and shooting before my eye
across the several little glades and alleys that I pass
through. I think there are as many kinds of gardening
as of poetry: your makers of parterres and flower
gardens are epigrammatists and sonneteers in this
art; contrivers of bowers and grottos, treillages and
cascades, are romance writers. Wise and London
are our heroic poets; and if, as a critic, I may single
out any passage of their works to commend, I shall
take notice of that part in the upper garden at
Kensington, which was at first nothing but a gravel-pit.
It must have been a fine genius for gardening that
could have thought of forming such an unsightly
hollow into so beautiful an area, and to have hit the
eye with so uncommon and agreeable a scene as
that which it is now wrought into. To give this
particular spot of ground the greater effect, they
have made a very pleasing contrast; for, as on one
side of the walk you see this hollow basin, with its
several little plantations, lying so conveniently under
the eye of the beholder, on the other side of it there
appears a seeming mount, made up of trees, rising
one higher than another, in proportion as they approach the centre. A spectator, who has not heard
this account of it, would think this circular mount was
not only a real one, but that it had been actually
scooped out of that hollow space which I have before
mentioned. I never yet met with any one, who has
walked in this garden, who was not struck with that
part of it which I have here mentioned. As for myself,
you will find, by the account which I have already
given you, that my compositions in gardening are
altogether after the Pindaric manner, and run into
the beautiful wildness of nature, without affecting the
nicer elegancies of art. What I am now going to
mention, will perhaps deserve your attention more
than any thing I have yet said. I find that, in the

discourse which I spoke of at the beginning of my
letter, you are against filling an English garden with
evergreens; and indeed I am so far of your opinion,
that I can by no means think the verdure of an
evergreen comparable to that which shoots out
annually, and clothes our trees in the summer season.
But I have often wondered that those who are like
myself, and love to live in gardens, have never
thought of contriving a winter garden, which should
consist of such trees only as never cast their leaves.
We have very often little snatches of sunshine and
fair weather in the most uncomfortable parts of the
year, and have frequently several days in November
and January that are as agreeable as any in the finest
months. At such times, therefore, I think there could
not be a greater pleasure than to walk in such a
winter garden as I have proposed. In the summer
season the whole country blooms, and is a kind of
garden; for which reason we are not so sensible of
those beauties that at this time may be every where
met with; but when nature is in her desolation, and
presents us with nothing but bleak and barren
prospects, there is something unspeakably cheerful in
a spot of ground which is covered with trees that
smile amidst all the rigours of winter, and give us a
view of the most gay season in the midst of that which
is the most dead and melancholy. I have so far
indulged myself in this thought, that I have set apart
a whole acre of ground for the execution of it. The
walls are covered with ivy instead of vines. The
laurel, the horn-beam, and the holly, with many other
trees and plants of the same nature, grow so thick in
it, that you cannot imagine a more lively scene. The
glowing redness of the berries, with which they are
hung at this time, vies with the verdure of their
leaves, and is apt to inspire the heart of the beholder
with that vernal delight which you have somewhere
taken notice of in your former papers. It is very
pleasant, at the same time, to see the several kinds of
birds retiring into this little green spot, and enjoying

themselves among the branches and foliage, when my great garden, which I have before mentioned to you, does not afford a single leaf for their shelter.

"You must know, Sir, that I look upon the pleasure which we take in a garden as one of the most innocent delights in human life. A garden was the habitation of our first parents before the fall. It is naturally apt to fill the mind with calmness and tranquillity, and to lay all its turbulent passions at rest. It gives us a great insight into the contrivances and wisdom of Providence, and suggests innumerable subjects for meditation. I cannot but think the very complacency and satisfaction which a man takes in these works of nature to be a laudable, if not a virtuous habit of mind. For all which reasons, I hope you will pardon the length of my present letter.

"I am, Sir," &c.

COFFEE-HOUSE OPINION

Uti non
Compositus melius cum Bitho Bacchius. In jus
Acres procurrunt.   HOR. *Sat.* I. vii. 19.

Who shall decide when doctors disagree,
And soundest casuists doubt like you and me?
POPE.

IT is sometimes pleasant enough to consider the different notions which different persons have of the same thing. If men of low condition very often set a value on things which are not prized by those who are in a higher station of life, there are many things these esteem which are in no value among persons of an inferior rank. Common people are, in particular, very much astonished when they hear of those solemn contests and debates, which are made among the great upon the punctilios of a public ceremony; and wonder to hear that any business of consequence should be retarded by those little circumstances, which they represent to themselves as trifling and insignificant. I am mightily pleased with a porter's decision in one of Mr Southern's plays, which is founded upon that fine distress of a virtuous woman's marrying a second husband, while the first was yet living. The first husband, who was supposed to have been dead, returning to his house, after a long absence, raises a noble perplexity for the tragic part of the play. In the meanwhile the nurse and the porter conferring upon the difficulties that would ensue in such a case, honest Samson thinks the matter may be easily decided, and solves it very judiciously by the old proverb, that, if his first master be still living, "the man must have his mare again." There is nothing in my time which has so much surprised and confounded the greatest part of my honest country-men, as the present controversy between Count Rechteren and Monsieur Mesnager, which employs the wise heads of so many nations, and holds all the affairs of Europe in suspense.

Upon my going into a coffee-house yesterday, and lending an ear to the next table, which was en-compassed with a circle of inferior politicians, one of them, after having read over the news very attentively, broke out into the following remarks: "I am afraid," says he, "this unhappy rupture between the footmen at Utrecht will retard the peace of Christendom. I wish the pope may not be at the bottom of it. His holiness has a very good hand at fomenting a division, as the poor Swiss cantons have lately experienced to their cost. If Monsieur What-d'ye-call-him's domestics will not come to an accommodation, I do not know how the quarrel can be ended but by a religious war."

"Why, truly," says a wiseacre that sat by him, "were I as the king of France, I would scorn to take part with the footmen of either side: here's all the business of Europe stands still, because Monsieur Mesnager's man has had his head broke. If Count Rectrum had given them a pot of ale after it, all would have been well, without any of this bustle; but they say he's a warm man, and does not care to be made mouths at."

Upon this, one that had held his tongue hitherto, began to exert himself; declaring, "that he was very well pleased the plenipotentiaries of our Christian princes took this matter into their serious consideration; for that lackeys were never so saucy and pragmatical as they are now-a-days, and that he should be glad to see them taken down in the treaty of peace, if it might be done without prejudice to the public affairs."

One who sat at the other end of the table, and seemed to be in the interests of the French king, told them, that they did not take the matter right, for that His Most Christian majesty did not resent this matter because it was an injury done to Monsieur Mesnager's footman; "for," says he, "what are Monsieur Mesnager's footmen to him? but because it was done to his subjects. Now," says he, "let me tell you, it would look very odd for a subject of France to have a bloody nose, and his sovereign not to take notice of it. He is obliged in honour to defend his people against hostilities; and if the Dutch will be so insolent to a crowned head, as in any wise to cuff or kick those who are under his protection, I think he is in the right to call them to an account for it."

This distinction set the controversy upon a new foot, and seemed to be very well approved by most that heard it, until a little warm fellow, who had declared himself a friend to the house of Austria, fell most unmercifully upon his Gallic majesty, as encouraging his subjects to make mouths at their betters, and afterward screening them from the punishment that was due to their insolence. To which he added, that the French nation was so addicted to grimace, that, if there was not a stop put to it at the general congress, there would be no walking the streets for them in a time of peace, especially if they continued masters of the West Indies. The little man proceeded with a great deal of warmth, declaring that, if the allies were of his mind, he would oblige the French king to burn his galleys, and tolerate the Protestant religion in his dominions, before he would sheath his sword. He concluded with calling Monsieur Mesnager an insignificant prig.

The dispute was now growing very warm, and one does not know where it would have ended, had not a young man of about one-and-twenty, who seems to have been brought up with an eye to the law, taken the debate into his hand, and given it as his opinion, that neither Count Rechteren nor Monsieur Mesnager had behaved themselves right in this affair. "Count Rechteren," says he, "should have made affidavit that his servants had been affronted, and then Monsieur Mesnager would have done him justice, by taking away their liveries from them, or some other way that he might have thought the most proper; for, let me tell you, if a man makes a mouth at me, I am not to knock the teeth out of it for his pains. Then again, as for Monsieur Mesnager, upon his servants being beaten, why, he might have had his action of assault and battery. But as the case now stands, if you will have my opinion, I think they ought to bring it to referees."

I heard a great deal more of this conference, but I must confess with little edification; for all I could learn at last from these honest gentlemen was, that the matter in debate was of too high a nature for such heads as theirs, or mine, to comprehend.

UNCHARITABLE JUDGMENT

Nec deus intersit, nisi dignus vindice nodus
    Inciderit.   HOR. *Ars Poet.* 191.

Never presume to make a god appear,
But for a business worthy of a god. ROSCOMMON.

WE cannot be guilty of a greater act of uncharitableness than to interpret the afflictions which befal our neighbours as punishments and judgments. It aggravates the evil to him who suffers, when he looks upon himself as the mark of Divine vengeance, and abates the compassion of those towards him who regard him in so dreadful a light. This humour, of turning every misfortune into a judgment, proceeds from wrong notions of religion, which in its own nature produces good-will towards men, and puts the mildest construction upon every accident that befals them. In this case, therefore, it is not religion that sours a man's temper, but it is his temper that sours his religion. People of gloomy uncheerful imaginations, or of envious malignant tempers, whatever kind of life they are engaged in, will discover their natural tincture of mind in all their thoughts, words, and actions. As the finest wines have often the taste of the soil, so even the most religious thoughts often draw something that is particular from the constitution of the mind in which they arise. When folly or superstition strike in with this natural depravity of temper, it is not in the power even of religion itself, to preserve the character of the person who is possessed with it from appearing highly absurd and ridiculous.

An old maiden gentlewoman, whom I shall conceal under the name of Nemesis, is the greatest discoverer of judgments that I have met with. She can tell you what sin it was that set such a man's house on fire, or blew down his barns. Talk to her

of an unfortunate young lady that lost her beauty by
the small-pox, she fetches a deep sigh, and tells you,
that when she had a fine face she was always looking
on it in her glass.   Tell her of a piece of good fortune
that has befallen one of her acquaintance, and she
wishes it may prosper with her, but her mother used
one of her nieces very barbarously.   Her usual remarks
turn upon people who had great estates, but never
enjoyed them by reason of some flaw in their own or
their father's behaviour.   She can give you the reason
why such a one died childless; why such a one was
cut off in the flower of his youth; why such a one
was unhappy in her marriage; why one broke his leg
on such a particular spot of ground; and why another
was killed with a back-sword, rather than with any
other kind of weapon.   She has a crime for every
misfortune that can befal any of her acquaintance;
and when she hears of a robbery that has been
made, or a murder that has been committed, enlarges
more on the guilt of the suffering person, than on that
of the thief, or the assassin.   In short, she is so good
a Christian, that whatever happens to herself is a
trial, and whatever happens to her neighbours is a
judgment.

The very description of this folly, in ordinary life,
is sufficient to expose it: but, when it appears in a
pomp and dignity of style, it is very apt to amuse
and terrify the mind of the reader.   Herodotus and
Plutarch very often apply their judgments as imper-
tinently as the old woman I have before mentioned,
though their manner of relating them makes the folly
itself appear venerable.   Indeed, most historians, as
well Christian as Pagan, have fallen into this idle
superstition, and spoken of ill success, unforeseen
disasters, and terrible events, as if they had been let
into the secrets of Providence, and made acquainted
with that private conduct by which the world is
governed.   One would think several of our own historians in particular had many revelations of this kind
made to them.   Our old English monks seldom let

any of their kings depart in peace, who had endeavoured to diminish the power or wealth of which the ecclesiastics were in those times possessed. William the Conqueror's race generally found their judgments in the New Forest, where their father had pulled down churches and monasteries. In short, read one of the chronicles written by an author of this frame of mind, and you would think you were reading a history of the kings of Israel or Judah, where the historians were actually inspired, and where, by a particular scheme of Providence, the kings were distinguished by judgments, or blessings, according as they promoted idolatry, or the worship of the true God.

I cannot but look upon this manner of judging upon misfortunes, not only to be very uncharitable in regard to the person on whom they fall, but very presumptuous in regard to him who is supposed to inflict them. It is a strong argument for a state of retribution hereafter, that in this world virtuous persons are very often unfortunate, and vicious persons prosperous; which is wholly repugnant to the nature of a Being who appears infinitely wise and good in all his works, unless we may suppose that such a promiscuous and undistinguishing distribution of good and evil, which was necessary for carrying on the designs of Providence in this life, will be rectified, and made amends for, in another. We are not therefore to expect that fire should fall from heaven in the ordinary course of Povidence; nor, when we see triumphant guilt or depressed virtue in particular persons, that Omnipotence will make bare his holy arm in the defence of the one, or punishment of the other. It is sufficient that there is a day set apart for the hearing and requiting of both, according to their respective merits.

The folly of ascribing temporal judgments to any particular crimes, may appear from several considerations. I shall only mention two. First, that, generally speaking, there is no calamity or affliction, which is

supposed to have happened as a judgment to a vicious
man, which does not sometimes happen to men of
approved religion and virtue. When Diagoras the
atheist was on board one of the Athenian ships, there
arose a very violent tempest: upon which, the mariners
told him, that it was a just judgment upon them for
having taken so impious a man on board. Diagoras
begged them to look upon the rest of the ships that
were in the same distress, and asked them whether or
no Diagoras was on board every vessel in the fleet.
We are all involved in the same calamities, and subject
to the same accidents; and, when we see any one of
the species under any particular oppression, we should
look upon it as arising from the common lot of human
nature, rather than from the guilt of the person who
suffers.

Another consideration, that may check our presumption in putting such a construction upon a misfortune, is this, that it is impossible for us to know
what are calamities and what are blessings. How
many accidents have passed for misfortunes, which
have turned to the welfare and prosperity of the
persons to whose lot they have fallen! How many
disappointments have, in their consequences, saved a
man from ruin! If we could look into the effects of
every thing, we might be allowed to pronounce boldly
upon blessings and judgments; but for a man to give
his opinion of what he sees but in part, and in its
beginnings, is an unjustifiable piece of rashness and
folly. The story of Biton and Clitobus, which was in
great reputation among the heathens (for we see it
quoted by all the ancient authors, both Greek and
Latin, who have written upon the immortality of the
soul), may teach us a caution in this matter. These
two brothers being the sons of a lady who was priestess
to Juno, drew their mother's chariot to the temple at
the time of a great solemnity, the persons being absent
who, by their office, were to have drawn her chariot
on that occasion. The mother was so transported
with this instance of filial duty, that she petitioned

her goddess to bestow upon them the greatest gift that could be given to men; upon which they were both cast into a deep sleep, and the next morning found dead in the temple. This was such an event as would have been construed into a judgment, had it happened to the two brothers after an act of dis-obedience, and would doubtless have been represented as such by any ancient historian who had given us an account of it.

ON GIVING ADVICE

Lectorem delectando, pariterque monendo.
                HOR. *Ars Poet.* 344.

Mixing together profit and delight.

THERE is nothing which we receive with so much reluctance as advice. We look upon the man who gives it us as offering an affront to our understanding, and treating us like children or idiots. We consider the instruction as an implicit censure, and the zeal which any one shows for our good on such an occasion as a piece of presumption or impertinence. The truth of it is, the person who pretends to advise, does, in that particular, exercise a superiority over us, and can have no other reason for it, but that, in comparing us with himself, he thinks us defective either in our conduct or our understanding. For these reasons, there is nothing so difficult as the art of making advice agreeable; and indeed all the writers, both ancient and modern, have distinguished themselves among one another, according to the perfection at which they have arrived in this art. How many devices have been made use of, to render this bitter portion palatable! Some convey their instructions to us in the best chosen words, others in the most harmonious numbers; some in points of wit, and others in short proverbs.

But, among all the different ways of giving counsel, I think the finest, and that which pleases the most universally, is fable, in whatsoever shape it appears. If we consider this way of instructing or giving advice, it excels all others, because it is the least shocking, and the least subject to those exceptions which I have before mentioned.

This will appear to us, if we reflect, in the first place, that upon the reading of a fable, we are made to believe we advise ourselves. We peruse the author for the sake of the story, and consider the precepts rather as our own conclusions than his instructions. The moral insinuates itself imperceptibly; we are taught by surprise, and become wiser and better unawares. In short, by this method, a man is so far overreached as to think he is directing himself, while he is following the dictates of another, and consequently is not sensible of that which is the most unpleasing circumstance in advice.

In the next place, if we look into human nature, we shall find that the mind is never so much pleased, as when she exerts herself in any action that gives her an idea of her own perfections and abilities. This natural pride and ambition of the soul is very much gratified in the reading of a fable; for, in writings of this kind, the reader comes in for half of the performance; everything appears to him like a discovery of his own; he is busied all the while in applying characters and circumstances, and is in this respect both a reader and a composer. It is no wonder, therefore, that on such occasions, when the mind is thus pleased with itself, and amused with its own discoveries, that it is highly delighted with the writing which is the occasion of it. For this reason the Absalom and Achitophel was one of the most popular poems that ever appeared in English. The poetry is indeed very fine: but had it been much finer, it would not have so much pleased, without a plan which gave the reader an opportunity of exerting his own talents.

This oblique manner of giving advice is so inoffensive, that, if we look into ancient histories, we find the wise men of old very often chose to give counsel to their kings in fables. To omit many which will occur to every one's memory, there is a pretty instance of this nature in a Turkish tale, which I do not like the worse for that little oriental extravagance which is mixed with it.

We are told that the Sultan Mahmoud, by his perpetual wars abroad and his tyranny at home, had filled his dominions with ruin and desolation, and half unpeopled the Persian empire. The vizier to this great sultan (whether a humorist or an enthusiast, we are not informed) pretended to have learned of a certain dervise to understand the language of birds, so that there was not a bird that could open his mouth but the vizier knew what it was he said. As he was one evening with the emperor, in their return from hunting, they saw a couple of owls upon a tree that grew near an old wall out of a heap of rubbish. "I would fain know," says the sultan, "what those two owls are saying to one another; listen to their discourse, and give me an account of it." The vizier approached the tree, pretending to be very attentive to the two owls. Upon his return to the sultan, "Sir," says he, "I have heard part of their conversation, but dare not tell you what it is." The sultan would not be satisfied with such an answer, but forced him to repeat word for word every thing the owls had said. "You must know, then," said the vizier, "that one of these owls has a son, and the other a daughter, between whom they are now upon a treaty of marriage. The father of the son said to the father of the daughter, in my hearing, 'Brother, I consent to this marriage, provided you will settle upon your daughter fifty ruined villages for her portion.' To which the father of the daughter replied, 'Instead of fifty, I will give her five hundred, if you please. God grant a long life to Sultan Mahmoud! Whilst he reigns over us, we shall never want ruined villages.'"

The story says the sultan was so touched with the

fable, that he rebuilt the towns and villages which
had been destroyed, and from that time forward consulted the good of his people.

To fill up my paper, I shall add a most ridiculous
piece of natural magic, which was taught by no less
a philosopher than Democritus, namely, that if the
blood of certain birds, which he mentioned, were
mixed together, it would produce a serpent of such
a wonderful virtue, that whoever did eat it should be
skilled in the language of birds, and understand every
thing they said to one another.   Whether the dervise
above mentioned might not have eaten such a serpent,
I shall leave to the determination of the learned.

THE DEATH OF SIR ROGER

Heu pietas ! heu prisca fides !
VIRG. Æn. vi. 878.

Mirror of ancient faith !
Undaunted worth ! Inviolable truth ! DRYDEN.

WE last night received a piece of ill news at our
club, which very sensibly afflicted every one of us.
I question not but my readers themselves will be
troubled at the hearing of it.   To keep them no
longer in suspense, Sir Roger de Coverley is dead !
He departed this life at his house in the country,
after a few weeks' sickness.   Sir Andrew Freeport
has a letter from one of his correspondents in those
parts, that informs him the old man caught a cold at
the county-sessions, as he was very warmly promoting
an address of his own penning, in which he succeeded
according to his wishes.   But this particular comes
from a whig justice of peace, who was always Sir
Roger's enemy and antagonist.   I have letters both
from the chaplain and Captain Sentry, which mention
nothing of it, but are filled with many particulars to

the honour of the good old man. I have likewise a
letter from the butler, who took so much care of me
last summer when I was at the knight's house. As my
friend the butler mentions, in the simplicity of his
heart, several circumstances the others have passed
over in silence, I shall give my reader a copy of his
letter, without any alteration or diminution.

" Honoured Sir,

" Knowing that you was my old master's good
friend, I could not forbear sending you the melancholy
news of his death, which has afflicted the whole
country, as well as his poor servants, who loved him,
I may say, better than we did our lives. I am afraid
he caught his death the last county-sessions, where
he would go to see justice done to a poor widow
woman, and her fatherless children, that had been
wronged by a neighbouring gentleman ; for you know,
Sir, my good master was always the poor man's
friend. Upon his coming home, the first complaint
he made was, that he had lost his roast-beef stomach,
not being able to touch a surloin, which was served
up according to custom; and you know he used to
take great delight in it. From that time forward he
grew worse and worse, but still kept a good heart to
the last. Indeed we were once in great hopes of his
recovery, upon a kind message that was sent him from
the widow lady whom he had made love to the forty
last years of his life; but this only proved a lightning
before death. He has bequeathed to this lady, as a
token of his love, a great pearl necklace, and a couple
of silver bracelets set with jewels, which belonged to
my good old lady his mother. He has bequeathed
the fine white gelding that he used to ride a hunting
upon to his chaplain, because he thought he would be
kind to him; and has left you all his books. He has,
moreover, bequeathed to the chaplain a very pretty
tenement with good lands about it. It being a very
cold day when he made his will, he left for mourning
to every man in the parish a great frieze-coat, and to
every woman a black riding-hood. It was a most

moving sight to see him take leave of his poor servants, commending us all for our fidelity, whilst we were not able to speak a word for weeping. As we most of us are grown gray-headed in our dear master's service, he has left us pensions and legacies, which we may live very comfortably upon the remaining part of our days. He has bequeathed a great deal more in charity, which is not yet come to my knowledge; and it is peremptorily said in the parish, that he has left money to build a steeple to the church: for he was heard to say some time ago, that, if he lived two years longer, Coverley church should have a steeple to it. The chaplain tells everybody that he made a very good end, and never speaks of him without tears. He was buried, according to his own directions, among the family of the Coverleys, on the left hand of his father Sir Arthur. The coffin was carried by six of his tenants, and the pall held up by six of the quorum. The whole parish followed the corpse with heavy hearts, and in their mourning suits; the men in frieze, and the women in riding-hoods. Captain Sentry, my master's nephew, has taken possession of the Hall-house, and the whole estate. When my old master saw him a little before his death, he shook him by the hand, and wished him joy of the estate which was falling to him, desiring him only to make a good use of it, and to pay the several legacies, and the gifts of charity, which he told him he had left as quit-rents upon the estate. The captain truly seems a courteous man, though he says but little. He makes much of those whom my master loved, and shows great kindness to the old house-dog, that you know my poor master was so fond of. It would have gone to your heart to have heard the moans the dumb creature made on the day of my master's death. He has never enjoyed himself since; no more has any of us. It was the melancholiest day for the poor people that ever happened in Worcestershire. This being all from,

"Honoured Sir, your most sorrowful Servant,

"EDWARD BISCUIT.

"P. S. My master desired, some weeks before he died, that a book, which comes up to you by the carrier, should be given to Sir Andrew Freeport in his name."

This letter, notwithstanding the poor butler's manner of writing it, gave us such an idea of our good old friend, that upon the reading of it there was not a dry eye in the club. Sir Andrew, opening the book, found it to be a collection of acts of parliament. There was in particular the Act of Uniformity, with some passages in it marked by Sir Roger's own hand. Sir Andrew found that they related to two or three points which he had disputed with Sir Roger, the last time he appeared at the club. Sir Andrew, who would have been merry at such an incident on another occasion, at the sight of the old man's hand-writing burst into tears, and put the book into his pocket. Captain Sentry informs me that the knight has left rings and mourning for every one in the club.

PROJECT OF A NEW CLUB

Quid dignum tanto feret hic promissor hiatu?
                    HOR. *Ars Poet.* 138.

In what will all this ostentation end?   ROSCOMMON.

SINCE the late dissolution of the club, whereof I have often declared myself a member, there are very many persons who, by letters, petitions, and recommendations, put up for the next election. At the same time I must complain, that several indirect and underhand practices have been made use of upon this occasion. A certain country gentleman began to *tap* upon the first information he received of Sir Roger's death; when he sent me up word that if I would get him chosen in the place of the deceased, he would present me with a barrel of the best October I had ever tasted in my life. The ladies are in great pain to know whom I intend to elect in the room of Will Honeycomb. Some of them indeed are of opinion that Mr Honeycomb did not take sufficient care of their interests in the club, and are therefore desirous of having in it hereafter a representative of their own sex. A citizen who subscribes himself Y. Z., tells me that he has one-and-twenty shares in the African company, and offers to bribe me with the odd one in case he may succeed Sir Andrew Freeport, which he thinks would raise the credit of that fund. I have several letters dated from Jenny Mann's, by gentlemen who are candidates for Captain Sentry's place; and as many from a coffee-house in Paul's churchyard of such who would fill up the vacancy occasioned by the death of my worthy friend the clergyman, whom I can never mention but with a particular respect.

. Having maturely weighed these several particulars, with the many remonstrances that have been made to me on this subject, and considering how invidious an office I shall take upon me if I make the whole election depend upon my single voice, and being unwilling to expose myself to those clamours, which on such an occasion will not fail to be raised against me for partiality, injustice, corruption, and other qualities, which my nature abhors, I have formed to myself the project of a club as follows :—

I have thoughts of issuing out writs to all and every of the clubs that are established in the cities of London and Westminster, requiring them to choose out of their respective bodies a person of the greatest merit, and to return his name to me before Lady-day, at which time I intend to sit upon business.

By this means, I may have reason to hope, that the club over which I shall preside will be the very flower and quintessence of all other clubs. I have communicated this my project to none but a particular friend of mine, whom I have celebrated twice or thrice for his happiness in that kind of wit which is commonly known by the name of a pun. The only objection he makes to it is, that I shall raise up enemies to myself if I act with so regal an air, and that my detractors, instead of giving me the usual title of Spectator, will be apt to call me the King of Clubs.

But to proceed on my intended project: it is very well known that I at first set forth in this work with the character of a silent man ; and I think I have so well preserved my taciturnity, that I do not remember to have violated it with three sentences in the space of almost two years. As a monosyllable is my delight, I have made very few excursions, in the conversations which I have related, beyond a Yes or a No. By this means, my readers have lost many good things which I have had in my heart, though I did not care for uttering them.

Now in order to diversify my character, and to show the world how well I can talk if I have a mind, I have thoughts of being very loquacious in the club which I have now under consideration. But that I may proceed the more regularly in this affair, I design, upon the first meeting of the said club, to have my mouth opened in form; intending to regulate myself in this particular by a certain ritual which I have by me, that contains all the ceremonies which are practised at the opening of the mouth of a cardinal. I have likewise examined the forms which were used of old by Pythagoras, when any of his scholars, after an apprenticeship of silence, was made free of his speech. In the mean time, as I have of late found my name in foreign gazettes upon less occasions, I question not but in their next articles from Great Britain they will inform the world, that " the Spectator's mouth is to be opened on the twenty-fifth of March next." I may perhaps publish a very useful paper at that time of the proceedings in that solemnity, and of the persons who shall assist at it. But of this more hereafter.

ON EGOTISM

Præsens, absens ut sies.
TER. *Eun.* Act. I. Sc. 2.

Be present as if absent.

"It is a hard and nice subject for a man to speak
of himself," says Cowley; "it grates his own heart to
say any thing of disparagement, and the reader's ears
to hear any thing of praise from him." Let the
tenour of his discourse be what it will upon this
subject, it generally proceeds from vanity. An osten-
tatious man will rather relate a blunder or an absurdity
he has committed, than be debarred from talking of
his own dear person.

Some very great writers have been guilty of this
fault. It is observed of Tully in particular, that his
works run very much in the first person, and that he
takes all occasions of doing himself justice. "Does he
think," says Brutus, "that his consulship deserves
more applause than my putting Cæsar to death,
because I am not perpetually talking of the ides of
March, as he is of the nones of December?" I need
not acquaint my learned reader, that in the ides of
March Brutus destroyed Cæsar, and that Cicero
quashed the conspiracy of Catiline in the calends of
December. How shocking soever this great man's
talking of himself might have been to his contemporaries, I must confess I am never better pleased
than when he is on this subject. Such openings of
the heart give a man a thorough insight into his
personal character, and illustrate several passages in
the history of his life: besides that, there is some
little pleasure in discovering the infirmity of a great
man, and seeing how the opinion he has of himself
agrees with what the world entertains of him.

The gentlemen of Port Royal, who were more
eminent for their learning and humility than any

other in France, banished the way of speaking in the first person out of all their works, as arising from vain-glory and self-conceit. To show their particular aversion to it, they branded this form of writing with the name of an egotism; a figure not to be found among the ancient rhetoricians.

The most violent egotism which I have met with in the course of my reading, is that of Cardinal Wolsey, *Ego et rex meus*, "I and my king;" as perhaps the most eminent egotist that ever appeared in the world was Montaigne, the author of the celebrated Essays. This lively old Gascon has woven all his bodily infirmities into his works; and, after having spoken of the faults or virtues of any other man, immediately publishes to the world how it stands with himself in that particular. Had he kept his own counsel, he might have passed for a much better man, though perhaps he would not have been so diverting an author. The title of an Essay promises perhaps a discourse upon Virgil or Julius Cæsar; but, when you look into it, you are sure to meet with more upon Monsieur Montaigne than of either of them. The younger Scaliger, who seems to have been no great friend to this author, after having acquainted the world that his father sold herrings, adds these words: *La grande fadaise de Montaigne, qui a écrit qu'il aimoit mieux le vin blanc——Que diable a-t-on à faire de sçavoir ce qu'il aime?* "For my part," says Montaigne, "I am a great lover of your white wines."—"What the devil signifies it to the public," says Scaliger, "whether he is a lover of white wines or of red wines?"

I cannot here forbear mentioning a tribe of egotists, for whom I always had a mortal aversion—I mean the authors of memoirs, who are never mentioned in any works but their own, and who raise all their productions out of this single figure of speech.

Most of our modern prefaces savour very strongly of the egotism. Every insignificant author fancies it of importance to the world to know that he writ his

book in the country, that he did it to pass away some
of his idle hours, that it was published at the importunity of friends, or that his natural temper, studies,
or conversations, directed him to the choice of his
subject.

> Id populus curat scilicet.

Such informations cannot but be highly improving to
the reader.

In works of humour, especially when a man writes
under a fictitious personage, the talking of one's
self may give some diversion to the public; but I
would advise every other writer never to speak of
himself, unless there be something very considerable
in his character: though I am sensible this rule will
be of little use in the world, because there is no man
who fancies his thoughts worth publishing that does
not look upon himself as a considerable person.

I shall close this paper with a remark upon such
as are egotists in conversation: these are generally
the vain or shallow part of mankind, people being
naturally full of themselves when they have nothing
else in them. There is one kind of egotists which is
very common in the world, though I do not remember
that any writer has taken notice of them, I mean
those empty conceited fellows who repeat, as sayings
of their own or some of their particular friends,
several jests which were made before they were born,
and which every one who has conversed in the world
has heard a hundred times over. A forward young
fellow of my acquaintance was very guilty of this
absurdity; he would be always laying a new scene for
some old piece of wit, and telling us, that, as he and
Jack Such-a-one were together, one or t'other of them
had such a conceit on such an occasion; upon which
he would laugh very heartily, and wonder the company
did not join with him. When his mirth was over, I
have often reprehended him out of Terence, *Tuumne,
obsecro te, hoc dictum erat? vetus credidi.* But
finding him still incorrigible, and having a kindness

for the young coxcomb, who was otherwise a good-
natured fellow, I recommended to his perusal the
Oxford and Cambridge jests, with several little pieces
of pleasantry of the same nature. Upon the reading
of them he was under no small confusion to find that
all his jokes had passed through several editions, and
that what he thought was a new conceit, and had
appropriated to his own use, had appeared in print
before he or his ingenious friends were ever heard of.
This had so good an effect upon him, that he is content
at present to pass for a man of plain sense in his
ordinary conversation, and is never facetious but
when he knows his company.

ON CONTENTMENT

Non possidentem multa vocaveris
Recte beatum. Rectius occupat
   Nomen beati, qui Deorum
   Muneribus sapienter uti.
Duramque callet pauperiem pati.
                              HOR. *Od.* IV. ix. 45.

Believe not those that lands possess,
And shining heaps of useless ore,
The only lords of happiness;
   But rather those that know
   For what kind fates bestow,
And have the heart to use the store
That have the generous skill to bear
The hated weight of poverty. CREECH.

I WAS once engaged in discourse with a Rosicru-
cian about "the great secret." As this kind of men
(I mean those of them who are not professed cheats)
are overrun with enthusiasm and philosophy, it was
very amusing to hear this religious adept descanting
on his pretended discovery. He talked of the secret
as of a spirit which lived within an emerald, and

converted every thing that was near it to the highest perfection it is capable of. "It gives a lustre," says he, "to the sun, and water to the diamond. It irradiates every metal, and enriches lead with all the properties of gold. It heightens smoke into flame, flame into light, and light into glory." He further added, "that a single ray of it dissipates pain, and care, and melancholy, from the person on whom it falls. In short," says he, "its presence naturally changes every place into a kind of heaven." After he had gone on for some time in this unintelligible cant, I found that he jumbled natural and moral ideas together into the same discourse, and that his great secret was nothing else but content.

This virtue does indeed produce, in some measure, all those effects which the alchymist usually ascribes to what he calls the philosopher's stone; and if it does not bring riches, it does the same thing, by banishing the desire of them. If it cannot remove the disquietudes arising out of a man's mind, body, or fortune, it makes him easy under them. It has indeed a kindly influence on the soul of man, in respect of every being to whom he stands related. It extinguishes all murmur, repining, and ingratitude, towards that Being who has allotted him his part to act in this world. It destroys all inordinate ambition, and every tendency to corruption, with regard to the community wherein he is placed. It gives sweetness to his conversation, and a perpetual serenity to all his thoughts.

Among the many methods which might be made use of for the acquiring of this virtue, I shall only mention the two following. First of all, a man should always consider how much he has more than he wants: and secondly, how much more unhappy he might be than he really is.

First of all a man should always consider how much he has more than he wants. I am wonderfully pleased with the reply which Aristippus made to one who condoled him upon the loss of a farm:

"Why," said he, "I have three farms still, and you have but one; so that I ought rather to be afflicted for you than you for me." On the contrary, foolish men are more apt to consider what they have lost than what they possess; and to fix their eyes upon those who are richer than themselves, rather than on those who are under greater difficulties. All the real pleasures and conveniences of life lie in a narrow compass; but it is the humour of mankind to be always looking forward, and straining after one who has got the start of them in wealth and honour. For this reason, as there are none can be properly called rich who have not more than they want, there are few rich men in any of the politer nations, but among the middle sort of people, who keep their wishes within their fortunes, and have more wealth than they know how to enjoy. Persons of a higher rank live in a kind of splendid poverty, and are perpetually wanting, because, instead of acquiescing in the solid pleasures of life, they endeavour to outvie one another in shadows and appearances. Men of sense have at all times beheld, with a great deal of mirth, this silly game that is playing over their heads, and, by contracting their desires, enjoy all that secret satisfaction which others are always in quest of. The truth is, this ridiculous chase after imaginary pleasures cannot be sufficiently exposed, as it is the great source of those evils which generally undo a nation. Let a man's estate be what it will, he is a poor man if he does not live within it, and naturally sets himself to sale to any one that can give him his price. When Pittacus, after the death of his brother, who had left him a good estate, was offered a great sum of money by the King of Lydia, he thanked him for his kindness, but told him he had already more by half than he knew what to do with. In short, content is equivalent to wealth, and luxury to poverty; or, to give the thought a more agreeable turn, "Content is natural wealth," says Socrates; to which I shall add, "Luxury is artificial poverty." I shall therefore recommend to the consideration of those who are always aiming after superfluous and imaginary enjoyments, and will not be at the trouble of contracting their desires, an excellent saying of Bion the philosopher; namely, that " no man has so much care as he who endeavours after the most happiness."

In the second place, every one ought to reflect how much more unhappy he might be than he really is. The former consideration took in all those who are sufficiently provided with the means to make themselves easy; this regards such as actually lie under some pressure or misfortune. These may receive great elevation from such a comparison as the unhappy person may make between himself and others, or between the misfortune which he suffers, and greater misfortunes which might have befallen him.

I like the story of the honest Dutchman, who, upon breaking his leg by a fall from the mainmast, told the standers-by, it was a great mercy that it was not his neck. To which, since I am got into quotations, give me leave to add the saying of an old philosopher, who, after having invited some of his friends to dine with him, was ruffled by his wife, that came into the room in a passion, and threw down the table that stood before them : " Every one," says he, " has his calamity, and he is a happy man that has no greater than this." We find an instance to the same purpose in the Life of Doctor Hammond, written by Bishop Fell. As this good man was troubled with a complication of distempers, when he had the gout upon him he used to thank God that it was not the stone; and when he had the stone, that he had not both these distempers on him at the same time.

I cannot conclude this essay without observing that there was never any system besides that of Christianity which could effectually produce in the mind of man the virtue I have hitherto been speaking of. In order to make us content with our present condition, many of the ancient philosophers tell us that our discontent only hurts ourselves, without being able to make any alteration in our circumstances; others, that whatever evil befalls us is derived to us by a fatal necessity, to which the gods themselves are subject; while others very gravely tell the man who is miserable, that it is necessary he should be so to keep up the harmony of the universe, and that the scheme of Providence would be troubled and perverted were he otherwise. These, and the like considerations, rather silence than satisfy a man. They may show him that his discontent is unreasonable, but are by no means sufficient to relieve it. They rather give despair than consolation. In a word, a man might reply to one of these comforters, as Augustus did to his friend who advised him not to grieve for the death of a person whom he loved, because his grief could not fetch him again: "It is for that very reason," said the emperor, "that I grieve."

On the contrary, religion bears a more tender regard to human nature. It prescribes to every miserable man the means of bettering his condition; nay, it shows him that the bearing of his afflictions as he ought to do, will naturally end in the removal of them; it makes him easy here, because it can make him happy hereafter.

Upon the whole, a contented mind is the greatest blessing a man can enjoy in this world; and if in the present life his happiness arises from the subduing of his desires, it will arise in the next from the gratification of them.

FALSE CRITICISM

Studium sine divite vena.

HOR. *Ars Poet.* 409.

Art without a vein. ROSCOMMON.

I LOOK upon the playhouse as a world within itself. They have lately furnished the middle region of it with a new set of meteors, in order to give the sublime to many modern tragedies. I was there last winter at the first rehearsal of the new thunder, which is much more deep and sonorous than any hitherto made use of. They have a Salmoneus behind the scenes who plays it off with great success. Their lightnings are made to flash more briskly than heretofore; their clouds are also better furbelowed, and more voluminous; not to mention a violent storm locked up in a great chest, that is designed for the Tempest. They are also provided with above a dozen showers of snow, which, as I am informed, are the plays of many unsuccessful poets artificially cut and shredded for that use. Mr Rymer's Edgar is to fall in snow at the next acting of *King Lear*, in order to heighten, or rather to alleviate, the distress of that unfortunate prince; and to serve by way of decoration to a piece which that great critic has written against.

I do not indeed wonder that the actors should be such professed enemies to those among our nation who are commonly known by the name of critics, since it is a rule among these gentlemen to fall upon a play, not because it is ill written, but because it takes. Several of them lay it down as a maxim, that whatever dramatic performance has a long run, must of necessity be good for nothing; as though the first precept in poetry were "not to please."— Whether this rule holds good or not, I shall leave to the determination of those who are better judges than myself; if it does, I am sure it tends very much to the honour of those gentlemen who have established it; few of their pieces having been disgraced by a run of three days, and most of them being so exquisitely written, that the town would never give them more than one night's hearing.

I have a great esteem for a true critic, such as Aristotle and Longinus among the Greeks; Horace and Quintilian among the Romans; Boileau and Dacier among the French. But it is our misfortune that some, who set up for professed critics among us, are so stupid, that they do not know how to put ten words together with elegance or common propriety; and withal so illiterate, that they have no taste of the learned languages, and therefore criticize upon old authors only at second-hand. They judge of them by what others have written, and not by any notions they have of the authors themselves. The words unity, action, sentiment, and diction, pronounced with an air of authority, give them a figure among unlearned readers, who are apt to believe they are very deep because they are unintelligible. The ancient critics are full of the praises of their contemporaries; they discover beauties which escaped the observation of the vulgar, and very often find out reasons for palliating and excusing such little slips and oversights as were committed in the writings of eminent authors. On the contrary, most of the smatterers in criticism, who appear among us, make it their business to vilify and depreciate every new production that gains applause, to decry imaginary blemishes, and to prove, by far-fetched arguments, that what pass for beauties in any celebrated piece are faults and errors. In short, the writings of these critics, compared with those of the ancients, are like the works of the sophists compared with those of the old philosophers.

Envy and cavil are the natural fruits of laziness and ignorance; which was probably the reason, that in the heathen mythology, Momus is said to be the son of Nox and Somnus, of darkness and sleep. Idle men, who have not been at the pains to accomplish or distinguish themselves, are very apt to detract from others; as ignorant men are very subject to decry those beauties in a celebrated work which they have not eyes to discover. Many of our sons of Momus, who dignify themselves by the name of critics, are the genuine descendants of these two illustrious ancestors. They are often led into those numerous absurdities in which they daily instruct the people, by not considering that, first, there is sometimes a greater judgment shown in deviating from the rules of art than in adhering to them; and, secondly, that there is more beauty in the works of a great genius, who is ignorant of all the rules of art, than in the works of a little genius, who not only knows but scrupulously observes them.

First, We may often take notice of men who are perfectly acquainted with all the rules of good writing, and notwithstanding choose to depart from them on extraordinary occasions. I could give instances out of all the tragic writers of antiquity who have shown their judgment in this particular; and purposely receded from an established rule of the drama, when it has made way for a much higher beauty than the observation of such a rule would have been. Those who have surveyed the noblest pieces of architecture and statuary, both ancient and modern, know very well that there are frequent deviations from art in the works of the greatest masters, which have produced a much nobler effect than a more accurate and exact way of proceeding could have done. This often arises from what the Italians call the *gusto grande* in these arts, which is what we call the sublime in writing.

In the next place, our critics do not seem sensible that there is more beauty in the works of a great genius, who is ignorant of the rules of art, than in those of a little genius, who knows and observes them. It is of these men of genius that Terence speaks, in opposition to the little artificial cavillers of his time:

Quorum æmulari exoptat negligentiam
Potius, quam istorum obscuram diligentiam.

Whose negligence he would rather imitate than these men's obscure diligence.

A critic may have the same consolation in the ill success of his play as Dr South tells us a physician has at the death of a patient, that he was killed *secundum artem*. Our inimitable Shakspeare is a stumbling-block to the whole tribe of these rigid critics. Who would not rather read one of his plays, where there is not a single rule of the stage observed, than any production of a modern critic, where there is not one of them violated! Shakspeare was indeed born with all the seeds of poetry, and may be compared to the stone in Pyrrhus's ring, which as Pliny tells us, had the figure of Apollo and the nine Muses in the veins of it, produced by the spontaneous hand of nature, without any help from art.

APPENDIX

THE SPECTATOR CLUB

By Sir Richard Steele

Haec alii sex
Vel plures uno conclamant ore.
Juv. *Sat.* vii. 166.

Six more at least join their consenting voice.

The first of our society is a gentleman of Worcestershire, of ancient descent, a baronet; his name Sir Roger de Coverley. His great-grandfather was inventor of that famous country-dance which is called after him. All who know that shire are very well acquainted with the parts and merits of Sir Roger. He is a gentleman that is very singular in his behaviour, but his singularities proceed from his good sense, and are contradictions to the manners of the world only as he thinks the world is in the wrong. However, this humour creates him no enemies, for he does nothing with sourness or obstinacy; and his being unconfined to modes and forms makes him but the readier and more capable to please and oblige all who know him. When he is in town, he lives in Soho Square. It is said he keeps himself a bachelor by reason he was crossed in love by a perverse beautiful widow of the next county to him. Before this disappointment, Sir Roger was what you call a fine gentleman, had often supped with my Lord Rochester and Sir George Etherege, fought a duel upon his first coming to town, and kicked bully Dawson in a public coffee-house for calling him youngster. But being ill-used by the above-mentioned widow, he was very serious for a year and a half; and though, his temper being naturally jovial, he at last got over it, he grew careless of himself, and never dressed afterwards. He continues to wear a coat and doublet of the same cut that were in fashion at the time of his repulse, which, in his merry humours, he tells us, has been in and out twelve times since he first wore it. It is said Sir Roger grew humble in his desires after he had forgot this cruel beauty: but this is looked upon, by his friends, rather as matter of raillery than truth. He is now in his fifty-sixth year, cheerful, gay, and hearty; keeps a good house both in town and country; a great lover of mankind; but there is such a mirthful cast in his behaviour that he is rather beloved than esteemed.

His tenants grow rich, his servants look satisfied, all the young women profess love to him, and the young men are glad of his company. When he comes into a house, he calls the servants by their names, and talks all the way up-stairs to a visit. I must not omit that Sir Roger is a justice of the quorum: that he fills the chair at a Quarter Session with great abilities, and three months ago gained universal applause by explaining a passage in the Game Act.

The gentleman next in esteem and authority among us is another bachelor, who is a member of the Inner Temple, a man of great probity, wit, and under-standing; but he has chosen his place of residence rather to obey the direction of an old humoursome father than in pursuit of his own inclinations. He was placed there to study the laws of the land, and is the most learned of any of the house in those of the stage. Aristotle and Longinus are much better under-stood by him than Littleton or Coke. The father sends up every post questions relating to marriage articles, leases, and tenures, in the neighbourhood; all which questions he agrees with an attorney to answer and take care of in the lump. He is studying the passions themselves, when he should be inquiring into the debates among men which arise from them. He knows the argument of each of the orations of Demosthenes and Tully, but not one case in the reports of our own courts. No one ever took him for a fool; but none, except his intimate friends, know he has a great deal of wit. This turn makes him at once both disinterested and agreeable. As few of his thoughts are drawn from business, they are most of them fit for conversation. His taste for books is a little too just for the age he lives in; he has read all, but approves of very few. His familiarity with the customs, manners, actions, and writings of the ancients, makes him a very delicate observer of what occurs to him in the present world. He is an excellent critic, and the time of the play is his hour of business: exactly at five he passes through New Inn, crosses through Russel Court, and takes a turn at Will's till the play begins; he has his shoes rubbed and his periwig powdered at the barber's as you go into the Rose. It is for the good of the audience when he is at the play, for the actors have an ambition to please him.

The person of next consideration is Sir Andrew Freeport, a merchant of great eminence in the city of London: a person of indefatigable industry, strong reason, and great experience. His notions of trade are noble and generous, and, as every rich man has usually some sly way of jesting, which would make no great figure were he not a rich man, he calls the sea the British Common. He is acquainted with commerce in all its parts; and will tell you it is a stupid and barbarous way to extend dominion by arms; for true power is to be got by arts and industry. He will often argue that, if this part of our trade were well cultivated, we should gain from one nation; and if another, from another. I have heard him prove that diligence makes more lasting acquisitions than valour, and that sloth has ruined more nations than the sword. He abounds in several frugal maxims, amongst which the greatest favourite is, " A penny saved is a penny got." A general trader of good sense is pleasanter company than a general scholar; and Sir Andrew having a natural unaffected eloquence, the perspicuity of his discourse gives the same pleasure that wit would in other men. He has made his fortunes himself; and says that England may be richer than other kingdoms by as plain methods as he himself is richer than other men; though at the same time I can say this of him, that there is not a point in the compass but blows home a ship in which he is an owner.

Next to Sir Andrew in the club-room sits Captain Sentry, a gentleman of great courage and under-standing, but invincible modesty. He is one of those that deserve very well, but are very awkward at putting their talents within the observation of such as should take notice of them. He was some years a captain, and behaved himself with great gallantry in several engagements and at several sieges; but having a small estate of his own, and being next heir to Sir Roger, he has quitted a way of life in which no man can rise suitably to his merit who is not something of a courtier as well as a soldier. I have heard him often lament that, in a profession where merit is placed in so conspicuous a view, impudence should get the better of modesty. When he has talked to this purpose, I never heard him make a sour expression, but frankly confess that he left the world because he was not fit for it. A strict honesty and an even regular behaviour are in themselves obstacles to him that must press through crowds, who endeavour at the same end with himself—the favour of a commander. He will, how-ever, in his way of talk, excuse generals for not disposing according to men's desert, or inquiring into it; for, says he, that great man who has a mind to help me has as many to break through to come at me as I have to come at him; therefore, he will conclude, that the man who would make a figure, especially in a military way, must get over all false modesty, and assist his patron against the importunity of other pretenders, by a proper assurance in his own vindica-

tion.　He says it is a civil cowardice to be backward
in asserting what you ought to expect, as it is a
military fear to be slow in attacking when it is your
duty.　With this candour does the gentleman speak of
himself and others.　The same frankness runs through
all his conversation.　The military part of his life has
furnished him with many adventures, in the relation of
which he is very agreeable to the company; for he is
never overbearing, though accustomed to command
men in the utmost degree below him; nor ever too
obsequious, from a habit of obeying men highly above
him.

But that our society may not appear a set of
humourists, unacquainted with the gallantries and
pleasures of the age, we have amongst us the gallant
Will Honeycomb, a gentleman who, according to his
years, should be in the decline of his life; but having
ever been very careful of his person, and always had
a very easy fortune, time has made but very little impression, either by wrinkles on his forehead or traces
in his brain.　His person is well turned, of a good
height.　He is very ready at that sort of discourse
with which men usually entertain women.　He is all
his life dressed very well; and remembers habits as
others do men.　He can smile when one speaks to him,
and laugh easily.　He knows the history of every
mode, and can inform you from which of the French
king's wives our wives and daughters had this manner
of curling their hair, that way of placing their hoods;
and whose vanity to show her foot made that part of
the dress so short in such a year.　In a word, all his
conversation and knowledge have been in the female
world.　As other men of his age will take notice to
you what such a minister said upon such and such an
occasion, he will tell you when the Duke of Monmouth
danced at court, such a woman was then smitten,
another was taken with him at the head of his troop
in the park.　In all these important relations, he has
ever about the same time received a kind glance, or a
blow of a fan, from some celebrated beauty, mother of

the present Lord Such-a-one. This way of talking of his very much enlivens the conversation among us of a more sedate turn ; and I find there is not one of the company, but myself, who rarely speak at all, but speaks of him as that sort of man who is usually called a well-bred fine gentleman. To conclude his character, where women are not concerned, he is an honest worthy man.

I cannot tell whether I am to account him whom I am next to speak of as one of our company; for he visits us but seldom, but when he does it adds to every man else a new enjoyment of himself. He is a clergy-man, a very philosophic man, of general learning, great sanctity of life, and the most exact breeding. He has the misfortune to be of a very weak constitution, and, consequently, cannot accept of such cares and business as preferments in his function would oblige him to ; he is, therefore, among divines what a chamber-counsellor is among lawyers. The probity of his mind, and the integrity of his life, create him followers, as being eloquent or loud advances others. He seldom introduces the subject he speaks upon ; but we are so far gone in years that he observes, when he is among us, an earnestness to have him fall on some divine topic which he always treats with much authority, as one who has no interest in this world, as one who is hastening to the object of all his wishes, and conceives hope from his decays and infirmities. These are my ordinary companions.

NOTES

p. 1. This paper and my next. Addison in the opening paper describes some traits of his own character. "My next" was the work of Steele (*vide* Appendix), to whom belongs the credit of creating the members of the Club. Addison's rather intemperate champion, Bishop Hurd, assumed that the second essay was "touched" by Addison.

p. 3. Will's. The Coffee-house in Russell Street, Covent Garden, made famous by Dryden and Congreve. It is mentioned in the first number of *The Tatler* as the address for an account of poetry.

Child's. Another celebrated Coffee-house in St Paul's church-yard frequented by the clergy.

The Postman. One of the imitations of Defoe's *Review of the Affairs of France* conducted by a "Politicus Gallo-Anglus" named Fonvive.

St James's. A fashionable resort in St James's Street from which the foreign and domestic news in *The Tatler* is dated.

The Grecian. A Coffee-house in the Strand. It was one of the earliest in England, being established about 1652 by the Greek servant of an English merchant. It is distinguished in *The Tatler* as the source of Learning.

The Cocoa-tree. A Tory resort in St James's Street.

Jonathan's. The favourite haunt of stock-jobbers. It was in Change Alley, Cornhill.

p. 4. Between the Whigs and Tories. The "strict neutrality" was not always observed, but Addison is careful to make the reservation "unless I shall be forced etc."

A looker-on. Steele and Addison were always happy in their choice of titles, as is seen by their continuance. "The Looker-On" was the title in recent years of a well-known series of articles in *Blackwood's Magazine* by Mrs Oliphant.

p. 5. Nicolini. Nicolino Grimaldi, referred to both as Signor Nicolini and as Signor Grimaldi, a famous Italian singer who first appeared in England in 1708.

Painted dragons etc. This refers to the staging of Handel's *Rinaldo*, 1711.

p. 6. Sir Martin Mar-all. An adaptation by Dryden of Molière's L'Etourdi (1667). The knight pretends to serenade while the music is really produced by his servant in an adjoining room.

p. 7. Armida. The heroine of *Rinaldo*.

Mynheer Handel. Georg Friedrich Haendel (1685—1759). He came to England in 1710, and after revisiting Hanover in the following year, he remained in England till his death.

A taste of the Italian. The libretto of *Rinaldo* was translated by Dr Aaron Hill from the Italian of Rossi.

p. 8. In a fortnight. Compare the fact that *The Messiah* was composed in twenty-three days.

The poet himself. *Rinaldo* was based on Tasso's *Gerusalemme Liberata*.

Monsieur Boileau. Satire IX.

Mr Rich. Christopher Rich (*d.* 1714), manager of Drury Lane, who at one time controlled the three chief London theatres.

p. 9. Pied piper. The legendary piper of Hameln who beguiled the children to follow him into a mountain cavern in 1284. The story is told in Browning's well-known poem which was written to amuse the son of W. C. Macready.

London and Wise. George London and Henry Wise, a famous firm of gardeners in the reign of Queen Anne. They introduced the formal Dutch style of gardening and are praised by Evelyn in his *Sylva*.—Cf. p. 199.

p. 10. Bacon observes. "Which surcharge nevertheless is not to be remedied by making no more books, but by making more good ones, which, as the serpent of Moses, mought devour the serpents of the enchanters." *Adv. of Learning*, Bk. II. Int. 14.

p. 13. Nicolini. See note for p. 5.

Hydaspes. An opera produced in 1710, by Giovanni Battista Buononcini (*d.* 1750). Inspired by love Hydaspes sings himself into such valour that he strangles the lion.

p. 16. Statue on the Pont-Neuf. A statue of Henri IV.

The London Prentice. The allusion has not been traced. It may refer to the character of Ralph, the ridiculous apprentice in Beaumont's burlesque, *The Knight of the Burning Pestle*. The latter, a general travesty of mock-heroic drama, was specially aimed against Heywood's *Four Prentices of London*.

p. 18. Socrates. *Phaedo*, sec. 40.

Aristophanes. *The Clouds*.

Catullus. *Carmina*, XXIX.

Quillet. The *Callipaedia* of Claude Quillet, 1655, one of the *Mazarinades* of which more than four thousand have been enumerated.

p. 19. Sextus Quintus. Felice Peretti (Sixtus V), 1521—1590. He was distinguished for many reforms and by his erection of the Vatican library. He came of a poor family and the tradition is that his sister had been a laundress.

Pasquin. The term Pasquinade is derived from Pasquino, a sharp-tongued Roman tailor of the fifteenth century. After his death a mutilated statue discovered near his shop was named after him and anonymous lampoons were exhibited upon it.

Aretine. Pietro Aretino (1492—1557), the satirical Italian poet whose writings gained him the title of "The Scourge of Princes."

Sophi of Persia. A title borne by the Shah from 1505—1725 during the reign of the Safavi dynasty.

p. 20. Sir Roger L'Estrange. The reference is to the translation of Æsop by L'Estrange in 1694. L'Estrange was a famous journalist who became licenser of the press in 1663. His *Observator* and other papers entitle him to rank as one of the most important pioneers of modern journalism.

p. 21. Dr Sydenham. Thomas Sydenham (1624—1689), after serving as a captain of cavalry with the Parliamentary forces, became a physician of European reputation. The treatise referred to is the *Methodus Curandi Febres* (1666).

Sanctorius. Santorio of Padua (d. 1636), author of a treatise *De Medicina Statica*, 1614, of which the earliest English translation appeared in 1676.

p. 23. Italian epitaph. "I was well: I would be better: and here I am." (Morley.) Professor Gregory Smith points out that Dryden quotes it in the dedication of his *Æneid*.

p. 24. Martial. *Epigrams*, x. 47.

p. 25. Glaucumque etc. *Aeneid*, VI. 483. The original is in the *Iliad*, XVII. 216.

p. 27. Sir Cloudesley Shovel. Sir Clowdisley Shovell (1650—1707) became commander-in-chief of the fleet in 1705. He was drowned in shipwreck off the Scilly Isles. Cf. *Spectator*, No. 329.

p. 28. When I see kings lying etc. This paper might be called a "tournament" essay as the subject has been handled by so many eminent writers. It recalls, as Mr Dobson points out, Raleigh's famous apostrophe. Probably Defoe had Addison's essay in mind when in 1722 he wrote his reflections on Marlborough's funeral: similarly Leigh Hunt reminds us of it in his essay "On the Deaths of Little Children."

p. 29. Will Honeycomb, Sir Andrew Freeport, the Templar. See Appendix and notes thereon.

NOTES 239

p. 80. Sir Roger de Coverley. See Appendix and note.

Captain Sentry, the Clergyman. See Appendix and note.

p. 31. The Roman Triumvirate. Octavius, Antony and Lepidus, 44 B.C.

Punch. This refers to the famous puppet-show established in 1710 at Covent Garden by Martin Powell.

p. 33. Counterfeit books. Cf. Lamb's *biblia-abiblia*.

Ogleby's Virgil. John Ogilby (1600—1676), author, printer, translator, dancing-master.

Dryden's Juvenal. Published in 1693.

Cassandra and Cleopatra. Two ten-volume romances by La Calprenède (1642 and 1647) of which there were several translations. The name should be *Cassandre* or *Cassander*, the son of Antipater, not the daughter of Priam.

Astraea. A pastoral romance by Honoré D'Urfé, translated 1657.

The Grand Cyrus. A ten-volume romance by Madame de Scudéri, 1653.

Pembroke's Arcadia. "The Countess of Pembroke's Arcadia" was published in 1590, four years after Sir Philip Sidney's death.

Locke. The original reading is "Lock of Human Understanding," which, as Professor Gregory Smith points out, gives force to what follows.

Sherlock. Dr William Sherlock (1641?—1707), Dean of St Paul's, author of a "Practical Discourse Concerning Death," 1689.

The Fifteen Comforts of Matrimony. An English version (1682) of a fifteenth century French work, *Quinze Joies de mariage* by Antoine Lasale.

Temple's Essays. The Essays were published in 1680 and 1692, those of the latter date being the more important.

p. 34. Malebranche. The *Recherche de la Vérité* was translated in 1694.

Book of Novels. Novels in the older sense, *i.e.* short 'merry tales.'

Academy of Compliments. "The Academy of Compliments, or a New Way of Wooing," 1685.

Culpepper. Nicholas Culpeper (1616—1654), a writer on medicine and astrology.

The Ladies' Calling. By the author of *The whole Duty of Man*. The author is still unidentified.

Mr Durfey. *Tales, Tragical and Comical* by T. D'Urfey, 1704, a Huguenot poet and dramatist (1653—1723).

Elzevirs. The name of a celebrated family of Dutch printers (father and five sons), whose work is practically synchronous with the seventeenth century. The name is associated with beautifully printed editions of the ancient classics in 12mo., 16mo., and 24mo.

Clelia. Another romance in ten volumes by Madame de Scudéri, translated into English 1656—61.

Baker's Chronicle. Sir Richard Baker (1568—1645), last of the Chroniclers and immortal as Sir Roger de Coverley's 'historian.' His *Chronicles* appeared in 1643.

Advice to a Daughter. *The Lady's New Year Gift*, or *Advice to a Daughter*, 1700, the most popular work of George Savile, first Earl of Halifax. The book was enormously successful, and in its morality is curiously like his grandson's masterpiece, the Letters of Lord Chesterfield.

The New Atlantis. By Mrs Mary Manley, 1709. She was one of the first professional women of letters and succeeded Swift as editor of *The Examiner*. The *New Atlantis* was a disguised *chronique scandaleuse* of the English court.

Mr Steele's Christian Hero. A volume of practical ethics written by Steele in 1701 to fortify him against "a strong propensity to unwarrantable pleasures."

Sacheverell's Speech. This was Sacheverell's speech on his trial before the House of Lords, 1710.

Fielding's Trial. Robert ("Beau") Feilding was convicted in 1706 of bigamously marrying the Duchess of Cleveland.

Seneca's morals. Translated by Sir Roger L'Estrange.

Taylor. The two portions of Jeremy Taylor's great work were published in 1650 and 1651.

La Ferte. A dancing master of the time who advertises in the *Spectator*. (Gregory Smith.)

p. 36. Venice Preserved. The most famous of Thomas Otway's tragedies (1682).

p. 37. Hamlet. Act I. 4, 38.

p. 38. That dreadful butchering. Cf. Dryden's *Essay of Dramatic Poesy* where Lisideius (Sedley) says the English stage is "too like the theatres where they fight prizes," and quotes Horace's

"Nec pueros coram populo Medea trucidet."

p. 39. Corneille. *Horace* (1639).

Sophocles. *Electra.*

p. 41. Bullock. William Bullock (1657?—1740?), comedian. He is referred to in the *Tatler* along with his rival, Pinkethman. Bullock had a son, Christopher, who was acting in comedy also at this time and the reference may be to him.

Norris. Henry Norris (1665—1730?), a comedian who won fame in the part of Dicky in Farquhar's comedy, *The Constant Couple*, or *A Trip to the Jubilee*. Hence he was known as "Jubilee Dicky."

One of the first wits. *The Comical Revenge, or Love in a Tub* by Sir George Etherege, 1664.

p. 44. Betterton. Thomas Betterton (1635?—1710), the chief actor of his time. He was associated with Sir John Davenant in revolutionising the theatre. He acted the part of Macbeth soon after the Restoration and as late as 1707.

Balloon. The allusion remains unexplained. Perhaps it was a popular nickname for some well-known understudy.

p. 46. Tully. Cicero, *De Amicitia*, ch. VI.

Bacon. In his essay *Of Friendship*.

Apocryphal treatise. *Ecclesiasticus: the wisdom of Jesus, the son of Sirach.*

p. 48. Epictetus. The famous Stoic philosopher of the second half of the first century A.D. His pupil, Arrian the historian, collected his maxims in the *Enchiridion*.

p. 49. Boileau. In his *Réflexions sur Longin*.

p. 50. Sidney. In his *Apologie for Poetrie*, 1595.

Antiquated song. The version known to Addison was of later origin than that praised by Sidney.

Greatest modern critics. Addison seems to have had Le Bossu chiefly in mind. (Gregory Smith.)

p. 51. Valerius Flaccus. In the *Argonautica*, c. 70 A.D.

Statius. In the *Thebaid*, c. 92 A.D.

p. 60. In Hudibras. Pt. I. 3, 94.

p. 63. "Speak, that I may see thee." Attributed to Socrates by Apuleius. (Gregory Smith).

A very ingenious author. Probably, as Professor Gregory Smith suggests, Giambattista della Porta, the famous Neapolitan author of *De Humana Physiognomonia*, 1586. He is referred to by Dryden in his *Preface to the Fables*.

Life of Condé. A translation of a French memoir by Nahum Tate, 1693.

p. 64. A great physiognomist. Zopyrus. Cicero is the authority for the story in his *De Fato*, V. and *Tusc. Disput.* IV. 37.

p. 65. An ancient author. Plato's *Symposium*, 215, A.

Dr Moore. Henry More (1614—1687), one of the Cambridge Platonists, philosophical writer in prose and verse. Author of *Enchiridion Ethicum*, 1669.

242 NOTES

Prosopolepsia. Προσωπολημψία in this sense means the fallacy of judging by appearance.

p. 66. "As grasshoppers." A free rendering of *Numbers* xiii. 33.

p. 67. Paradin. Guillaume Paradin's *Annales de Bourgogne* (1566).

Fontanges. A mode of head-dress named after its inventor, Mlle. de Fontagne, in 1679.

p. 68. Conecte. Thomas Conecte, a Breton preacher who inveighed against the luxury of his times and died at the stake in 1434.

Commode. A fashionable head-dress at the end of the seventeenth century. "'At that time,' says St Simon (quoted in Littré's *Dict.*), 'head-dresses were worn called *commodes*, which had no fastenings to them.' Hence evidently the origin of the word; it was a *conveniency*" (T. Arnold).

M. d'Argentre. Bertrand d'Argentré, author of *Histoire de Bretagne*, 1582. This reference, like the foregoing, is taken by Addison from the article on Conecte in the celebrated *Dictionnaire Historique et Critique* of Pierre Bayle, 1696.

p. 74. A game of ombre. The *locus classicus* on this card game is in *The Rape of the Lock*. From Spanish *hombre*, a man.

p. 75. A mere courtier etc. This was the favourite style of title used by the old writers of "characters." But the word *mere* had by this time lost its earlier sense of 'true' and had acquired the slighting significance 'this and nothing else.'

p. 76. Sir Roger de Coverley. See Appendix and note.

Humour. A use of the word that retains much of the older Jonsonian sense. Cf. "humorist" on p. 78.

p. 79. Bishop of St Asaph. The reference is uncertain. It must be either to William Fleetwood, Bishop of St Asaph (1708—1714), whose preface to some sermons of later date was published by Steele in No. 384 of *The Spectator* or to his predecessor, William Beveridge, whose sermons were published in the year of his death, 1708.

Dr South. Robert South (1634—1716), a preacher famous for his wit.

Tillotson. John Tillotson (1630—1694), Archbishop of Canterbury, noted for the perspicuity of his style which places him with Dryden and Temple among the pioneers of modern prose.

Sanderson. Robert Sanderson (1587—1663), professor of divinity in Oxford and Bishop of Lincoln.

Barrow. Isaac Barrow (1630—1677), Master of Trinity, 1672, having previously been professor of Greek and later of mathematics at Cambridge. The latter post he relinquished in favour of his pupil, Isaac Newton. He was also "a great preacher in an age of great preachers, and a great theologian in an age of great theologians" (Saintsbury).

Calamy. Edmund Calamy (1600—1666), a famous Puritan divine, chiefly remembered now by the fact that his initials form part of the word *Smectymnuus*.

p. 80. Mr William Wimble. This character was identified in the eighteenth century with Thomas Morecraft, a Baronet's younger son who died in 1741. Many editors have noted the resemblance between Will Wimble and Mr Thomas Gules of *The Tatler*, No. 256.

p. 83. Twenty-first speculation. *Spectator* No. 21 is a dissertation by Addison on the professions.

p. 88. The perverse widow. This is the "perverse beautiful widow" described by Steele in *The Spectator*, No. 2 (see appendix) and in No. 113. She has been identified with Mrs Catharine Bovey (or Boevey), a philanthropic widow to whom Steele dedicated a volume of his *Ladies Library*. The widow is one of Steele's happiest additions to the *Spectator* portrait gallery, particularly in No. 113 where we are told of Sir Roger's wooing and of her having "the finest Hand of any Woman in the World."

p. 89. Sydenham. See note for p. 21.

Medicina Gymnastica. A work by Francis Fuller of St John's, Cambridge, 1704.

A Latin treatise. *Artis Gymnasticae apud Antiquos*, (1569), by Hieronymus Mercurialis, an Italian.

p. 91. Otway. *The Orphan*, Act II, Sc. IV.

p. 98. Galenic way. Claudius Galenus, the famous Greek physician, 131—201 A.D.

p. 100. Latin proverb. *Lupus est homo homini*, Plautus, *Asinaria*, II. 4, 88.

p. 105. A white witch. A kind of oxymoron, meaning one using supernatural gifts for a good end. Mr W. H. Wills compares Dryden's line, "like white witches mischievously good."

p. 106. A Jesuit. Mr Spectator's taciturnity had led before to his being taken for a Jesuit. Professor Gregory Smith cites Nos. 4 and 77 by Steele and Budgell respectively.

p. 109. One of the greatest geniuses. Jonathan Swift, who had written on the same subject in the *Tatler*, No. 230. In his *Proposal for Correcting, Improving, and Ascertaining the English Tongue*, published a few months after this essay of Addison, Swift says that he had already communicated much of what he had to say "by the hands of an ingenious gentleman, who for a long time did thrice a week divert or instruct the kingdom by his papers...under the title of *Spectator*."

p. 110. Rep. That is, *reputation*.

Pos. For *positive*.

The signs of our substantives. The omission of the article, cf.

> "When pulpit, drum ecclesiastic,
> Was beat with fist instead of a stick."

L'Estrange. "Swift had very much to do with the rescuing of Style, by the hands of Addison and the rest, from the vulgarisation which it was undergoing at the close of the seventeenth century, not merely in common writers, not merely in the hands of an eccentric like L'Estrange, but in those of scholars like Collier and Bentley." See note to p. 20.

p. 111. An academy. This project is referred to by Dryden, Swift, Goldsmith and other essayists.

p. 112. Grand Cairo. Cf. the description of Mr Spectator, p. 3.

p. 120. Dryden. *Absalom and Achitophel*, Pt. I. 544.

In a late paper. Referring to No. 161 by Budgell.

p. 122. Namur. Taken by King William in 1695.

Milton's *Death. Par. Lost*, II. 846.

p. 123. "Human face divine." *Par. Lost*, III. 44.

p. 124. One of my last week's papers. No. 169 by Addison.

Mr Dryden calls. *Cleomenes*, I. 1, 119.

p. 127. The epitaph of a charitable man. The epitaph of Edward Courtenay, Earl of Devonshire (*d.* 1556), was:

> What we gave, we have;
> What we spent, we had;
> What we left, we lost.

In the *Gesta Romanorum* (XVI) is the epigram, "What I formerly expended, I have; what I gave away, I have."

p. 131. Passage in Waller. From his lines "Upon the Earl of Roscommon's Translation of Horace."

Your discourse upon...grinning. See p. 120.

Pickled-herring. "A set of merry drolls, whom the common people of all countries admire and seem to love so well, *that they could eat them*, according to the old proverb: I mean those circumforaneous wits whom every nation calls by the name of that dish of meat which it loves best. In Holland they are termed Pickled Herrings; in France, Jean Pottages; in Italy, Maccaronies; and in Great Britain, Jack Puddings." (*Spect.* No. 47.)

p. 135. Nicolini. See p. 236.

Dogget. Thomas Doggett, *d.* 1721, an Irish actor, joint-manager of Drury Lane. He founded Doggett's Prize for the Thames Watermen.

Virgil's ruler.

> "Aeolus...cavum conversa cuspide montem
> Impulit in latus; ac venti, velut agmine facto,
> Qua data porta, ruunt."
>
> *Aeneid,* I. 85.

p. 139. Which Hudibras has given.

> "But still his tongue ran on, the less
> Of weight it bore, with greater ease."
>
> Pt. III. Bk. 2, 443.

p. 140. "Quoth Thomas." The Apostle, in the old ballad, atters this opinion while opposing the Wife of Bath's entrance into heaven.

Pippin-Woman. The indomitable lady of Gay's *Trivia,* whose head, after being cut off in the frozen Thames,

> "Chopt off, from her lost shoulders flies;
> Pippins she cried, but death her voice confounds,
> And Pip-Pip-Pip along the ice resounds."

The story of the Pippin-Woman appears to be the work of *Anon.* in the first decade of the eighteenth century. Gay's *Trivia* is five years later than Addison's essay.

p. 141. A modern philosopher. Thomas Hobbes (1588—1679), quoted by Addison in *Spectator,* No. 47, "The passion of laughter is nothing else but sudden glory arising from some sudden conception of some eminency in our selves by comparison with the infirmity of others, or with our own formerly."

p. 143. The Dispensary. A burlesque poem (1699) by Sir Samuel Garth, poet and physician, to ridicule the Apothecaries' opposition to the introduction of out-patients departments.

p. 150. Philomot. *Filemot* from *feuillemorte,* faded-leaf colour.

p. 152. Old Greek poet. Menander.

p. 153. Sir Roger de Coverley. See Appendix and Note.

Prince Eugene. Prince Eugene of Savoy, 1663—1736, who shared the military renown of Marlborough. He visited London in 1712 to induce the English government to continue the War of the Spanish Succession.

Scanderbeg. The Albanian chief (= Alexander Bey) who deserted the Turkish side in 1443, and, embracing Christianity (with the name of George Castriot), defeated the Turks repeatedly till his death in 1468.

p. 154. Dr Barrow. Isaac Barrow, the distinguished mathematician, divine and classical scholar (1630—1677). See p. 79.

Thirty marks. Twenty pounds. The mark was both a standard and a coin, the latter, as early as 1194, having the value of thirteen shillings and fourpence.

Will Wimble. See p. 80.

Tom Touchy. See p. 94.

Moll White. See p. 92.

p. 155. Sir Andrew. See Appendix and notes.

p. 156. Baker's Chronicle. See p. 34 and note.

Squire's. A coffee-house near Lincoln's Inn haunted, Steele tells us, by "young fellows who rise early but for no other purpose but to publish their laziness."

We have already. *Spectator*, Nos. 267 and 273.

p. 160. Zoïlus. The Greek rhetorician of the third century B.C. who gained the name of Homeromastix by his attacks on the Iliad.

Perrault. Charles Perrault, the French fabulist, whose poem *Le Siècle de Louis le grand* in 1687 started the famous controversy of the Ancients and the Moderns.

p. 166. Mr Maundrell. Henry Maundrell (1665—1701), chaplain to the Levant merchants at Aleppo. Addison's quotation, which was inserted in the revised edition of the *Spectator*, is taken from Maundrell's *Journey from Aleppo to Jerusalem*.

p. 169. Monsieur Perrault. See note for p. 160.

Boileau. From Boileau's *Réflexions sur Longin*. Boileau took the side of the Ancients against Perrault although Swift represents him as an advocate of the Moderns in *The Battle of the Books*.

p. 170. My paper. *Spectator*, No. 26. See p. 25.

Baker's Chronicle. See p. 34 and note.

p. 172. Sir Cloudesly Shovel. See note for p. 27.

Dr Busby. Headmaster of Westminster 1638—95.

p. 173. Martyr to good housewifery. A legend told of Elizabeth Russell of the Bedford family.

Jacob's Pillar. The stone built into the Coronation chair which Edward I removed from Scone to Westminster.

p. 173. The casualties of that reign. At the end of his account of each reign Sir Richard Baker gives an edifying list of "casualties."

Without a head. The head of the statue of Henry V was stolen at the Reformation.

p. 174. The Committee. A comedy by Sir Robert Howard, c. 1662.

The new tragedy. Ambrose Philips's tragedy *The Distressed Mother*, 1712, an adaptation of Racine's *Andromaque*.

Mohocks. Gangs of 'genteel' hooligans who infested the

streets of London in the reign of Queen Anne. They are constantly referred to in the literature of the time.

p. 175. Captain Sentry. See Appendix.

Steenkirk. When King William was defeated in 1692 by Marshal Luxemburg.

p. 183. St James's. See p. 236.

Giles's. A coffee-house frequented by foreigners.

Jenny Man's. The "Tilt Yard Coffee-house" opposite the Banqueting House in Whitehall.

p. 184. Will's. See p. 236.

p. 185. Garraway's. A coffee-house in Change Alley famous for its wine sales.

p. 186. Gratian. Baltasar Gracian, a Spanish Jesuit, author of various critical and popular ethical works in the seventeenth century. One of the latter was translated into English in 1694 under the title of *The Courtier's Oracle.*

p. 189. An essay upon wit. *Spectator*, Nos. 58—63.

Next Saturday. *Spectator*, No. 411.

p. 191. Words of the wise man. *Ecclesiastes* ix. 14.

In holy writ. *Proverbs* xxx. 7.

p. 192. A play by Aristophanes. *Plutus.*

p. 197. Lately read your essay. *Spectator*, No. 411.

p. 199. Treillages. Trellises.

Wise and London. See p. 237.

p. 202. One of Mr Southern's plays. *The Fatal Marriage* by Thomas Southerne, 1694.

The present controversy. The negotiations leading to the Treaty of Utrecht (1713) were hindered by the quarrel between the servants of the Dutch deputy, Rechteren, and of the French plenipotentiary, Mesnager.

p. 208. Diagoras. Cicero, *De Natura Deorum*, iii. 77.

Biton and Clitobus. The story of Biton and Cleobis occurs in Herodotus, I. 31 and is given by Cicero, *Tusc. Dis.*, I. 47, 113.

p. 211. A Turkish Tale. *Turkish Tales*, published by Tonson, 1708.

p. 216. Jenny Mann's. See note for p. 183.

A coffee-house in Paul's. Child's Coffee-house.

p. 218. Gentlemen of Port Royal. Port-Royal des Champs, near Versailles, was first famous for its Cistercian convent and in the second half of the seventeenth century for its lay community which rendered distinguished services to education by the preparation of books on grammar and logic etc.

p. 222. **Aristippus.** From Plutarch, *On Tranquillity*, VIII.

p. 223. **Pittacus.** From Diogenes Laertius, *Lives of the Philosophers*.

p. 224. **Dr Hammond.** Henry Hammond (*d.* 1660), chaplain to Charles I. His life was written by Bishop Fell, the subject of Tom Brown's famous adaptation of Martial's epigram.

p. 226. **The new thunder.** Supposed to be the invention of John Dennis of whom the well-known story is told that he recognised his "stolen thunder" in the theatre of an unfriendly manager.

Salmoneus. The son of Æolus, who imitated lightning with burning torches. (*Aeneid*, VI. 585.)

Mr Rymer's Edgar. A hard hit at Thomas Rymer who had attacked Shakespeare in his *Tragedies of the Last Age Considered*. Hence the fate to be meted out to his unsuccessful tragedy *Edgar*— to "fall in snow at the next acting of *Lear*."

p. 228. **Terence.** From the prologue to the *Andria*.

p. 229. **Dr South.** Robert South, the witty divine of the end of the seventeenth century (1634—1716).

Pyrrhus's ring. Pliny's *Natural History*, XXXVII. 3.

p. 230. **The Spectator Club.** This, the second number of the *Spectator*, was written by Steele. It is necessary for the student of the Coverley papers to keep this clearly in mind, as it is only by reference to this essay that the shares of Steele and Addison in the development of the club portraits can be traced and estimated. It will be noticed that Addison frequently gives a loose rein to his political irony.

Sir Roger de Coverley. The name as applied to a tune is found as early as 1648 and is referred to in the *Tatler* as *Roger de Caubly*. Sir Roger and the other members of the club have been not very satisfactorily identified with various real personages.

Lord Rochester. John Wilmot (1647—80), the typical Restoration wit and profligate.

Sir George Etherege. The Restoration dramatist (1635—1691), whose play, *The Comical Revenge*, 1664, is counted the first of the English Comedy of Manners.

Bully Dawson. According to Oldys, this bravo was the original of Shadwell's *Captain Hackum*. Shadwell's *Squire of Alsatia* (1688) is the *locus classicus* on low life in London towards the end of the seventeenth century.

p. 231. **Littleton or Coke.** Sir Edward Coke (1552—1634), author of the famous commentary on the *Tenures* of Sir Thomas Littleton (1402—81).

p. 232. **The Rose.** A rowdy tavern near Drury Lane Theatre.

For EU product safety concerns, contact us at Calle de José Abascal, 56–1°,
28003 Madrid, Spain or eugpsr@cambridge.org.

www.ingramcontent.com/pod-product-compliance
Ingram Content Group UK Ltd.
Pitfield, Milton Keynes, MK11 3LW, UK
UKHW012328130625
459647UK00009B/150